Cities
and structural adjustment

Cities
and structural adjustment

Nigel Harris & Ida Fabricius

University College London

UCL
PRESS

First published in 1996 by UCL Press

UCL Press Limited
University·College London
Gower Street
London WC1E 6BT

and
1900 Frost Road, Suite 101
Bristol
Pennsylvania 19007-1598

The name of University College London (UCL) is a registered trade mark used
by UCL Press with the consent of the owner.

British Library Cataloguing in Publication Data
A catalogue record for this book is available from the British Library.

Library of Congress Cataloging-in-Publication Data are available

ISBNs: 1-85728-618-9 HB
        1-85728-619-7 PB

Typeset in Zapf Elliptical.
Printed and bound by
Biddles Ltd, Guildford & King's Lynn, England.

Contents

Contents

Contents

Contents

Foreword

It gave me great pleasure to welcome the Indian and foreign experts to a symposium in Mumbai (Bombay) in October 1995, and now to welcome the publication of the results of their discussions. India has, over the past few years, been undergoing a process of macroeconomic reform, and opening up to world markets, a process with profound implications for a city such as Mumbai. The contributions to the symposium on how cities have managed these changes elsewhere in the world are thus of particular importance to us in understanding what is happening and what may happen to the great cities of India, and how we, the public authorities, ought to react to these changes. In turn, from our experience in managing this giant city, we may have something to contribute to the deliberations. Out of this mutual pooling of experience, we can all gain a much clearer perception of the way forwards.

Mumbai was proud to host this event and is proud to support an initiative that will be, in part, one of the city's contributions to the second United Nations Conference on Human Settlements, the City Summit. The new world economic order is upon us and it obliges us to learn new lessons about the contribution our cities can make.

R. T. Kadam
Mayor of Bombay

Preface

This volume records the contributions made, and some of the city case studies presented, at an international symposium, held in Bombay in October 1995. The symposium was designed as a contribution to the discussions at the second United Nations Conference on Human Settlements (Habitat II or the City Summit) at Istanbul in June 1996. The symposium was initiated and organized by the Development Planning Unit (University College London) and Bombay First, with the active support of the Housing Development Finance Corporation and the British Council. The Mayor and City Corporation sponsored the occasion. The organizers of the symposium are very grateful for the financial and material support making the event possible given by the Overseas Development Administration, the management of the Leela Kempiniski Hotel and Bombay First. None of the views expressed in the discussions or the papers can be construed as representing those of the ODA or any of the other organizations involved.

Nigel Harris & Ida Fabricius
Development Planning Unit, UCL

For the symposium, the DPU commissioned case studies of the experiences of the following cities in economies undergoing structural adjustment: Accra, Barcelona, Birmingham, Bogotá, Dortmund, Glasgow, Johannesburg, Kingston (Jamaica), Lille, London, Lyons, Milan, Monterrey, Rotterdam, Santiago de Chile, Sheffield and Turin. Not all case studies were ready in time for the symposium, and it was not possible to publish all those completed. Those published here (Chs 6–13) were included either because they adhere most closely to the original terms of reference or they reflect particular aspects of the diversity of experience. The range of the studies commissioned is still narrow, excluding North American cities, those of East Europe or Russia, East and Southeast Asia and much of Africa.

Notes on contributors

Joaquim Clusa is Economic Adviser to the Barcelona Metropolitan Regional Agency for Urban Development and Infrastructure. Until recently he was a senior adviser to the Association of Municipalities of the Barcelona Metropolitan Area. He has worked on consultancies involving urban and regional planning, public finance assessments and the reorganization of local government, and has published extensively on these issues.

Antonio Daher is a professor and researcher at Instituto de Estudios Urbanos of the Catholic University in Santiago, Chile, and currently a member of the Consultative Committee at the Centre for Environmental Research and Planning (CIPMA), and the Environmental Commission at the Centre for Public Policy Studies (CEP), and faculty associate at the Lincoln Institute of Land Policy, Cambridge, Massachusetts. He has undertaken consultancies and lectured in Argentina, Bolivia, Brazil, Colombia, Jamaica, Mexico, Paraguay, Peru and Uruguay.

Julio Dávila is a lecturer at the Development Planning Unit, University College London. He was formerly a policy research officer with the National Planning Department in Colombia, and a researcher with the International Institute for Environment and Development, London and Buenos Aires. Founder and co-editor of the journal *Environment and Urbanisation*, he has worked as a consultant in Latin America, Africa and Poland and is the author of several essays and articles on urban economic development, urban environment and gender issues.

Lalit Deshpande, former Professor of Economics and Head of Department of Economics at the University of Bombay is currently Professor in Personnel Management and Industrial Relations at the Tata Institute of Social Sciences in Bombay, and a member of the Advisory Group on Labour Market Policy at the International Labour Organisation in Geneva, of the Development Board for Maharashtra, Government of Maharashtra, and a consultant of Bombay First. His areas of specialization are labour, market issues and urbanization.

Ida Fabricius is a lecturer at the Development Planning Unit, University College London, and is a social scientist specializing in housing in development and gender issues. She has worked for the EU, the DPU and with international NGOs in Europe and overseas.

Gustavo Garza is a faculty member of the Centre for Demographic and Urban Development Studies at El Colegio de Mexico, and is Scientific Adviser to the Nuevo León Institute for Urban Studies (INSEUR-NL)

Cheryl Gopaul is the National Geographic Information Systems Coordinator for Jamaica, Office of the Prime Minister, and she is an urban/environmental planner. She is a part-time lecturer at the University of the West Indies, and Technical Consultant for the United Nations Fund for Population Activities (UNFPA), Caribbean Office, Jamaica. Previously she worked as Permanent Secretary for the Ministry of Agriculture in Guyana and on research and consultancies in USA and Canada.

Nigel Harris, Professor of Development Planning at UCL, is an economist specializing in the economic and industrial base of metropolitan areas. He was formerly a research fellow at the Indian Statistical Institute, Calcutta and Deputy Director of the Centre for Urban Studies, UCL. He was a research fellow at Queen Elizabeth House, Oxford, Director of the DPU, 1982–89, and a policy consultant to the World Bank and to UNDP on the urban environment. He has had assignments in Taiwan, Indonesia, Sri Lanka, India, Kenya, Nepal, Brazil and Mexico and is the author of numerous works.

William J. Lever, Professor of Urban Studies at the University of Glasgow, has written books on industrial change in Britain, globalization, urban development on Clydeside and European cities. He has an interest in West Africa and Southeast Asia and is a consultant to national and local government in Britain, to OECD and the UN. He is the editor of the journal *Urban Studies*.

Anick Loréal, a research associate of the Agence de Développement et d'Urbanisme (ADU) of Lille, is in charge of economic research. Publications include *Lille, devenir une métropole internationale* and *Renforcer les conditions et les moteurs du développement économique: schéma directeur de l'arrondissement de Lille.*

Zilton Macedo, Senior Economist to EMPLASA, Metropolitan Planning Agency of São Paulo, took his doctoral degree at the Development Planning Unit, University College London. He is a senior lecturer at the Catholic University of São Paulo, a consultant on economic and environmental impact of larger projects and has published widely on the evolution of São Paulo industrial economy.

Om Prakash Mathur, Professor at the National Institute of Public Finance and Policy in New Delhi, has been the Director of the National Institute of Urban Affairs and worked for many years at the United Nations Centre for Regional Development in Nagoya, Japan.

Frank Moulaert, Professor of Economics at the University of Lille I, did his PhD in regional science at the University of Pennsylvania. His publications include *Cities, enterprises and society on the eve of the 21st century* (with Allen Scott), *Towards global localization* (with P. Cooke and others), *The changing geography of advanced producer services* (with P. Daniels) and *Regional analysis and the new international division of labour.*

Ricardo Samaniego, Chief Economic Advisor to the Secretary of Finance of México City, earned his degree in economics at the University of Chicago. He worked as General Director of the México City Planning Committee of the Department of the Federal District, as visiting scholar at MIT and UCLA, as economist at the IMF and as a consultant to the World Bank. He is the author of several essays and articles in the field of economics.

Jean-Francois Stevens, Doctor in Economic Science, is an Associate Professor at the University of Lille II. He is the research director of the Agence de Développement et d'Urbanisme (ADU) of Lille. His publications include *Lille Euro-cité* and *Les chances du Nord – Pas-de-Calais.*

Sandy Taylor, Head of the Economic Information Bureau, Economic Development Department at Birmingham City Council, earned his degree in economics at Aberdeen University. He is involved in aspects of strategic local economic development policy in Birmingham and has advised on recent initiatives on the regeneration of the city centre, major events and the Highbury Initiative.

Richard Tomlinson, consultant in urban and regional development, is managing a team preparing an urban infrastructure investment programme for South Africa and leading the government's research team into local economic development. As Professor at the Graduate School of Public Development Management, University of Witwatersrand, he has written several books on urban and regional issues.

Peter Townroe, Professor of Urban and Regional Studies, is Director of the School of Urban and Regional Studies at Sheffield Hallam University. For the World Bank and the UNDP he has undertaken consultancies in Pakistan, São

Paulo, Swaziland and Indonesia and recently for the Rural Development Commission and the Department of the Environment in Britain. He has published widely on issues of industrial location and urban and regional economic development.

Inauguration of the symposium

The management of cities during structural adjustment

Anupan Dasgupta

Additional Municipal Commissioner

I have been working as one of the Municipal Commissioners of Greater Bombay Municipal City Corporation for the past two and a half years, and therefore what I am going to say must be qualified in two ways. First, it does not purport to reflect the political views of the corporation and, secondly, I speak as a practising administrator in the city government, without any claim to being as expert as the distinguished group here.

Bombay's overall position can very roughly be described by way of a strength and weakness analysis. It has a very large population and therefore a very large market. It has highly skilled manpower and, by Indian standards, well developed infrastructure facilities. For many decades, perhaps a century, it has been the premier financial and commercial centre of India, a fairly modern and progressive political and administrative centre and, by way of a natural endowment, as it were, a good harbour. These have contributed in various measures to the growth of Bombay to reach its present status as the premier city of India. In the context of globalization of the country's economy and the structural adjustment that India is undergoing at the moment, these are important plus points, but the story is not one of unmixed blessings. We are acutely aware, particularly in the city government, of the large number of problems that beset Bombay.

I mentioned population as a very important economic advantage, providing a very large market. It also constitutes a major problem in as much as roughly 50 per cent of the population lives in squatter colonies, or "slums". The infrastructure facilities, which were developed with much foresight and considerable investment 50–100 years ago, are gradually becoming inadequate and do not keep pace or bear the strain imposed by this growing population. Because Bombay has always been a premier city, offering important opportunities, it has attracted many people from practically all parts of the country, and this has resulted in haphazard growth of the city in slums. Not only that, but it has a had a set of difficult implications for the economic, social and political life of the city. It is with this mixed bag of endowments and problems that we have entered the phase of globalization of the country's economy.

I will, as I said at the beginning, try to present to you a picture from below, from the bottom of the ladder as it were, in terms of what if looks like in the city government. The structure of government in India is essentially three tier: the Union government, the state government and the local government. It is the local government, the city government, that is responsible for providing the various civic services (the infrastructure) that normally keep the city going.

Bombay city government is one of the oldest in India. The Act that established the corporation dates back to 1888. It has, of course, undergone many amendments to keep pace with the changing needs over time, but at any given time the city government (I guess like city governments in other countries) is governed by a statute that cannot be altered or amended without the express approval of the state legislature. This ensures a degree of continuity and stability in the government, as well as in the instruments of government in the city. But from a different angle, it imposes severe constraints in terms of flexibility. What is already written in the Act cannot be changed by anyone within the city government. It has to be done by a group of people sitting outside. This is an important fact that must be considered when we discuss various strategies in the sessions to come.

The second aspect is that there is a politically elected element in this government, and it is large. We have as many as 221 Municipal Corporatists, who, together, constitute the Municipal Corporation. The Corporation is then subdivided for the purposes of day-to-day activities into separate committees.

Finally, there is a large administrative workforce, headed by the Municipal Commissioner. So this particular structure also has its advantages and disadvantages in terms of the ability of the city government to respond to situations or problems, and to innovate or stay on course.

The third important aspect is the factor of public participation. It might sound a little odd that we have an elected body consisting of as many as 220 people, but we specifically raise the question of public participation. It is important because of two recent developments (or rather one recent development with two aspects). The 74th Amendment to the Indian Constitution made it mandatory that, apart from the general body of the Corporation, or any administrative body like ours, there has to be ward-level committees of municipal councillors who will have a wide range of quasi-administrative and quasi-deliberative functions and powers. The second important aspect is that, for the first time perhaps, there is a recognition that, apart from the organized forms of public participation, there is room (and indeed need) for participation by non-governmental organizations (NGOs).

These are not the issues before this symposium; it is more about globalization. But one of the major concerns should be to examine how the process of globalization is likely to affect the life, the economy, and the style of functioning of various units of government in the context of a city like Bombay.

Globalization, the history of globalization, or structural adjustment across the globe, has been well documented. Unfortunately, I have not had time to go through the material, but the shared wisdom is that cities around the world have undergone a metamorphosis because of the forces released by the process of globalization at different times. Cities have responded differently, although there are certain common strategies, but the responses have been appropriate to local circumstances and geographical locations. In the context of opening up the economy of a country, it is necessary to see what the process amounts to from the point of view of a city such as Bombay and from the perspective of a "bottom–up" approach.

The responses of various cities to these changing scenarios are often characterized by innovation. Those cities that have been able to innovate successfully have been better able to address the issues and problems and get on top of them. This process of innovation calls for a flexible structure. How far is it possible for an organization such as the Municipal Corporation of Greater Bombay to be flexible in its approaches, when it is the creature of a statute that runs to over 500 sections and 20 schedules, listing in great detail what is to be done or not done under given sets of circumstances?

Every city government has broadly two groups of functions or responsibilities. One is regulatory and the other is developmental in character, to meet the need for utilities. Now, is the same form of city government responsive for both types of functions? In other words, is the same corporate structure the best instrument on one hand for handling the problems of traffic offences, of this or that breach of the norms, and on the other for undertaking to manage and operate installations such as water supply and sewerage, which have to be run on a commercial basis so that they generate enough surpluses not only for upkeep, but for future growth and development?

Another issue is the promotion of local initiative if the major problems facing the city are to be effectively handled. One of the syndromes of developing societies is over-dependence on organized government. Globalization and the forces that globalization unleashes run in a quite different direction. There is much talk about what private participation can do in, say, infrastructure projects. But it is not simply infrastructure that makes a large city tick. More essential is how the services and facilities are run and maintained. If garbage collection is a major problem, can people do something themselves? How can they constitute themselves into local groups that will assist the municipal machinery in efficient collection and disposal of garbage? These are issues that are important even in a complete market economy.

In the twenty-first century, Bombay will be part of an age of information technologies, and services will be the mainstay of Bombay's economy (or, for that matter, any city's economy) instead of traditional manufacturing. But is it possible for us to attain that status while we persist with our usual forms of city government?

Nasser Munjee

HDFC and Bombay First

It was Nigel Harris who, three years ago, sparked off a great debate on Bombay. His whirlwind tour of the city and his lecture at the Bombay Municipal Commission generated much interest, and the British Council organized a series of seminars stimulated by that debate on various aspects of Bombay – housing, telecommunications, transport. As a result of these seminars, the seeds of the idea of Bombay First were sown. We have taken it a little further now by actually establishing it, using the concept of London First (the concept, not the details) to create an institutional forum to start thinking about, and systematically investigating, some of the key issues that this city faces.

It is important in this part of the world because Asia is changing so dramatically. I was at a seminar in Vienna two weeks ago on cities and structural change. I learned that Hong Kong is investing nearly US$25 billion in its new airport and infrastructure services, which could change the face of that city. The people concerned understand the importance of the connectedness of Hong Kong to the rest of the world. In shipping, Hong Kong handles 11 million containers each year. Six berths are added to the port every six months. When I asked the chairman of Bombay Port Trust how long it takes to add a berth to our new port, he said about six years. That is the relative pace of change we seem to have here. China is setting up, or is thinking of setting up, very efficient ports (14 new cities on the eastern seaboard) to enhance its connectedness, and three new ports around Hong Kong. Now, that is the pace of change.

Last October, Jordan and Israel signed a peace agreement, and now a new city is being planned on the Gulf of Aquaba, jointly, as a commercial port city. Beirut is now emerging from the ashes, and in the next five years, if there is a sustained peace, Beirut will compete very dramatically as a financial centre for that part of the world. Shanghai is changing day by day and, when China takes over Hong Kong in 1977, there will have to be two major financial centres operating. And when one thinks of Bombay and its tremendous potential advantages as a port city, a financial centre, a commercial centre and an entertainment centre, it has so many economic strengths that we need to ask the question: who is going to think about its future, draw up the strategies and give it a sense of direction? And then who is going to implement these ideas? What is the mechanism, the governing system, to see that things actually happen?

We are in a city that is basically frozen because of our land laws, rent control laws, development control rules and zoning regulations. There is a development control rule saying that you cannot build a single square foot of office space on the island city of Bombay while India is going through a dramatic economic reform. Real estate prices, as a consequence, have risen from US$200 per square foot, in 1991, to US$1200 per square foot today, i.e. in the past five years of economic reform. As a result, office space for rental or purchase has become more expensive than Tokyo, more expensive than Hong Kong, and we do not have the competitive advantages of Tokyo or Hong Kong. These are scarcity rents that have been driven up because the city is frozen. We have not taken a view as to how we are going to adapt to this future. We are still stuck in the old philosophical paradigm of decongestion. We must unfreeze our cities.

So we face various problems, and I do not pretend that Bombay First is going to solve them, but it will create the basic paradigm for thought and public debate. We will not produce solutions but stimulate informed public debate and, if we can create informed public debate, play a major role. This seminar is just the beginning. I am grateful to Nigel for coming to Bombay and having this meeting here. We are going to listen to you very attentively, and we hope that as a result of this we will have many new ideas at the end of the day.

Coming away from Vienna, one of the things that you hear happening throughout cities in Europe (perhaps we hear it a little here too) is that planners now are the instruments of citizens. Citizen participation, people's participation in their own cities as far as the environment and services are concerned, is extremely important. That participative process must be permitted through the mechanism of local government, private partnerships, non-governmental organization partnerships and new institutional forms that will need to emerge.

Introduction

Nigel Harris

"Structural adjustment" – or "macroeconomic reform" – has become an obsession of the world's governments, in both the richest and the poorest countries. As a policy stance, it has become as universal as import-substituting protectionism was in the developed countries in the 1930s and 1940s, and in the developing countries in the 1950s and 1960s.

Furthermore, the agenda of reforms has become strikingly uniform, both among economists and between countries, summarized in John Williamson's "Washington Consensus" (1990). The reform programme has become the target for what Bergstein and Williamson call "a global stampede in the last quarter of the twentieth century" (Williamson 1994: 3). They continue:

> Countries of every geographical region, income level and ideology, have joined the rush. Asians, Europeans, Latin Americans and Africans: countries once among the richest in the world (such as Argentina, Australia and New Zealand) and countries near the bottom: capitalists, socialists and those in between.

The political diversity of the reforming governments is indeed remarkable. The range includes overtly communist regimes (China from 1978, Vietnam from 1989, Laos from 1990, apart from the much older attempts at market reform in the former Soviet Union and eastern Europe), social democratic or Labour (Australia, New Zealand, Spain, Portugal, France), liberal conservative (President Reagan's USA, Mrs Thatcher's Britain), Leftist–populist regimes (Menem's Peronists in Argentina, the PRI in Mexico under the last three presidents), and the newly democratizing Russia and eastern Europe.

Structural adjustment is supposedly unpopular. It has the reputation of requiring authoritarian regimes. Yet only a handful of countries have experienced a military coup preceding and dictatorship during the reforms – Suharto in Indonesia (1966), Pinochet in Chile (1973), Turkey in 1980, Ghana in 1983 and South Korea in 1980 (by contrast, most military coups have not led to reform – witness the cases of Argentina, Uruguay, Nigeria, etc.). On the contrary, in so far as the reform package can be seen as both the result and the means to achieve global integration, it can be credited with the destruction of some important authoritarian regimes, strikingly so in the case of both the old Soviet Union and apartheid South Africa.

In some cases, a dedicated minority have fought to come to power in order to reform. But more often, it is the old order that has been forced to reform by the exigencies of the short-run management of the economy. Indeed, in some cases, political leaders have come to power with one set of aims (or one reputation) and have been converted in office – most strikingly in the cases of President Mitterand in France in the early 1980s, of President Menem in Argentina, Finance Minister Kwesi Batchwey in Ghana, and Finance Minister Manmohan Singh in India.[1]

Furthermore, so universal has the new orthodoxy become, if its opponents come to power, they rarely seek to return to the *status quo ante*. Even in Chile, where the reform regime came to power through violence, leaving a legacy of at least anguish, at most a demand for retribution, President Aylwin has modified only marginally the policy framework put in place by General Pinochet (Bosworth et al. 1994).

The universality of the change, acting upon an immense diversity of national situations, suggests common causes external to each country – the demands made upon each national economy by the emergence of an integrated, as opposed to an interdependent, global economy. Thus, the shift is not an ephemeral turn of intellectual fashion nor the temporary dominance of a particular group of political leaders. Each national economy is being reshaped to a new phase in the development of the system, having enforced upon it common disciplines regardless of local circumstances. As a result of the new global economy, governments have become increasingly unclear as to what their national economy is, what the national interest is, since they appear to be administering no more than a fragment of a much larger whole, which is outside their control. This is one of the factors in the dissolution of the traditional political alignments of the corporatist Right and the *dirigiste* Left, which shared a belief in a powerful state.

The change has undermined the old certainties of national policy. Economic nationalism offered a set of relatively clear criteria as to what the national interest was – in imports as opposed to exports, in capital inflows and outflows, in the ownership of capital, and so on. The new order in these matters has become opaque.

The national economy is embodied in its territorial parts, and the cities play a peculiar role within that, a role of extraordinary importance. They are the most dynamic centres of modern production, and it is understandable that the changes in the national relationship to the world economy as a result

---

1. Mr Manmohan Singh had a reputation for great caution, but once in office, acted "with unprecedented boldness and speed" – Little et al. 1993: 127.

of structural adjustment could have the most radical effects on the urban economy. This can be seen most dramatically in the countries of East and Southeast Asia – particularly in China – as the by-products of rapid economic growth, itself in part the result of macroeconomic reform.

However, the more local the economy, the more peculiar its disaggregated output of goods and services, and, therefore, the more unique its relationship to the national and world economies. Each city has a different starting point, a different historical inheritance, a different resource endowment (and each city's unique location is one of its resources), and it operates in a different political and policy framework. Thus, reactions to the uniform programme would be peculiar to each city, even if we could isolate the effects of reform as opposed to other changes; for example, sudden increases in oil prices, the general fluctuations of the business cycle, and so on. Often, reforms are precipitated precisely by these types of shock rather than adopted as a considered choice of policy. If, as in China, reform promotes or supports rapid economic growth, then the growth itself is likely to produce rapid structural change. Thus, the temptation to draw quick "lessons" from the contemporary record of the restructuring of city economies must be resisted, since it so easily becomes a superficial exercise. But even with this qualification, something can perhaps be learned from the history of the past two decades of economic restructuring even if, most frequently, these are negative lessons: what should not be attempted, rather than what should.

Perhaps one of the lessons is the importance of "flexibility" (Killick 1995; on cities, cf. Harris 1994), the capacity of markets and institutions to adjust with reasonable speed to changes in the economic environment.[2] Rigidities seem to force delayed responses and then, as a result, sudden rupture; a city that has incrementally adjusted over a long period to changes in the demand for its output then suddenly faces a crisis in which adjustment is somehow paralyzed. Inner-city dereliction is one vivid demonstration of the incapacity to make incremental adjustments (illustrated well in several of the later chapters in this book). At the other extreme, Hong Kong's successive self-transformations offer an example of impressive flexibility, capable at each stage of capturing and exploiting opportunities. In looking at cities, one is

---

2. There are grave difficulties in measuring "flexibility". Caneri for Turkey (in Williamson 1994) seeks to illustrate the increase in flexibility as a result of reform in the following way:

> It took six years for the government to react to the first oil price increase, over six months to the major financial crisis of 1983, six weeks to the exchange crisis of 1987, six days to the 1990 Gulf War, and now six hours to major external changes.

Ricardo Samaniego, at the Bombay symposium, offered a Mexican parallel – Mexico was able to return to the international bond market only 70 years after the largest financial crisis of the country in the nineteenth century; seven years after the crisis of 1982 (which led the debt crisis of the developing countries in the 1980s); but only seven months after the financial crisis of early 1995.

thus concerned not just with the scale of threat posed by changes in the economic environment, but why some cities find such difficulties in reacting appropriately, or take such a long time to draw appropriate lessons and search for new alternatives.

Recession is the time when economies – and their flexibility – are most tested, when, as Peter Townroe puts it in his chapter on Sheffield, there is a "whirlwind blowing". Managing the city in crisis is, to change the imagery, like planning on horseback: the sheer pace of events overwhelms the capacity to be clear-headed. The developed countries, with some variations, have experienced three major downturns in the past two decades, and they have had important but differing effects on cities. To oversimplify, the first (in the mid-1970s) hit very hard a set of heavy industrial cities that had long been in some decline (the prototypes might include Glasgow, Hamburg and the Ruhr, Pittsburg, etc.). The second, at the end of the 1970s and the beginning of the 1980s, afflicted the high-growth manufacturing cities of the postwar period, those that in the immediate past had seemed so prosperous, they could not be affected severely (e.g. Birmingham and the West Midlands in Britain, Detroit in the USA). Finally, the third in the early 1990s affected many of the new servicing activities that had grown so swiftly in the 1980s. Increasingly cities were required to reorganize both their economies and their institutions, and with speed. It was an approach to city management that was quite incompatible with the old forms of city planning, with their calm expectation of being able to shape the city over 20 years.[3] The shocks were different, the speed of change and of learning very different, although those managing cities learned much from each other in trying to react sensibly to these waves of destruction and creation. In many manufacturing cities, much time and treasure was initially devoted to trying to sustain or expand industry: industrial estates, enterprise zones and advance factories, with associated incentives, proliferated. As cities competed, such responses became increasingly expensive and risky; they had poor results if judged by the criterion of reducing unemployment. Cities shifted almost universally from seeking to facilitate the development of a wide array of servicing activity, to making themselves international centres of culture and major transport junctions.

A small part of this story is told in the selection of case studies presented herein. But often the experience of particular cities is difficult to evaluate.

---

3. Henning et al. (1991) cite in this connection the decline of the Urban Policy Unit in the Dortmund City Council:

> Once an influential policy unit attached to the Chief City Manager, [it] has lost most of its importance . . . due to a vanishing belief in the manageability and efficiency of comprehensive urban development planning and programming, and to the strengthened line departments and the "rise of semi-public institutions" – Chambers of Commerce, Trade and Crafts, the Land Development Corporation, the Labour Office, trade unions, universities and polytechnics, political parties, and other organizations, in sum representing a new form of urban governance.

There have been few attempts by national or local governments to evaluate the outcome. The criteria for so doing are not always apparent, nor is the time period over which the evaluation should be undertaken; when has a city successfully made the transition from the old to the new? Just under a decade after the 1973 downturn, military coup and introduction of the radical reform programme, Santiago de Chile experienced a very severe economic crisis; an evaluation taken then would have cast grave doubts on the merits of "structural adjustment". High unemployment persisted in the city, and the country, up to 1986, 13 years after the reform project began.

Furthermore, issues of growing severity – the decline in the real incomes of the lowest quarter of the US labour force and the persistent tendency for unemployment levels to rise higher in Europe at each point in the business cycle, as well as the growing inequality of incomes – undermine the proud claims of city fathers to have made the successful transition from a manufacturing to high-value-added service centre. On the other hand, Guangzhou in southern China bursts with prosperity; never before have so many people been employed there.

Macroeconomic reforms and cities

What are some of the key policy pointers in the reform package for cities? Some of them can be listed as follows:

The decline in a differentially discriminating protectionist regime, affecting differently the range of outputs from the city, its exporting capacities, and the prices of both domestically produced and imported inputs to the city's output, with knock-on effects both in terms of employment and incomes and in the relative physical deterioration of some areas while others expand. Exchange rate policy plays a key role here in damping down or enhancing these effects.

It is difficult to separate the effects here of liberalization and other forces of structural change (including the impact of new technology), but the decline of protection must have had some important effects on the composition of output of European and American cities, perhaps forcing or accelerating urban deindustrialization. Comparable processes in the decline of manufacturing can also be seen in Accra and Santiago de Chile but, on the other hand, the decline of industry, and the growth of "sick industries" in Indian cities (and its spread beyond metropolitan boundaries), long pre-dates the reform programme.

The opportunities for manufactured exports (and, later, labour-intensive service exports) have received the most attention and there are some remarkable performances here, nowhere more dramatic than in southern China (on another dramatic case, the expansion of Bangladesh textiles, see Rhee 1990;

the literature on the industrialization of the Mexican border with the US is vast, but see Sklair 1989). Expansion in labour-intensive manufacture for exports has had dramatic effects in terms of employment, again with ramifications for the expansion of the domestic market, for increased inmigration of particular types of workers and for the generation of capital.

Expanded exports test the existing and often already inadequate infrastructure to the limit. Poor services in the city can neutralize any comparative advantage in production for export and hence can damage both jobs and incomes in the city.

There are some important reservations here. For example, it appears that developing countries currently have a comparative advantage in energy-intensive manufactured exports, that is, those forms of production that impose maximum strain on the natural environment. Given that the proportion of output moved is expanding faster than the growth of production, a disproportionate growth of freight movement is also implied by the export orientation, further tending to damage environmental quality (particularly air). Thus, in the absence of a suitably strengthened environmental governance, two by-products of expanded exports can have a severe deleterious effect (Harris 1992), and can thereby make more difficult the expansion of service exports or tourism.

Opening up the economy forces the modernization of the transport system to make the movement of goods and people reach international standards of cost and speed. In the case of old ports, the implications of unitization/ containerization are well known in terms of rapid declines in dock employment, as productivity rises at extraordinary rates, and the radical contraction in the space requirements for port facilities (particularly where, as usually happens, the docks are relocated to greenfield sites, leaving inner-city docks derelict). Often, the demand for land in old railway systems also declines, making considerable areas available for redevelopment. Some cities have embraced the opportunity of declining dock and railway areas (with associated decline in inner-city industrial areas) to initiate major urban redevelopment schemes that support new economic roles – as in Hamburg, New York, Yokohama (the Minato Mirai 21 Plan), Sydney (Darling Bay), or London's Docklands or proposed King's Cross scheme.

The need for greater reliability and speed – as the unit weight of goods declines (economizing on materials and energy to move goods) – epitomized in just-in-time stock policies, will tend to shift cargo to airfreight, implying a major expansion in airfreight facilities (warehousing, custom processing, air docking facilities, etc.) and in the access points and surface transport management leading to the airport. There are other opportunities for associated free trade zones, air services centres, and so on. Increases in tourism and in the export of labour-intensive services accentuates the vital role of air terminals in the city economy, and explains the intensified competition by cities in the provision of airports (exemplified in East Asia with new airports being developed in Hong Kong and Seoul, and planned in Shanghai and Taipei, following the opening of Kansai and, in Southeast Asia, the upgrading of Bangkok and, earlier, Singapore's Changi).

Improved air services make an expansion in tourism possible, with ramifications in the manufacturing and agricultural supply sectors. Furthermore, important local services can then become export sectors – as, for example, with health or educational facilities – by taking in foreign clients. The development of cultural activities becomes of economic significance in supporting this expansion in tourism. The quality of life in the city, including its environmental standards and the maintenance of security, become important economic factors in sustaining service exports and tourism.

The increasing role of foreign capital has important effects in accelerating the technical upgrading of city output and the volume of flows through financial centres. Where local authorities recognize the importance of foreign capital, it can also force competitive upgrading of infrastructure (to attract investment) and competitive debureaucratization: southern China's local authorities compete to facilitate the entry of foreign capital and, in doing so, deregulate. Some Indian states (e.g. Andhra, Karnataka, West Bengal) are already competing strongly for foreign investment, and the larger cities are likely to follow suit, as in China

Changes in public finance have important implications for cities. The decline in consumer subsidies, or their more accurate targeting, and the reform of public service provision can affect both general consumption and the position of the poor. The reform of local authority finances, from increased privatization of services to increased local taxes, and in some cases increased local authority debts, have implications for public employment, living standards and markets.

The city economy, like the national economy, is also less protected against external fluctuations and shock. The rapidity with which financial flows can enter and leave countries in an integrated system can threaten the underlying stability of the economy, as occurred in Mexico in January 1995. In one particular sector, real estate prices, Renaud (1995) has shown how Japanese credit policy in the late 1980s was most important in inflating land prices in many major cities in the world, and then led the way in the collapse of prices. Land pricing, particularly in the downtown area, has a key role in shaping urban development, the effectiveness of public intervention, and the pattern and location of economic activity.

It seems that an increased proportion of city economic activity is slipping below the threshold of statistical recording: it is "informalizing". For example, Bombay's textile industry, located in the central city area, employed some 220000 workers 25 years ago, but now there are possibly no more than 60000; at the same time as this decline in the formal sector, on the periphery of the metropolitan region, the informal "power loom industry" has developed and now possibly employs as many as 150000. If this general trend is real and universal, it is still not clear how far the phenomenon is related to the opening up of economies and the intensification of competition, as opposed to the growth in formal sector labour costs and regulation, or the effect of new technology, and so on. However, from the point of view of national and local governance, the change implies increasing difficulty in monitoring and managing the economy, a larger part of which is not recorded in the existing data. It becomes impossible to make inferences from the official data series; or at least, what is happening in official output figures, for example, must be matched against electricity consumption (as happened in Italy in the late 1970s to assess the size and growth of the black economy) or other indirect indices of activity. Increased unemployment or decreased real incomes no longer indicate degrees of hardship and have to be matched against the much rarer sample surveys of household consumption (see the anomalies in 1980s Mexico in this question, in Lustig 1992: 61–95). None the less, whether city activities are fully recorded or not, they are part of the system that generates the employment and incomes of the citizens, and are therefore no less deserving facilitation and support than activities that are recorded.

It also appears to be the case that the processes of reform are forcing *de facto*, if not always *de jure*, decentralization of government. Formal legislative changes have been important in some countries (e.g. for example, France, Colombia, India), but even without such changes, local areas – states in federal systems, provinces or cities – seem to be acquiring greater powers of initiative and responsibility for local economic management. That initiative can promote disaster, as with the debts of French local authorities, each borrowing to compete to become a "Eurocultural metropolis". Decentralization permits greater degrees of flexibility in relation to external shocks and allows the reshaping of external demands to fit local potential more closely. But it requires a more sophisticated approach to world events at the local level, and the backing of much more local data. Part of that sophistication is in evaluating the effect of national policies on the city, and pressing the city's case for policy reform by the national government.

Not all these issues are equally related directly to the reform package; but in sum, they constitute a new context within which cities operate and a new agenda of urban policy issues.

How have cities reacted?

City reactions

Different cities have reacted in different ways and at different speeds, but in general, this process culminated, as we have seen, in abandoning the attempt to protect or restore the old industrial economy in order to absorb unemployment. For the first time for a long time, city managers endeavoured to see the city economy as a whole rather than seeing only a few priority sectors (of which manufacturing was traditionally the main one) and a bundle of inter-dependent activities, to see it in an international context rather than a national or regional one, to think of the future (and there was a flood of reports on various cities in the new millennium) in terms of flexible scenarios founded in a consensus of city interests rather than the technically expert master plan. Local government shifted its role from being a public provider of services to being part of the leadership of the city: the political overtook the technical and infrastructural.

The city was now conceived as essentially a centre of service provision and flows for markets and audiences far outside the control or even the knowledge of the local or national governments. What were these services?

- the traditional if ill defined complex of business or producer and pro-fessional services, part of which is related to manufacturing activity, located outside the urban economy (as for example in the case of Lyons)
- personal services, part of which is closely related to the quality of life and tourism in the city
- financial services
- along with commercial, retail and wholesale trade, hotels and restau-rants.

London, peculiar in this respect, recorded a decline in manufacturing employment of some 800 000 over the preceding two decades, and an increase in financial and business services to reach roughly 800 000. Given this com-plex, what specifically export-orientated activities can be built upon it?

Tourism, both local and international, is an obvious favourite, and cities set about creating comparative advantages in this field through the obvious tactics of developing local amenities, from waterside facilities to the rehabil-itation (or invention) of historical quarters, museums, and so on. The old industrial cities required general rehabilitation if they were to exploit their potential, and much ingenuity has been directed to renovating old buildings and localities to perform a modern role. But there were other key sectors con-tributing to specialized tourism, as well as other important cultural exports. London discovered in the early 1990s that it had 215 000 workers employed in the manufacture and delivery of "culture": everything from music, drama and museums to the antiques and book trades (Kennedy 1991). The cultural complex underpinned the substantial international movement to participate in London's financial activities; that is to say, the two were mutually self-reinforcing. Cities also developed export sectors in the provision of special-ized medical care (Singapore, London, San Diego, Tijuana, Barcelona, Bogota, etc.), and this was often, although not invariably, related to a complex of teaching and research hospitals, clinics and university medical facilities, which in turn, by attracting foreign students, made local higher educational institutions an export sector. Most cities came to aspire to have a local uni-

9

versity, to add to or expand the existing ones (as Hamburg created its Technical University), and to exploit them both as exporters but as also centres of innovation and research for local commercial and manufacturing enterprises. Yet other cities endeavoured to use sports as a means to sustain local markets, as with Indianapolis (Smith-Heimer 1993: 18–25) or Sheffield, and in the case of Barcelona, a successful bid for the 1992 Olympic Games was exploited to seek to transform the whole city and position it for a new complex of roles long after the Games had been held.

Cities might abandon the attempt to protect the old assembly industries, with their mass employment, but they sought to retain a key role in industrial innovation, linking to universities and research centres, science parks and technopoles. The models were American, whether in the formal initiative of North Carolina's Research Triangle, or the spontaneous grouping of innovatory companies in Silicon Valley (associated initially with Stanford University) or outside Harvard–MIT in Cambridge and Boston. Many technopoles were developed in Japan. In Europe, Berlin, with a long history of massive subsidies from the old West Germany, was particularly ambitious in this respect. Fos in France, Cambridge in Britain and many others were developed not as instruments to sustain employment (the objective of the old industrial policies) but as means to capture the rewards of innovation. In time, everyone seemed to have a science park, many of them not linked to any institutionalized research capacity; others were empty of activity or financially driven to accept warehousing in lieu of the elusive "high tech". However, the more advanced required high-level communications, so the development of telecommunications, airports and motorway networks or high-speed trains were key elements reinforcing this effort.

Just as manufacturing processes had been "unbundled" earlier in order that different parts of the final output could be made in different countries, the same thing has been happening in services. Many cities in developing countries have thus been able to develop labour-intensive service exports – as with software programming for California in Bombay and Bangalore, data loading and processing for American and Canadian public and private agencies and companies in the Caribbean and East Asia, and for Japanese clients in China and the Philippines (where British police records are also loaded and processed). It is likely that this kind of activity will expand in the future in much the same way as manufactured exports led the growth in developing countries, and cities will benefit from this in so far as they are able to provide a favourable environment and an appropriately skilled labour force.

The elements of the favourable environment have been mentioned in the earlier discussion, and they range from the effectiveness of the local and national government, to the quality of life of the city, through to the transport and other infrastructural service provisions. Innovations here – for example, the creation of new airports, the introduction of high-speed trains, improvements in telecommunications – can have strong effects in expanding the rest of the economy. The role of government in managing and maintaining this environment thus becomes very much more important in securing the facilitating context without which the area will decline.

Earlier it was mentioned that decentralization of governmental power seemed to be forced by the liberalization of economies, but this is not simply between the established tiers of the existing public powers. In many cities, new coalitions of urban interests have emerged to assume a responsibility for thinking about the future of the city, including, as well as the city authorities, the chamber of commerce and other business associations, craft associations and trade unions, universities, non-governmental organizations, the political parties and citizen groups. This is the forum upon which the consensus for the plan is created. It is also the focus both for efforts to promote the city for the immediate purposes of attracting capital or talented people, and facilitating their relocation to the city, and for pressurizing or representing the interests of the city to higher levels of government and to international agencies (in Europe, all larger cities maintain some lobbying capacity in the headquarters of the European Union in Brussels).

In some cases, the development of a forum has promoted research on the city and more systematic means to create, on a continuing basis, the relevant data (and to produce in some cases a statistical yearbook for the city). Adequate and timely information is the key both to flexibility and to being able to exploit opportunities that may occur only momentarily; the key to creating an entrepreneurial city. Timely intelligence is the key to increasing speed and accuracy of reactions, of the increased awareness by the city authorities of the city's strengths and weaknesses, and of the opportunities and threats confronting them. It is also a vital factor in promoting the city and in supplying the arguments for persuading the national government and other agencies of the validity of the city's case. In the old order, few city officials had much idea of their city's comparative strengths and weaknesses, and almost no incentive to find them out; they have now become of vital importance if the city is to have some chance of shaping its destiny.

Endnote

We live in contradictory times, times of great intellectual confusion, in which the old order of separate semi-closed national economies is far from gone, the new globally integrated economy only dimly sensed. The city, traditionally fearsome and magnificent, the stuff of great terrors and hopes, remains a spectacular achievement in terms of the concentration of intelligence, an intelligence that manages much of the global system. If anything, that role is being enhanced rather than reduced by the processes of restructuring and enhancement of services. The process of change is painful as much for its impact on employment and incomes as on inherited ways of life and long-standing expectations, but it also allows the emergence of a new level of creativity in the city, of experiment and innovation – after the long night of almost complete state domination and the tyranny of state rivalries. There are grounds for optimism as well as for fears.

References

Bosworth, B. P., R. Dornbusch, R. Labán (eds) 1994. *The Chilean economy: policy lessons and challenges*. Washington DC: The Brookings Institution.

Harris, N. 1992. Wastes, the environment and the international economy. *Cities* **9**(3), 177–85.

—1994. *Structural adjustment and cities: three papers*. Working Paper 63, Development Planning Unit, University College London.

Henning, W., W. F. Kahnert, K. R. Kunzmann 1991. Restructuring and industrial economy: breaking up traditional structures in Dortmund, Germany. In *Urban regeneration in a changing economy*, E. F. Fox-Przeworski, J. Goddard, E. de Jong (eds), 1–17. Oxford: Oxford University Press.

Kennedy, R. et al. 1991. *London: world city moving into the twenty-first century*. London Planning Advisory Committee and others. London: HMSO.

Killick, T. (ed.) 1995. *The flexible economy: causes and consequences of the adaptability of national economies*, London: Routledge / Overseas Development Institute.

Little, I. M. D., R. Cooper, W. M. Corden, S. Rajapatirama 1993. *Boom, crisis and readjustment: the macroeconomic experience of developing countries*. New York: World Bank / Oxford University Press.

Lustig, N. 1992. *Mexico: the remaking of an economy*. Washington DC: Brookings Institution.

Renaud, B. 1995. *The 1985–94 global real estate cycle: its causes and consequences*. Policy Research Working Paper 1452, World Bank (Financial Sector Development Department), Washington DC.

Rhee, Y. W. & T. Belot 1990. *Export catalysts in low-income countries: a review of eleven success stories*. Discussion Paper 72, World Bank, Washington DC.

Sklair, L. 1989. *Assembling for development: the maquila industry in Mexico and the United States*. Boston: Unwin Hyman.

Smith-Heimer, J. 1993. *Contemporary economic development in US cities: five case studies* [mimeo; report prepared for the US Agency for International Development and the City of Warsaw: seminar on economic development issues and options]. USAID, Warsaw:

Williamson, J. 1990. *Latin American adjustment: how much has happened?* Washington DC: Institute of International Economics.

Williamson, J. (ed.) 1994. *The political economy of policy reform*. Washington DC: Institute of International Economics.

CHAPTER ONE
New economic roles

The changing structure of the city economy

Peter M. Townroe

Introduction

The physical fabric of cities, once established, changes only slowly. But the nature of the economic and social activity undertaken within that fabric may be transformed rapidly – within decades rather than over decades. And in any case the overall balance of that activity may shift as the physical fabric is extended, pushed ahead as the population and the income of each city increases. These changes will reflect a redefinition of the role played by each city within the wider national society and within the international economy.

At the end of the twentieth century, coming from a variety of circumstances in their individual histories, cities in both the richer and poorer countries of the world find themselves facing a new degree of exposure to external social and economic forces. Their internal forces for change, forces of growth, of marketplace inventiveness, of developmental investments and of evolving local policies and institutions are being reinforced by a particularly strong set of external pressures. These pressures are coming both from the impact of worldwide new technologies and from related international policy developments. The relevant technologies have to do with transport and communication, and the policy developments have to do with the reduction of barriers between nations in the traded flow of goods and services and in the varying flows of finance capital.

This introduction offers a brief reflection on this new context of the international economy for the cities of the world in the last quarter of the twentieth century. The evolving economic environment may be seen as pushing the economies of the major cities in a country towards playing new roles in their relationships with other cities, as well as in their linkages with their hinterlands. These new roles are redefining urban policy agendas across the world, requiring a broadening of perspective by urban governments. For in this new world, cities can be seen to fail, at least not to maintain real income per head, or perhaps to lose population. The adjustments required to the structures of the urban economies for the new roles have a tendency to result in losers as well as winners in the inhabitants of each city.

Changing roles for cities are coming at a time of a worldwide explosion in city growth. United Nations population estimates (UN 1994) indicate that, by 1990, 43% of the population of the world (or 2.3 billion people) lived in urban areas.[1] The urban population is growing some two and a half times faster than its rural counterpart. By the year 2025, the forecast is for a worldwide urban population of well over 5 billion, three-quarters of whom will be living in countries currently regarded as "developing". By the year 2010, 26 urban agglomerations will have a population in excess of 10 million, 21 of these being in developing countries. A further 33 or so cities will lie in the population range of 5–10 million. To a greater or lesser degree, the growth of these cities is fuelled by their participation in the international economy.

Taking the term "structural adjustment" in its conventional meaning – of liberalization of economies to market forces; of a relative withdrawal of government from price setting and marketplace control, of movement towards orderly public finances, and of an opening up towards an export focus in international trade relations – there is a danger in seeing it as a one-off change. After all, a given regulation can only be removed once without being re-imposed, a public sector budget can only move from deficit to balance once without moving back into deficit. Present discussions of macroeconomic reforms, especially in relation to poorer nations, have the danger of seeing the adjustments as a process to be passed through, to come out on the other side into a new, and more desirable, steady state. Although that may be a justifiable perspective in terms of policy regimes, it may blind observers to the obvious truism that economic structures will continue to change, under the new policy regime as under the old. And indeed, one of the prime consequences of the new policy regime is that, other things being equal, economic structures henceforth will tend to change more rapidly than hitherto. In this sense, the message for city governments is that structural adjustment is never ending.

Human creativity combines with the rich random and planned information environments of cities to ensure a continuing dynamism. And although this dynamism is obviously more active in some cities than in others, no city stands still. Its economy, its society, its institutions and culture – all are in continuous movement. The concept of "management" in cities in relation to structural adjustment has therefore to be based on an evolutionary view of strategy and on a flexibility of response to changing circumstance. City governments are necessarily working in a tension: to provide specific infrastructures and required urban services, while trying not, in so doing, to impose

---

1. The statistics quoted in this chapter, with the exception of the UN population figures presented here, are all taken from (World Bank 1995).

rigidities of response in the future. As a city develops, certain options for the future close off; or can only be reopened at great expense. The location of the city airport is one example; reclaiming built land for public parks is another; widening key arterial roads another. At the same time city governments face a further tension. On the one hand, this is between supporting the producer interest in the city economy, seeking to facilitate change to meet opportunity and to raise the productivity of land, labour and capital; and, on the other hand, defending the consumer interest, an interest buffeted by changes in incomes, in access to services and facilities and in possible degradations to the local natural environment.

It might be argued that the idea of city and national governments seeking to re-intervene in order to manage the forces released by policies of disengagement and liberation involves a contradiction. But experience shows that management is needed. This is demonstrated in the case study cities in this volume. The opportunities provided by the policies of structural adjustment, of greater international involvement and faster aggregate economic growth require governmental responses. This is most clear in the provision of infrastructure, of facilities, of necessary public services. At the same time, the relative losers in the process require protection, or at least a framework for reorientation and redeployment. And for many cities in the world there is a severe management requirement imposed by increases in population, and in levels of income, increases that would be there with or without the particular national economic policy changes termed structural adjustment that have been introduced since the mid-1970s.

In the next section, some points are made in relating *new* economic roles in cities to the continuation of *existing* roles. The fundamental reasons for the existence and maintenance of cities have not changed. Contrasts are then briefly drawn between dominant characteristics of cities in richer and in poorer countries. *The context of the world economy* enlarges on the comments made above in relation to the changing context of the world economy, in particular the forces of "globalization".

New roles for cities in MDCs and *New roles for cities in LDCs* explore the implications of these external economic changes for cities in the more and less developed countries, in both cases pointing to opportunities as well as problems. A conclusion here is that, in both cases, the changes in the world economic system are exposing the urban economies to a requirement for repeated change as perhaps never before: a need for dynamic response, with failure to respond resulting in relative economic decline.

Emerging urban geographies and *Emerging structural issues* point towards emerging urban geographies and structural profiles in major cities. It is then from these geographies and profiles and the questions they generate that the urban policy agenda is emerging. Reflection on the experience of the past two decades or so demonstrates how in so many cities the rapidity of change seems to have pushed city governments into a policy of "coping incrementalism" rather than of pursuing a bold-but-informed strategy. There are important lessons to be learned here from the exchange of experience between cities.

The final section of this introduction underlines a tension that is fairly recent on the agenda of city governments worldwide. A combination of rising public awareness and concern, and international pressures from agreements such as Agenda 21 (reached at the Rio Earth Summit in 1992) require city governments to confront the grosser environmental consequences of urban growth. Conflicts between producer and consumer interests, and between rising GDP income and a quality-of-life adjusted income, were always present for city governments. Arguably, structural adjustment towards more open and market-orientated economies will force urban governments, and their national counterparts, to respond to these conflicts, openly and explicitly, as never before.

Cities, rich and poor

Cities reflect a tension between centripetal and centrifugal forces. The abstractions of the standard urban economic model highlight the resulting balance (Henderson 1977). On the production side of the urban economy there are, relative to the size of the city, both internal and external economies of scale, which encourage spatial agglomeration. These economies of scale are particularly strong in many of the infrastructure services in the city, both in "hard" infrastructures such as transportation networks and utilities as well as in the "soft", such as universities and hospitals. These economies typically (but not always) build upon an initial natural advantage – a harbour, a river crossing, a water supply – an advantage that can possibly turn out to be a disadvantage as the city becomes over time very much larger.

The centripetal forces of agglomeration are countered by centrifugal forces that encourage dispersal of both residence and workplace from the earlier growing urban core. These are, for example, the forces of commuter costs in time and money, and of land costs at the centre, which rise faster than other factor costs for both housing and industrial and commercial activity. The costs rise with a rising population, but especially with rising real incomes in the city. At the same time there are non-market costs in both production and consumption, which encourage decentralization. These may be, for example, the costs of congestion and pollution.

In both rich and poor cities, policy-makers have frequently sought to reinforce these centrifugal forces by land-use controls or financial incentives. The basic but sometimes unspoken rationale for this lies in an imbalance between the advantage of private cost and benefit for the marginal household or industrial or commercial producer, and the social costs and benefits of the existing or average household or producer already located in the city. However, the arithmetic here is problematic. Such policy regimes have had mixed success, often with what have come to be considered deleterious side effects for the strength and flexibility of the urban economy.

Fundamentally, cities exist and grow around a core dynamic scale-economy. This core advantage rests in the economic value that results from the exchange of information and knowledge. It is an advantage that builds upon the accumulation of all forms of capital in the city, both physical and human. This simple notion, which reflects a complex reality, provides a basis for understanding the relative growth and decline of cities in richer countries, as well as in the newly emergent industrializing and in the poorer and predominantly agricultural countries.

Worldwide, the sharing of the essential economic forces of concentration and deconcentration in cities is also seen in the sharing of the essential technologies that support both the centripetal and the centrifugal forces. For all of their differences, the major cities of the world share broadly similar technologies of transportation, of energy supply and of services such as education and health care. The major technological differences lie in the degrees of capital intensity (metro systems, water-borne sewerage, etc.), rather than in fundamentally different technologies. They also share the characteristic of dependence upon external trade linkages for their prosperity. The linkages are with their immediate hinterlands, with other cities across the country and, increasingly, with other cities across the world. A city's capability to sustain and to develop these linkages, whether the city is rich or poor, in per capita terms, is fundamental to its economic sustainability and growth.

Given the comments above, with their emphasis on the similarities of the forces within the cities of both rich and poor countries, wherein lie the major differences? At the risk of sweeping and inappropriate generalization, the following six differences are important to bear in mind when considering a global picture.

Size

Until the middle of the twentieth century, the global experience of large cities, of a population in excess of one million, was very much concentrated in North America, Europe and Japan. This is now rapidly changing, as the world gains many more cities of this size, principally in developing countries, in both middle- and very low-income countries. As noted earlier, the number of cities in poorer countries with populations in excess of 5 million and 10 million is also increasing.

Rates of population growth

The historical experience of most cities in developed countries was of a period of rapid growth, fostered by both high rates of in-migration and a young and fertile resident population (as seen in England: Williamson 1990). This experience translates to the cities of the developing world in the late twentieth century, but with a dimension of greater speed (discussed by, for example, Gilbert 1992, or modelled by Kelley & Williamson 1994, or related to two specific cities in Colombia by Mohan 1994). Population growth rates of 5% or 6% per annum in Third World cities have not been unknown since the mid-1960s, almost twice as fast as rates reached in mid-nineteenth century England for example. It remains true that in the USA, in particular, high growth rates in metropolitan areas in southern and western states are still being experienced, reflecting a very mobile society, but this pattern is uncommon in other industrialized countries.

Income levels and distributions

Average incomes in the cities of poorer countries, whether measured on a household or a GDP per capita basis, are by definition lower than in cities in richer countries; but also for those poorer cities:

- incomes are higher in the city than in the rural areas
- incomes exhibit extremes in distribution between high and low
- real household incomes, allowing for public services and so on, are closer to money incomes than in richer countries
- over time there is considerable mobility of individuals and individual households between income categories, especially in rapidly growing cities
- even in the cities that are very poor on an average per capita basis, there will be a sizeable middle class, with expectations in their patterns of consumption approaching world standards.

Formal and informal activities

Even cities in the richest countries have a proportion of their economic activities centred in what may be regarded as the "informal" sector: unlicensed, untaxed, unprotected and without involvement in legal contracts. But this proportion is higher in poorer cities, and is particularly high in rapidly growing poorer cities. It is high in Sub-Saharan Africa for example.

Manufacturing activity

The proportion of the labour force engaged in both formal sector and informal sector production of goods rather than of services tends to rise as income levels rise as a city grows within an industrializing economy. The proportion then falls away again at higher levels of income, as manufacturing is decentralized or moved offshore and the export base of the rich city becomes concentrated on the provision of services.

Urban bias in public expenditure

Large cities in poorer countries receive larger amounts of the available public expenditure on a per capita basis than do surrounding towns and villages.[2] This seems to hold true in many countries, for both investment expenditure and revenue expenditure on public services, perhaps reflecting the relative productivity of the spending. The reverse has been true for many large cities in the richer countries, particularly if income support expenditure is set to one side and a comparison is made between spending in core areas and in the outer suburbs of metropolitan areas.

The list of contrasts could be extended: to norms and standards applied in public services for example, or the role played *vis-à-vis* rural hinterlands. In many developing countries, the single largest city plays a particularly dominant and significant role in terms of acting as the key hub for all forms of communication and interlinkage with the rest of the world. This dominance is less marked in all but the smallest of the richer countries.

The context of the world economy

New economic roles for an individual city emerge as it grows, in terms of both population and income. These new roles also emerge as the national economy within which the particular city economy is located grows and structurally evolves. And these evolving roles in turn respond to economic growth in other countries, both rich and poor, as trade links extend and modify. All of this would happen just as a result of overall economic growth. But the picture is in fact more complex, as suggested earlier. A combination of new technologies and new worldwide policy regimes is adding pressures for the emergence of new roles. These pressures have economic consequences for the structure of urban economies. Four particular categories of added pressure may be noted as providing a new context for urban development at the end of the twentieth century. These are the falling costs of transport and communication, the reduction in barriers to international trade, the globalization of capital, and a widespread philosophy of deregulation and withdrawal of governmental involvement in key market decisions.

The past three decades have seen the introduction of three new major tech-

---

2. This effect has been reinforced by an implicit taxation bias against agriculture in many developing nations, often by an over-valued currency or by industrial protection. The expenditure bias is implied by the relative access to electricity, mains water supply and sanitation provision in developing countries. In urban areas of developing countries the percentages of the population with access to these services were of the order of 73%, 85% and 73% in 1990, up from 70%, 74% and 60% in 1980. This compares with 32%, 58% and 40% in 1990 in rural areas, up from 27%, 33% and 31% in 1980. (World Bank 1994: 27).

nologies that have transformed the costs of communication between cities around the world. The first is the jumbo jet and its derivatives. (1000 Boeing 747 jumbo models have been sold since 1969, carrying over 1.5 billion passengers.) The second is the sea-freight container. This is a low technology item supported by high-technology logistics in its management. (Maritime transport costs were one third of their 1920 level by 1960 and have continued to fall since.) The third new communications technology is the international telephone network, supported by the microprocessors of the desktop-but-networked computer. (International telephone calls dropped in price sixfold between 1940 and 1970; and then tenfold between 1970 and 1990.) All three of these technologies have required huge investments to support their full worldwide effectiveness. For the vast majority of countries, the essential components of this investment (the technologies and their supporting infrastructures) are now in place. The international costs of trade and exchange using these technologies are set now to fall even further.

The second new factor influencing the changing structure of the economies of cities is the dramatic removal of barriers to the international trade in goods and services. Such barriers were low in the colonial period of industrialization of Europe and North America up to the end of the last century. They then started to rise, with major increases in the case of many countries after the First World War. Progressively, under the various GATT rounds since the Second World War they have come down, culminating in the Uruguay Round of 1994.[3] Worldwide agreements have been reinforced by agreements within free trade areas (as in the European Union and the North American Free Trade Area), as well as in bilateral agreements, of "favoured nation status", and so on. Under this freeing up of restrictions, there has been a very strong growth in international trade in goods and services, from 25% of the world GDP in 1970 to 45% in 1990. And the share of manufactured goods in the exports of developing countries has risen from 20% to 60% in the same period.

The opening up of so many economies to greater import penetration, but also to far-reaching export opportunities, has had a radical and rapid effect on industrial enterprises in some cities, as the case studies of Santiago de Chile and Monterrey demonstrate in this volume. Consumers in countries both rich and poor have tended to gain from the changes, whereas producers in rich countries have faced new low-cost competition, and producers in poor countries have faced competition from new technologies and new levels of consumer responsiveness to choice and quality. Low-skill workers in rich

3. Since 1986, 24 developing countries have joined GATT, and a further 21 are joining its successor, the World Trade Organization. At the same time over 60 developing countries have reported unilateral trade liberalization measures to the GATT. The Uruguay Round reduced average tariffs on industrial goods to 3.9% (the figure was over 40% in 1947); and begins a phased removal of subsidies and quantitative restrictions on agriculture, textiles and clothing.

cities in competing sectors have lost out, in both income and employment opportunities. Their high-skill counterparts in poorer cities have tended to gain on both counts (Wood 1994). There will be an added pressure for income distributions to widen in both cases. The political angst of these changes has been felt in many cities.

The third particular pressure of the past decade has been the transformation of the world capital market. This is now well documented (see, for example, Amin & Thrift 1994). Using the global communications networks between financial centres, trade in foreign exchange, for example, has grown in excess of 20% per annum since the early 1980s, and international trade in bonds and equities by nearly 10% per annum, both well in excess of growth in world trade or world output. Recently the flows of private capital to low- and middle-income countries have risen from US$42 billion (in 1989) to US$175 billion (in 1994), on a net basis. Of these flows 30% involve foreign direct investment, mainly located in major cities. Capital mobility has accounted for some 11% of capital formation in developing countries between 1970 and 1990. The importance of major cities as nodes in this global marketplace for capital and finance is clear, as is the competition for the status of being the host location of major institutional players.

"Deregulation" is a term used to encompass both the privatization of state assets and the drawing back of the state from innumerable interventions in many marketplaces. When combined with falling barriers to imports, the impact upon cities seems to be threefold. Changes in the overall structure of the local economy are accelerated in cities in both rich and poor countries. Prices of utility services initially rise as the companies come out of state ownership; but then, depending upon the competitive and regulatory regime and the need to catch up on backlog in investment, prices fall. Market forces encouraging metropolitan decentralization of economic activities are given added momentum (as argued by Krugman 1991, 1995). In many countries new flows of foreign investment are supporting these changes.

The impact of all four of these particular pressures on cities, when combined with the continuing pressures of growth and economic development, pushes cities rich and poor into an environment of greater social and economic turbulence than hitherto (Pugh 1995). Turbulence in this sense is not new to the urban realm, whether in the north of England 150 years ago or in newly independent colonial states in Asia and Africa of four decades ago. But current pressures are impacting upon rich and poor cities alike. They are pressing a changing *use* of the city faster than the fabric of the city can respond, and indeed faster than the mix of labour skills and related attitudes and expectations can respond. The result is unemployment and under-employment, high adjustment costs in the physical fabric, and a lack of certainty of direction in the design of urban development strategies. The "exposed city", whether in the USA or on the Indian subcontinent, has a problem in deciding wherein lies its future advantage relative to its future burdens of cost.

21

New roles for cities in MDCs

The political systems of the richer countries of the world put a high premium on the maintenance of real per capita or household incomes. They also put a high premium on notions of broad geographical equity in material prosperity between regions. There is therefore, in many if not most major cities of the developed world, a political will to seek to ensure urban economic sustainability. This may be defined as the maintenance over time of a level of output and income per head in the city that retains the position of that city relative to other cities in the national urban hierarchy.

With the exception of "government" cities focused around a military facility or government offices, present-day cities maintain themselves by trading, in both goods and services. The challenge of the late twentieth-century trading environment is particularly strong for those cities that built up their economic base on the export, nationally and internationally, of manufactured goods. Three pressures are at work: new levels of import competition, rising levels of labour productivity supported by increased capital intensity, and the movement of labour-intensive production activities off shore to lower labour-cost locations. Employment in manufacturing in these cities therefore falls, and with it household incomes and local levels of expenditure. The employment that is left in manufacturing is either in local support enterprises or it has to seek a premium from continuing invention and innovation in both product and process. The knowledge component of the goods for export has to increase (Nijkamp 1990, Knight 1995).

New roles for such cities therefore emerge. This may be in high value-added manufacturing. Or it may be that the economic base of the city can move to service activities, exporting services in finance and banking, or tourism, health care, education, the law, or in media and design. This trend is well documented for many North American and European cities, particularly those that act as regional capitals (e.g. Hall 1993). Often it is associated with a sector specialism. However, relative competitive success in exporting these services places similar requirements on the city, as does the related new role in manufacturing. Four broad requirements may be identified. To be able to respond flexibly and profitably to the new external environment, such a city will need:

- an educated and skilled labour force, which can offer the characteristics of flexibility and entrepreneurialism as well as life-time learning
- a rich local knowledge-base built upon a range of information providers
- a breadth in the portfolio of external communication linkages, securing access to new technologies
- an institutional flexibility, particularly in those private- and public-sector support activities that stand in behind the performance of the exporting sectors of the local economy.

The case studies in this volume demonstrate how, in relatively little time, major industrial cities in Europe have redefined themselves and their role within the national and international economy. There has been a danger in policy terms in seeing the process of economic regeneration away from a declining heavy industrial base, or from sectors such as textiles, subject to new competition from low-cost producers elsewhere, as a one-off process (as noted in the introduction to this chapter in relation to structural adjustment policies). The policy support is seen as needed just to put the city onto a new and apparently secure trajectory of prosperity. However, as in cities in poorer nations, the adjustment process is in fact continuing. There is little sign of the perceived need for policy support coming to an end.

New roles for cities in LDCs

One understandable feature of structural adjustment cities in richer countries has been a desire to associate industrial change with environmental improvement. Increasing attention is therefore being paid to trade-offs between the production and consumption of goods and services and the external consequences for both the local natural environment and for local "society" in terms of many aspects of non-material quality of life. In contrast there has perhaps been a temptation in cities in poorer countries to feel that close attention to these trade-offs is something that cannot be afforded, when poverty is widespread and support services to the population are so inadequate, and when the local businesses have to compete in both import and export markets with the more experienced and larger companies of the rich countries. The role of environmental flag-carrier is not one that has been eagerly grasped in poorer cities.

In the poorer countries of the world, the prime roles for cities in the past half century may be said to have been twofold. First, to establish the core infrastructure of a modern industrial state: key energy supplies, communication infrastructures, central health care and education systems, legal and governmental institutions, supports for private sector and parastatal industrial and commercial investments (e.g. World Bank 1994). Secondly, to absorb a rising population, as the country goes through the demographic transition from high to low birth and death rates, with associated pressures on rural labour markets. Demand for labour in the cities pulls in migrants, who then need to be brought into income-generating functions that serve a modern industrial city. The challenge of policies to relieve urban poverty remains close to the top of all city government agendas (Lipton & van der Gaag 1993). The more successful of the poorer countries of 50 years ago have fulfilled these two roles over two generations and they have succeeded in raising real per capita incomes.

In the new international economic context of the late twentieth century, new roles are now being added to these two prime roles. First, there is the defence of the gains made so far, particularly in the export industries in the manufacturing sector. Supported by the capital of large multinational companies, very low labour cost countries provide new competition for the low- and medium-cost nations. There is therefore a role for the city in supporting the progressive upgrading of quality and value for money in the export sectors. This requires investment and improved labour skills to secure rising labour productivity and falling unit labour costs. The city has to facilitate access to capital (domestic and foreign), and to new technology. This requires the renewal and the upgrading of the existing physical infrastructure.[4]

The second role lies in fostering new lines of economic activity, in the externally traded sectors in both manufacturing and in services. These new activities may come from existing local companies and organizations or from inward investors from elsewhere.[5] The problem here is that inward investors frequently have an expectation of developed country standards of support services and facilities; and for offshore manufacturing plants that export to other countries rather than serve the local market, there is a wide range of choice of low labour-cost locations now emerging internationally. This is particularly true for the countries of the Pacific Rim.

A third role lies in providing for the consumption aspects of a modern state. Even in poor cities the media and entertainment sectors of the local economy will be large and significant. This is especially so in large cities serving a regional or national audience. Activities such as printing, publishing, film-making, professional sports and tourist-related services grow in importance with income, but also independently of income as communications media improve and local travel becomes easier.

For all of these new roles, study after study emphasizes the significance of education and skill training. The world as a whole has experienced a transformation in this respect since the mid-1960s. Since 1960, enrolments in all levels of education have increased fivefold. Workers with more education are more productive and earn higher wages, with a larger wage premium where there is a relative scarcity of educated workers. This will tend to be particularly true in fast-growing cities in fast-growing economies, and can therefore act as a constraint on economic transformation.

---

4. The costs of falling behind in the provision of infrastructure may be illustrated by the finding that 92% of a sample of firms in Nigeria and 64% of a sample in Indonesia had incurred the cost of installing private electrical generating capacity in order to guarantee a supply of power. In contrast, in Thailand the comparable figure was only 6%. In a sample of 95 developing countries, more than one third in 1992 were found to have a waiting time for a telephone connection of more than six years. (World Bank 1994: 31).
5. Between 1985 and 1992, 5 million of the 8 million jobs created in investments by multinational companies were in developing nations; bringing a world total in these nations to 12 million, with more than the same number of workers again linked to these companies through subcontracting. One third of world trade involves cross-border flows within companies, increasingly from low labour-cost locations.

The difficult challenge for governance in these cities is how to secure economic transformation in the face of the new international competition while managing the continuing extensive pressures of growth imposed by rising population levels and by increases in real incomes (World Bank 1991, 1992, Pugh 1995). Old systems of city management are being found wanting. The legislative and tax-raising powers of city governments are felt to be inadequate, and pressures of local democracy and accountability call for greater transparency in decision-making and decentralization of authority. These governments face the task of providing services for a rapidly growing population, a large proportion of which is poorly educated or illiterate, at the same time as seeking to lock their city into the benefits of the global economy.

Emerging urban geographies

Rapidly growing cities can find disjunctures in their geographies. In other words, the geography of land uses that was appropriate for a city of one million people is likely to be inappropriate when the population reaches ten million. Growth generates inefficiencies when, by its nature, it is incremental around the edges of the city. New areas may not link well with existing areas. At the same time, transformations are required in the "old" land area of the previously smaller city. And this may be difficult if there are rigidities in the land market and extensive bureaucratic controls. Structural change in the city economy may well further underline inappropriateness and consequent inefficiency. Difficult terrain (the island in Bombay or Lagos for example) may compound the problem.

Rising real incomes and a switch in emphasis in the urban economy from manufacturing to service-sector activities place a new emphasis on the central business district. There is little sign yet that modern communications technologies have done more than support limited decentralization of some back-office functions from CBDs in large cities. And yet a high-rise high-density financial, commercial and governmental core to a city is extremely expensive in supportive infrastructures as the city grows. Incremental private sector investment will seek rising rental levels in CBD offices; but few cities have a property tax system that can yield the required rising revenues to pay for the needed transportation links. The consequence is either a disjuncture between transport demand, and transport supply, or a gross excess of office floorspace supply relative to demand swinging in a cycle to severe shortage. Present structural adjustment pressures add to the uncertainties of both the private sector investors and the decision-makers in the public sector.

In richer countries much of the focus of urban policy since the mid-1960s has been on the doughnut ring around the central core, termed the "inner city". This has often been a zone of transition, characterized by older high-density housing and small industrial and commercial premises. It provides homes and employment for recent in-migrants and for the less affluent in the city. Much attention has been paid to the physical upgrading of such areas and the relative improvement of the socio-economic circumstances of the residents. In cities in poorer countries such a "collar" zone is typically less easily delineated, but the function of such areas, for migrants, for the poor, for petty trading and for the striving to be upwardly mobile, is present in the slum areas. Structural adjustment growth added in-migrant pressure on these areas.

The patterns of development in the outer areas of growing cities, rich and poor, are very much determined by the patterns of landownership and of investment in transport infrastructure. The suburban impact of changes in the structure of the city economy will be influenced therefore by land-use control policies, by property taxation and changing regimes for transport, and by policies to promote decentralization to outer areas and employment regeneration in inner areas. Such policies are discussed in the case studies (and for a longer-run pattern in Europe, see Drewett et al. 1992). What is noteworthy, however, is the similarity of the underlying economic dynamic in cities both rich and poor.

Emerging structural issues

The economic policy agenda in a strategic sense, for cities in both rich and poor countries experiencing change imposed by the new world economic environment, revolves around four sets of key questions:

- Is there to be a future place in the city economy for internationally competitive export-orientated manufacturing activity? Can the appropriate sector or sectors be identified? What support can the city as an overall entity offer to the corporate players within that activity?
- For service sector activities in the city economy, what are the implications of the new levels and lower costs of communication with other cities domestically and internationally? Can the city ensure that the relevant property possibilities (in offices, etc.) and their supportive infrastructures are in place?
- Can the responses made by the city to the above questions take advantage of the new openness of capital markets while providing the necessary discipline for raising local tax revenues and for the repayment of interest and debt?
- What is to be the balance in city expenditures between supportive investments and services to the emerging growth sectors of the urban economy, and spending to facilitate adjustment by sectors in relative decline? And what is to be the balance between support to producer interests in the city and expenditures on services to residents in general and support for the poor and disadvantaged in particular?

One dimension of reply to all four of these sets of questions currently found in many countries is a movement to decentralize both the requirement to find answers and the capability to act upon them at the city level. The movement towards greater devolved powers of both revenue raising and expenditure decisions to city authorities is widespread, in both rich and poor countries (World Bank 1992).

Economic and environmental sustainability

The pressures of structural adjustment pushing cities forwards into new economic roles are coming at a time when a new level of awareness is growing in the world community of the negative environmental consequences of the present path of urbanization and the associated industrialization for a growing world population. The 1992 Rio Conference was a mark of this growing awareness, and the Habitat II conference will take the awareness further forwards, specifically in relation to cities. The concerns are both global and local, and they are voiced by policy-makers, non-governmental organizations and individual citizens in both rich and poor countries (see Hardoy et al. 1992, for example; and Haughton & Hunter 1994).

City policy-makers find themselves forced into uneasy compromise. Citizens, voters, look to a rising material standard of living, from whatever their current standing. They also look for security of income and for a good standard of public services. Hence, the need for city authorities to embrace the requirement of economic sustainability: policies to maintain the output per capita of the city at levels comparable with competitor or reference cities elsewhere in the national economy. At the same time, achievement of that economic sustainability may only be possible with environmental damage.

"Environmental damage" is difficult to identify in terms of human welfare. Some damage is recoverable through natural processes (organic matter pollutants in a water course). Other apparent damage may be securely hidden (as in a sealed landfill). Other damage may be aesthetic (loss of countryside or noted architecture). Some damage may be narrowly confined to certain plants or non-human animals (loss of a particular habitat). In contrast, within the city, the prime environmental concerns have always been the negative consequences of activities of both firms and households for human health. But here also, although gross immediate impacts (from a sewage polluted water supply) are easy to identify, the longer-term incremental delayed impacts (benzene compounds in air pollution from vehicles) provide difficulties in the identification of unambiguous cause and effect.

City governments in both rich and poor countries are presently ill equipped to fulfil the new role being pressed upon them by a concerned public: that of environmental arbiter. In that role, judgements have to be made between the apparent requirements for economic sustainability and the dangers thereby for environmental sustainability. This is true whether the criterion adopted for environmental sustainability is simply not to allow matters to deteriorate or whether a strong stand is taken in respect of a precautionary principle relating to conditions to be faced by later generations. Not only do judgements have to be made between relativities and absolutes, between the short run and the long, and between the local and the global, but those judgements have to be conveyed to a sceptical public.

The changes now emerging for the major cities of the world in the light of the policy regimes of structural adjustment, as noted earlier, add a new degree of turbulence to the definition of their economic roles. It is clear that material prosperity in this new context is not secured simply by deregulation and a greater reliance upon market forces. The case studies in this volume demonstrate very active city governments seeking to sustain prosperity for local citizens while fostering a competitive reorientation of local economic structures. Taxpayer support is seen for education and training, for product and process innovation, for the attraction of inward investment, for the provision of required infrastructures, for many services. The environmental factor adds a further requirement for governmental action. The city policy agenda for the immediate decades ahead therefore is not merely one of coping with rising population levels in the poorer countries and of maintaining living standards in the richer ones, but is also an agenda of new environmental understanding, requiring both new technologies and new policies.

References

Amin, A. & N. Thrift 1994. *Globalisation, institutions and regional development in Europe*. Oxford: Oxford University Press.

Drewett, R., T. Hoehn, S. Sacks 1992. The "crowding and uncrowding" of European cities: secular population trends 1750–1986. In *Innovation and urban population dynamics: a multi-level process*, K. P. Strohmeier & C. W. Matthiessen (eds), 57–75. Avebury: Aldershot.

Gilbert, A. G. 1992. Third World cities: the changing national settlement system. *Urban Studies* **30**(4/5), 721–40.

Hall, P. 1993. Forces shaping urban Europe. *Urban Studies* **30**(6), 883–98.

Hardoy, J. E., D. Millon, D. Satterthwaite 1992. *Environmental problems in Third World cities*. London: The International Institute of Environment and Development.

Haughton, G. & C. Hunter 1994. *Sustainable cities in Europe*. London: Earthscan.

Henderson, J. V. 1977. *Economic theory and the cities*. Oxford: Oxford University Press.

Kelley, A. C. & J. G. Williamson 1994. *What drives Third World city growth: a dynamic general equilibrium approach*. Princeton, New Jersey: Princeton University Press.

Knight, R. V. 1995. Knowledge-based development: policy and planning implications for cities. *Urban Studies* **32**(2), 225–60.

Krugman, P. R. 1991. *Geography and trade*. Cambridge, Mass.: MIT Press.

—1995. Urban concentration: the role of increasing nations and transport costs. In *Pro-*

ceedings of the World Bank Annual Conference on Development Economics 1994, M.
Bruno & B. Pleskovic (eds), 241–63. Washington DC: World Bank.

Lipton, M. & J. van der Gaag 1993. *Including the poor*. Washington DC: World Bank,

Mohan, R. 1994. *Understanding developing metropolises: lessons from the city study of Bogotá and Cali, Colombia*. Oxford: Oxford University Press.

Nijkamp, P. (ed.) 1990. *Sustainability of urban systems: a cross-national evolutionary analysis of urban innovation*. Avebury: Aldershot.

Pugh, C. 1995. International structural adjustment and its sectoral and spatial impacts. *Urban Studies* **32**(2), 261–85.

UN 1994. *World urbanisation prospects*. New York: United Nations.

Williamson, J. G. 1990. *Coping with city growth during the British Industrial Revolution*. Cambridge: Cambridge University Press.

Wood, A. 1994. *North–South trade, employment and inequality; changing fortunes in a skill-driven world*. Oxford: Oxford University Press.

World Bank 1991. *Urban policy and economic development: an agenda for the 1990s*. Washington DC: The World Bank.

—1992. *Governance and development*. Washington DC: The World Bank.

—1994. *World Development Report 1994: infrastructure for development*. Washington DC: The World Bank.

—1995. *World Development Report 1995: workers in an integrating world*. Washington DC: World Bank.

The discussion

Chairman: Gustavo Garza
PARTICIPANTS: Gerson Da Cunha, A. D. Moddie, Zilton Macedo,
Amitabh Kundu, G. K. Virmani, Joaquim Clusa, Cheryl Gopaul,
William F. Lever

The discussion initially focused on the question of institutional rigidities. An example was given of measures originally introduced to assist the poor – rent controls in Bombay or the Indian urban land ceiling Act – which, in the course of time, became serious restrictions on flexible responses and made the position of the poor worse than before. Should one go around existing institutions that were no longer effective or were corrupt, by creating new ones, as the World Bank had done in the 1970s in setting up, for example, new metropolitan water agencies? The attempt was to make such organizations non-political and isolate them from the rest of the governmental organization in order to manage large infrastructural projects. However, this had all sorts of drawbacks, especially when development moved into operation and maintenance – it was important to work through the existing political forces and administrative machinery.

Rigidities were not only embodied in institutions. They were equally problematic in the mind-set of the elite of administrators and managers who claimed to know what was best for everyone else, so there was no need to consult either people in general or even each other. The attitudes started in university education, which would have to be completely reformed. Many of the problems of government were not the result of political differences, but of the conditioned reflexes of the bureaucracy and its relative permanence in India in comparison to the high turnover of politicians. This made for great discontinuities in implementing projects. Even politicians were not good at explaining policies in terms of popular interests – a good example of this was the failure to show what the macroeconomic reform programme entailed in terms of improved living conditions and the sustainable growth of employment and incomes.

If the administrative machinery had strong rigidities, this was not true to the same extent for the economy. The decline in manufacturing in cities received much attention from the participants. Monterrey in Mexico had experienced a sharp decline in manufacturing from the early 1980s, but, on the other hand, some sectors (e.g. beer and cement) had made a major expansion to become multinational in scope. The city had made major infrastructural investments to assist the transition from a manufacturing to a servicing centre. Data on Indian urban manufacturing showed a strong growth up to the beginning of the 1980s, and then a fairly consistent decline. This was possibly attributable to the differences in access to political power and resources, so a richer population could benefit from manufacturing while having it located somewhere else. The positive aspect of deindustrialization was that it allowed cities to take the issue of population much more seriously.

"Sustainability" was another fashionable term that needed to be explained in terms of popular interests. Different interests – government, the technicians, trade unions, employers and so on – interpreted the term in different ways in the short and long term. The politicians looked at issues in terms of the next election, but technicians wasted much time trying to persuade them of long-term remedies without much political pay-off. Sometimes the outcome contradicted our normal assumptions – in São Paulo, the government was trying to end the planning process and its own planning agency, but private business was coming to the defence of planning; the private club of bankers argued forcefully that, unless São Paulo was systematically improved, it would lose its central business district functions to Rio de Janeiro or Buenos Aires.

One participant asked what had been the experience of creating twin cities. As remedies to the problems of large cities, he argued, they had failed in both Bombay and Calcutta. A division of labour that was also competitive could develop between cities, it was also argued, as occurred between Barcelona and Madrid – the one had become specialized in Japanese investment and office headquarters, the other in American business, and both competed strongly in soccer. In Kingston, Jamaica, a period of intense insecurity in the 1960s and 1970s had led to the rapid deterioration of the downtown area. The government had mobilized private capital and non-government organizations in the task of rehabilitation, leading to a rapid increase in land prices. As a result of this, the government had initiated New Kingston, designed to be a commercial centre for Jamaica and the Caribbean at large. However, macroeconomic reform was simultaneously uprooting part of the rural population, so Kingston continued to grow rapidly in population; ultimately, the government decided to end the duplication of city administrations by merging new and old Kingston in a single metropolitan area. Another contributor noted that it was rare for a major city to create a complete "sister" city, although some had created a second central business district (CBD) – as in London (with Docklands), Tokyo, Paris (with La Défense), and the relocation of part of Manhattan's office sector to New Jersey. The distance between the two CBDs was usually small – 5 to 10 miles – and this was feasible because the rent gradient was steep, rapidly declining from the old CBD over a relatively short distance. To create a whole second city was extremely expensive. An alternative, and one financed by private capital, was, as in the USA, suburban sprawl, with mixed residential and commercial development. With the exception of new towns, public intervention rarely went beyond developing new commercial centres because the costs were so high. Furthermore, private business was conservative and unwilling to move from old locations without heavy subsidies or a legal ban on the old location. Clustering remained important for many businesses, and no amount of new telecommunications had overcome the need of certain businesses for face-to-face contact. Financial deregulation made this even more important – striking deals worth billions of dollars made it even more imperative to look the dealer in the face.

In his reply, Peter Townroe commented on a selection of issues. How could institutional rigidities be reduced to enhance flexibility in response to changing economic circumstances? In some cases, a determined political leadership had been able to override opposition here, even in the face of popular resistance. In other cases, new institutions had been created to get around the resistance of the old – there was a good example of this in the Lille case study. New institutions had been used to create new financial instruments and follow different policies, but this did not necessarily reform the old structures. There were inevitably tensions between old and new, and quite often only a major crisis could resolve these issues (as is shown in the Monterrey study). Holding this symposium, however, suggested that cities should not have to wait for a major crisis to reform – they ought to have created sufficient flexibility in advance to respond adequately and in time. Such flexibility required citizen participation, not just in terms of formal democracy, but also in terms of popular understanding about the overall challenges and the strategy. There was a paradox here. Although cities complained bitterly about the loss of their powers to national government, they in turn often resisted the redistribution of their power to raise and spend money to lower echelons of governance, to the citizens at large. But flexibility required the power to act at all levels – a traditional shipbuilding city such as Greenock in Scotland needed the power to attract alternative economic activities, as in fact it had done in getting IBM to invest there in computer manufacture.

One participant raised the issue of economic interactions between cities and their hinterlands, but there were many hinterlands, depending upon the communication system and market demand for the city's services – professional, business, consumer services, and so on. The source of migration might indicate another hinterland. The earlier example of what might be possible with the liberalization of service exports – a hospital in Minneapolis being cleaned by temporary contract workers from Mexico – changed both the city's hinterland and our normal concept of immigrants.

Land prices had raised much interest, especially in southern Bombay, and in the effect of the Olympic Games on Barcelona office rents and prices. But normally, land and property markets seemed to work well, and central business district prices and rents reflected accurately the relative rates of return to activity there. The problem was that expectations were so strong, the market continually tended to overshoot, producing great fluctuations that did not reflect supply and demand. Because of this instability, it was very easy for public authorities to get their policies wrong, and the Canary Wharf project in London was perhaps a good example of this.

Rapporteur summary

Zilton Macedo

In Nigel Harris's introduction he put a good question: how can a city respond quickly to structural changes? Plans do not relieve the government from being intelligent and fast in its responses. Here the experience of São Paulo is relevant. We had a plan for eight years from 1970, and in December of last year we launched a new one, which is completely different. Instead of being a physical plan for the city, it is an agenda listing 344 questions and challenges to be developed for the metropolitan region of São Paulo, whoever is mayor or whoever forms the government. They can choose from the list of 344 issues to respond to. It is a curious book, because all the statistics are in a separate chapter and all the questions are organized so that it is easy for any politician to understand what the issue is about.

Another point on this concerns the period of time within which we should react and the statistics we have to rely on. In São Paulo we are trying to produce a weekly index on the level of activity in the city. The index is based on the movement of cars, number of telephone calls, volume of mail, and so on. These are readily available statistics that nobody has tried to correlate with the level of activity in the immediate future, but this has proved to be a very efficient way of looking at city activity, mainly because it includes the informal sector.

A further point concerns the competition for the import of capital, and the deregulation and the dependence on this flow of international capital. Brazil was hit hard by the Mexican crisis in the last six to eight months, as well as domestically, because of a sudden decrease in inflation from 70% to 2% a month. The effect of the sharp decrease in inflation was that some industries that were decaying in São Paulo suddenly found their markets expanding rapidly. Industries producing popular consumer goods expanded because the income tax rate that was required by high inflation changed and suddenly the poorest were in a better position than the upper income groups. The effect was an enormous increase in jobs in the popular consumer industries and a decrease in, for example, the automobile industry. Certain parts of the city that were in rapid decline suddenly became fashionable places to locate a factory. Thus, it is not only external changes that affect cities; sometimes internal policies play an important role.

On the question of the informal sector, the only thing we know from indirect observation is that it is growing rapidly in Brazil as a whole. The main cause for this is that the social additions to labour costs that we have to pay in Brazil have reached 92% of the total wages paid. There are obligatory contributions for retirement, health, safety and housing. The fastest way to make a small or medium-size firm successful is to go for informality. This is a conclusion that even the unions in the more developed areas of the country accept.

Another important point of discussion was the idea of export services, from education to cultural services. Formerly we had no statistics on this, but we found that metropolitan São Paulo received 4.5 million people in business tourism in 1994, with an average stay of two days for events such as symposiums, industrial shows and fairs, and so on. That fact explained why, during the ten-year crisis from 1980 to 1990, shows, theatres and restaurants were the best investment in the city. If you want to have an event like this symposium these days in São Paulo, you have to book a room at least six months in advance. If you need a larger room, you have to book one year in advance, because otherwise there is no space. Thus, these sorts of services are replacing all the industrial jobs we are losing in metropolitan São Paulo. Industrial employment is moving to different parts of the state and the rest of the country. However, industrial production in metropolitan São Paulo is growing faster than in the past, so that what happened in the years of crisis was a renewal of the technology in the industrial bases. Thus, the second largest supplier of jobs in the state became the service sector.

Again, on the role of government, as I mentioned earlier, there is a fight between the state government, the metropolitan government and the private sector located in the city. The private sector is willing to support planning because it wants to escape from the Brazilian tradition of stop–go economic policies. It sees planning as a way to escape the likelihood that every day you have to play dice to know what is going to happen in economic policy.

There is an important issue on what lessons can be learned from rich and poor cities. From Singapore we learned an interesting point for shanty town settlements in São Paulo. Part of these shanty towns are situated on public land, part on private land. The aim of the project is to build homes for people living in each shanty town. This approach avoids major changes in the location of households, which is, in most cases, linked to the spatial distribution of jobs.

In the case of private land, owners are asked to give part of the land to the Municipal Housing Agency, which transfers the squatters there after finishing the buildings. The remaining cleared areas are returned to the landowners for development as they wish, but observing the ordinary legal and zoning procedures. This process favours private owners of squatted land because it is a faster way than any other procedure, legal or not, to recover property. This project has been successfully developed in São Paulo, based on the experience of a similar scheme implemented in Singapore.

On the other hand, we have learned from the Docklands experience in London. São Paulo has a prison for 5000 people, which is less than 1 km from the CBD. This piece of land has been offered to a company in return for building a new prison with twice the number of cells for prisoners 100 km from the city. The firm will be able to exploit the land for a hundred years. The other thing we learned from the Docklands project concerns the city airport. There is a military airport in São Paulo dating from the 1930s, when the city had 1 million inhabitants (now we have 16 million). It, too, is 1 km from the main bank in São Paulo. No-one uses the airport now, so the whole of it is to be redeveloped for hotels and a new airport (again, an inspiration from London Docklands). So, São Paulo will have an airport nearly within walking distance of the CBD (as Rio de Janeiro does). There is fierce competition between São Paulo and Rio to be the service centre for the country. São Paulo will have an airport 1 km, another 6 km, and a third, the international airport, 40 km from the CBD. Santos, the main Brazilian seaport for exports is 70 km to the southeast; 70 km to the west is the main airport for exports.

Will cities in developing countries be able to compete with those in the developed countries? One thing that caught my attention, when, in coming here, I passed through the Arab Emirates, was that the Emirates are investing a lot in Dubai airport. They are trying to compete in this part of the world as an international transport junction. Bombay can similarly compete because the city already has two or three airports and an important port, giving the city a strategic position, not only in India but in this region of the world's economy.

In Brazil, all politicians have had difficulty in understanding that election promises are less important than educating the voting public and the stable part of government. Instead of looking at physical infrastructural projects on the city's periphery all the time, we need to reshape the inner-city areas to improve the use of already existing infrastructure. This is the aim of the banker's club I mentioned before. They are interested in re-utilizing the inner-city area because it is becoming derelict, even though all the important banks are there, as is the rest of the financial sector. The banks own 50% of the buildings within a radius of 1 km from the main square in São Paulo, so it is understandable that the owners are pushing for improvements in the area. They are doing the job shop by shop. They have a meeting for each block, inviting people to attend the meeting and discuss improvement. They are working more effectively than all the government agencies put together.

CHAPTER TWO
The city as development agency

I The entrepreneurial city: promotion and development

Joaquim Clusa

Barcelona is an example of a strategy depending on a big event: the Olympic Games of 1992. The Games were the catalyst for a whole branch of public investment associated with general modernization. Even more important was the key role of the private sector in the process. Barcelona also illustrates how an investment such as that in the Olympics can have more benefits than the same amount of investment put in other cities – as with Seville, which hosted the Expo 1992.

First, I wish to explain the Barcelona restructuring and discuss whether it is a success story. Then I will explain the Olympic event in more detail, and the public–private partnership in the investment. Thirdly, I would like to stress the importance of good public–private partnerships in different policies in different cities.

In terms of entrepereneurship, how should a city be managed during a process of structural adjustment? We are probably agreed on the objectives and actions in different cities – the plans do not differ much. It is necessary to invest in ring roads, in new water facilities and, in some cities, in opera houses, technology parks, supertram lines or laser parks. On the one hand, we need to take advantage of the process of change to improve competitiveness, attractiveness and productivity of the city economy; on the other hand, this is to be done without increasing social polarization or compromising the ecological equilibrium. Just the opposite – economic change should be an opportunity to improve the living conditions for the majority of the citizens and reduce environmental risks.

The first goal can be quantified and summarized by an increase in the gross city product, and as a consequence of income per capita. The second goal is more generic, because it is more difficult to measure. The concept of an entrepreneurial city involves a particular mixture of agents, policies and strategies

36

in order to produce the best possible results during the processes of globalization and technological change. As an example of general objectives, let me quote from the last 1994 economic report for the Municipality of Barcelona:

Barcelona faces the next years to the end of the century with a consolidated position and, what is more important, with new projects for the future. In this context it is important to point out that there exists a city design, agreed in the second strategic plan of the city, as well as a public–private platform for the promotion of the city abroad. The second strategic plan and the quality of the services must be the basic characteristics of Barcelona for the year 2000.

The main lines of action for the Municipality are, according to this report:
• ease of interchanges between modes of transport (port, airport, roads, rail)
• sustainability
• the new horizon for the communication of infrastructures.

The quotation is about a municipality of 1.7 million inhabitants, the centre of a metropolitan area of 3.1 million and of a metropolitan region of 4.3 million, within a radius of about 40 km from the centre. It is also the capital of a European region called Catalonia, with 6.1 million inhabitants.

The case of Barcelona provides interesting insights into how a city can face a process of change with a fair degree of success in both fields: one, improving the economic position of the city, and two, improving the living conditions of its inhabitants and spreading the beneficial effects to a wider metropolitan and regional territory. Since the early 1970s Barcelona has experienced a sharp structural adjustment, characterized by, first, the reorganization of the industrial sector, in terms of employment, type of activities, size of the plants, productivity, spinning off of services, geographical relocation, the participation of multinational capital and export-orientated production. The industrial sector declined in employment by 16 per cent.

Secondly, tertiarization, with different consequences in the field of personal services, public administration and other services, through enterprises. The tertiary sector increased its share of employment by 21% in this 25-year period.

Thirdly, the decentralization of residents and employment with the consequent extension of the metropolitan area, an increase in rural land involved and a reduction in population densities in the centre. Despite the importance of strong annual adjustments, unemployment rates were consistently about 15% for most of this period. The GDP for the Barcelona area grew about 15% in real terms in 20 years and the income of the region of Catalonia reached approximately the average income level of the European Union, after having improved by 15 points in ranking over the period of the past 13 years. A recent Eurostat study of the economic regions of Europe gives Catalonia the status of a highly developed industrialized area, with solid and diversifying industrial structure, a wide range of salaries for the qualified working population, a high and increasing disposable income, a majority of medium-size companies and an increase in employment in the service sector.

Barcelona metropolitan area is ninth in the ranking of resident population of the European Union metropolitan areas, and third in population density after Paris and Athens. In terms of metropolitan regions it is the sixth in resident population, eighth in territorial extent and again third in density.

There are four urban agglomerations in what we call the metropolitan region. The use of urban land between 1978 and 1986 nearly doubled as a result of the decentralization and improvement in space standards.

A "globalization index": import plus exports as a proportion of GDP, reached 40% in 1988 compared to 29% in 1979. It has been nearly 40% for the past ten years or so. The Catalonia region has nearly 40% of the total foreign investment in Spain. There are more than 10 million visitors to the region every year, so that, for two or three months of the year, our population of 6 million reaches 8.5 million. The services that I mentioned are for this figure, rather than the 6 million. The metropolitan region has a share of about 70% of the population of Catalonia, and about 11% of Spain's resident population. It has 21% of the industrial employment in Spain, so it is an important industrial centre with an important share of GDP.

The second ring around the city (25 km from the centre), with three municipalities with more than 100 000 inhabitants, has an industrial tradition and employs 30% of the residential population. It has much of the urban growth of the metropolitan region, with shares of 56% of new housing, 57% of industrial land, 88% of the residential population growth, and 95% of the net creation of employment since the mid-1970s, in what has been called a diffused city.

The tertiarization process and the industrial restructuring meant a loss of nearly 500 000 industrial jobs with unemployment rates for a time of 25% according to the Active Population Enquiry, and of 21%, according to the Unemployment Register. The total employment decrease, which has been the most significant social cost of the adjustment process, was 25% in the first period, 1970 to 1988, but there was an increase of nearly 25% during the expansion and recovery period, which started in 1985–6.

Because of the industrial concentration, Catalonia grows faster than Spain in the expansion period, but also has deeper periodic crises. The expansion coincides with stagnation in the population and an increase in mobility. Nearly 38% of the employed population work in a different municipality from that of their residence, whereas it was only 32% five years ago. Nearly 250 000 people enter the municipality of Barcelona daily for work reasons, and more than 100 000 living in the city work elsewhere.

The expansion period did not reduce the unemployment rate below 15%. So, in relation to the figures from Sheffield or Glasgow, the situation was worse.

The process is parallel with the decentralization of population and economic activity. Barcelona municipality lost 5% of its employment during 1961–91 in four sectors. However, most of the industrial sector grew during the last decade after the restructuring of industry. The sectors performing well during this expansion period have been food, metal products and cars. At the same time, there is a concentration of workers in the service sector. There has been a certain decentralization of the different sectors, both industrial and service.

What are the lessons from Barcelona in relation to the Olympic Games? The process is of general interest for three main reasons: first, the use of a special event in order to modernize and promote the city and the metropolitan area; secondly, the key role played by public initiative to create the conditions for growth, infrastructure, industrial premises, housing at different prices; and thirdly, the strength of the economic system – the private sector – of the whole region in terms of investment, consumption, exports. Tourism is one of the principal sectors that has overcome most of the consequences of the economic crises of 1975–88.

The organization of an international event to promote and renew a city is today a rather well known strategy. Expos, Olympics, fairs and even religious celebrations have led to what is rightly named the "festivalization" of many urban policies. Barcelona used such a pretext.

The results

Let me present the main economic results of the experience. The process began in 1986, which is both the year of the nomination of the city as organizer of the Games and the year of Spanish entry to the European Union. It was also the first year with net creation of employment since 1975. From that time up to the opening of the doors of the Olympic Games, the city saw a period of fast economic growth. There were increases of nearly 25% in employment and 45% in real GDP per capita, coinciding with some decrease in residential population. The rapid economic growth was associated with an increase of 90% in the average price of new housing in the metropolitan region in a period of general boom in the real estate market – land, offices and industrial premises.

During the period, the Games played a crucial role as an instrument of urban and economic renewal. The new housing associated with the Olympic villages was 49% of all new housing in the municipality, but 26% of the metropolitan area and only 13% in the metropolitan region in two years. In terms of infrastructure, the Games led to an agreement to finance the new infrastructure among the three administrations – local, regional and central – as well as with the real estate sector of Spain and abroad. The new infrastructure has given new importance to the former disorganized metropolitan periphery.

The Olympics were an excuse and a catalyst to mobilize the investment needed to overcome part of the infrastructure deficiencies of the city. The total investment associated with the Olympics was equivalent to nearly 1000 km of motorway at current Spanish prices (1986–92). Only 9% of the investment accounts for sport facilities proper. The rest included the construction of new transport infrastructure: 75 km of new urban motorway, the new ring road of Barcelona crossing 13 municipalities, the airport and the railway renovation had a share of 42% of the total investment. Other important works were undertaken in the field of telecommunications, with 13% of the total investment, new housing in the Olympic villages of 15%, and new hotels 13%.

At the end of the investment, metropolitan Barcelona had developed an important infrastructure to compete with other cities to attract industry, services, and tourism. Office floorspace investment was specially located in the so called new centrality areas, managed by the local authority and private operators, and designed for the reorganization of the tertiary sector. There are 500 000 m^2 of vacant office floor space today.

The level of expenditure associated with the Olympic Games, which was only exceeded by Tokyo in 1964, had diverse impacts on employment. There are two estimates on the creation of jobs: 160 000 jobs and nearly 60 000 – rather different, representing 37% of net job creation in Catalonia or only 14%.

For our purposes it is important to understand the investment impact. The fiscal resources of the public sector used in the investment financed only 47% of the total, according to the most recent estimates. The share in terms of total expenditure, including the operational costs, was 40%. The rest (43%) was financed through commercial sources by private investors, the public companies of the central administration, railways and telephones, the Olympic holding company commercial investments and by services or sponsors associated with the Games. Private investment coming from abroad, one-third of the total private investment (excluding public companies' investment), had an additional mobilizing effect.

Despite its importance, the financing of the Games had a relatively small impact on the public budget and on the future debt levels of the municipality. According to one estimate, 47% of public participation in terms of resources managed (not in terms of origin) was contributed by central government (32%), municipality (18%), the regional government (32%) and other administrations (10%). The share of the investment expenditure from fiscal sources was more or less similar to the participation of the different tiers in the administration of Spain.

The share of the municipality in the Olympic investment represented 17% of the increase in the municipal debt in the period, and 16% of municipal investment in all types of infrastructure and civil works. The Olympic debt explains 42% of the total increase in the municipal debt of the period. But even so, the increase in debt was not very important. In 1993 it was only 1.9

times higher than the debt of 6 years before, and, according to the municipal forecasts, it will decrease in the coming years. The 1988 debt represented 1.9 times the current income of the municipality, whereas it represented 1.5 times in 1992.

If the share of infrastructural costs was not excessively high for the municipality, the same can be said for the regional and central government. The estimates point out that, for the regional government the share was 17%, and for central government the share was 40%. So the Olympic investment financed by public budget does not seem too heavy, especially if one takes into account the results of the event in terms of city marketing. The Barcelona municipality managed to produce a particular and unique concentration of public investment in the city, without producing much more increase in public spending than the normal tendencies in an expansionary period.

For the municipality of Barcelona, the benefits include the new central district for office and service location, the city marketing, and international promotion in the network of the six cities of the Mediterranean group. It is similar to the initiative of other regions – the Belgian parks, tourist plans, promotion of cultural and medical services, and joint ventures in private companies or new industrial premises in the metropolitan region.

At the regional level, there was also important initiatives – new industrial real estate in Catalonia with 60 new locations since the early 1980s, 10 of them in the metropolitan region, two new universities, investment in new infrastructure, special roads and the structure plan for the metropolitan region of Barcelona.

Let me just finish with four observations. The first relates to the explanation of the intensity of unemployment arising from the rigidity of the salary levels. Salaries did not change too much in the metropolitan area of Barcelona, but the way to restructure the labour market was through the closure of companies, producing a large decrease in employment.

The second identifies the role of public and local leadership in the adjustment process. A third point concerns whether there is always a need to introduce this kind of festivalization, to find a mobilizing event to get the infrastructure or the necessary agreement for investment: can it be done or could it produced by other means, such as strategic plans? And finally, in terms of administration one can wonder whether large cities need big governments, as *The Economist* tried to explain from the London experience last year. What we can say from the metropolitan institutions of Barcelona is that probably that there is no special need for a metropolitan tier of government, but there is a need to produce strategic agreements and partnerships between tiers of governments.

The discussion

Chairman: V. K. Phatak

PARTICIPANTS: P. S. A. Sundaram, Julio Dávila, Sandy Taylor,
Nigel Harris, William Lever, A. D. Moddie, G. K. Virman

The discussion concentrated on how a city could exploit the opportunities presented by a major event to set the city on the path of long-term structural change and economic growth. One speaker reflected on the failure to do this in the case of the Asian Games, held in Delhi in 1982. Delhi, he said, lacked a strong metropolitan authority capable of unifying the agencies involved and developing partnerships, using the proposed physical assets to be created as a means of involving private firms. Delhi failed in this respect because it viewed the Games as simply an issue of public provision and expenditure on sports facilities, not a means to push the city in a particular direction. In general in India, municipalities were not encouraged – or even allowed – to be entrepreneurial. Nor was it clear in India how far private firms were interested in participating in infrastructure investment and on what terms.

Birmingham had also made a bid to hold the 1992 Olympic Games but failed. The reason for the failure was that the bid started too late – it was developed over only 18 months, but it requires planning over a long period. Furthermore, unlike the Spanish government's strong support for Barcelona's bid, the Prime Minister in Britain, Mrs Thatcher, only gave late and half-hearted support for Birmingham's bid because the city was under the political control of the opposition party, Labour. Mrs Thatcher had little interest in sport – in contrast to the present Prime Minister, John Major, who was strongly backing Manchester's bid to be the location for a future Olympic Games. Birmingham's bid failed despite being one of the best locations in Britain for this kind of event, with the National Exhibition Centre (created through a 1969 partnership between the City Council and the Chamber of Commerce, and opened in 1976), an international convention centre, a national indoor arena, and so on.

"Festivalization" needed to be seen as not an end in itself, but rather as part of a long-term perspective; for example, it took 12 years campaigning for Birmingham to secure the agreement of the Lions International Organisation to hold its first European convention since 1962 in Birmingham in 1998. That event would bring 40000 visitors to the city for 10 to 14 days.

Another participant wanted to know how far the strong regional identity and regional governmental power in Catalonia was a precondition for making the Games a success as a leverage for economic development; was administrative and financial decentralization a necessary condition? Or was the success of the Games the result of a national and central government commitment? It seemed that it was the regional commitment that had been the key to the success of earlier events in Barcelona; for example, the 1928/9 international exhibition, where the central government had been reluctant to give support.

A speaker asked whether the strategy required a powerful charismatic local leader. That seemed to be so in some of the case studies, with Lille's emergence as an important transport junction being closely associated with the role of the former Prime Minister, Pierre Mauroy. Even Glasgow's success in being nominated as European City of Culture depended upon five or more years of dedicated efforts by the city leadership to change the image of the city. Stockholm, due to make a bid for the 2004 Olympic Games, seemed to lack such a leadership, and this might undermine its efforts.

The issue was also raised of the precise mechanism whereby a one-off event could be converted into a long-term strategy, After all, if "festivals" were sufficient condition of city development, Mecca – with over 10 million pilgrims per year in the brief Haj season – would have long been a very developed metropolis. What were the discussions in Barcelona surrounding the bid; did the city authorities conceive of the Games as the pretext for a long-term strategy rather than a one-off moment of glory with short-term high income generation?

Furthermore, after the event, a participant asked, had there been an evaluation of the net benefits of the Games in terms of revenue and permanent employment generated? In the case of Glasgow's City of Culture – an "event" that lasted a full year – there were various estimates of the jobs created, depending on whether part-time jobs were included. It seems that something like 10000 jobs were created at any one time during the year, and 2000 of these lasted beyond the year itself. This was felt to be quite satisfactory. What was less satisfactory was the distribution of the jobs; those in serious need were not the beneficiaries. Hence, there were suspicions that the events benefited only the cultured middle classes, not the unemployed. However, a less easily quantifiable benefit was the transformation of the image of the city, so that, in Glasgow's case, the subsequent decision to hold the annual conference of the Confederation of British Industry (the main organization of employers in Britain) there for two years was possibly a more important result for the city's economy than the City of Culture event itself. Chief executives discovered it was quite safe to walk the streets, and there were investment opportunities without high risks.

However, it was also important to note that there were risks in seeking to develop through a large event. If the city fails to do it well, the reputation for failure stays with the city much longer than the image of success lasts when an event is done well. Montreal is saddled with both the debts incurred in holding the Olympic Games and with a reputation for financial mismanagement. Beijing's hosting of the World Women's Conference – which the government saw as a great opportunity to publicize a new more liberal image for the regime – patently failed, making the image even worse than it had been before. One cannot make mistakes here. Another speaker raised the addi-

43

tional point of other negative consequences in terms of the under-utilization of the facilities created for the event, as, he said, occurred in the case of Delhi.

In reply, Joaquim Clusa pointed out that private investment during the preparation for the Barcelona Olympic Games went into hotels and offices, which were not directly related to the Games, and into the Olympic villages, which were sold off after the Games were over. So far as it concerned public infrastructure, where costs were fully recovered from consumers – for example, telephones, water, railways, and so on – the new investment was operated on a commercial basis, without drawing on public subventions. The role of the municipality was to acquire land, much of it derelict industrial and port land, service it with new infrastructure and sell it at a relatively low price, usually with a better internal rate of return than in comparable private development schemes.

Was the success attributable to Catalonia's peculiarities? But other Spanish cities had done similar things. Seville had used the World Expo in the same way. In fact, the regional government's share in total investment for the Games, about 35% (compared to the central government's 45%) was not the dominant element, and it was directed at permanent infrastructure additions – the new ring road and railway station, new airport facilities, and so on. Seville saw from early on the importance of obtaining the first high-speed train service in Spain, from Madrid to Seville. On the other hand, local government finance in Barcelona was only a small element in the whole, going into small local infrastructure projects – parks, roads, and so on. However, its leverage over the spending of a mass of different agencies, regional and central, was considerable, so there was an inconsistency between the predominance of non-local funding with local political and administrative leadership.

Were there important negative aspects? Since most of the infrastructure was needed, regardless of whether the Games were held or not, there were not specific negative side effects. In most cities, holding the Games increased investment only in sports facilities. Only in Tokyo and Barcelona were there major infrastructure projects. Some of the hotels were under-utilized after the Games, but this had tended to decline over time. However, the under-utilization of office space was more serious, but this was not necessarily attributable to the Games; after all, London and Paris suffered from this in the same period but without holding the Games.

The key issue is to see an event of this kind in long-term perspective. The Barcelona authorities began campaigning to hold the Games in 1981, so it was a long drawn-out process of lobbying and negotiation. Metropolitan leadership was – as in the Lille case study, where it needed a new and famous mayor for the City Council and Chamber of Commerce to meet for the first time in 10 or 15 years – undoubtedly important.

The work of evaluation of the impact of the Games in terms of the generation of permanent employment was still under way. Particular projects had been evaluated, although it was not always clear what the relevant criteria were. For example, evaluation of the new ring road gave a rate of return of an astonishing 70% per annum. This was because allowance was made for the savings in driving time. If one were to take it seriously, no other investments would take place except in ring roads! In terms of the long-term plan for the city, this is embodied in the second version of the strategic plan, which identified the continuing infrastructure deficits in relationship to a set of proposed objectives.

II Failures and successes: the balance sheet

L. K. Deshpande

If one is to draw up a balance sheet, one requires all the entries. The first thing I found, in looking at the case studies, was that it takes a long time to find out the population of each of the cities. I was told that no-one knows the size of the population of Johannesburg. There is much data that is missing but needed, if only to comment on qualitative judgements of successes and failures.

The second difficulty lies with what sort of criteria should be adopted for judging these successes or failures. The quantitative criteria are too sparse to make a judgement. Consider, for instance a city's structural adjustment experiences. Has the unemployment level gone down to an extent that is acceptable to society? I am sure the answer is no. One cannot say in Europe that people are happy with the levels of unemployment they have succeeded in achieving after going through this programme.

Consider shelter. Achievements in the renovation of housing stock appear to be the most successful, but this may be because of my ignorance: I do not know how dilapidated the stocks are that exist in many cities. But perhaps such renovation is something that, with the help of the developers, has, in fact, been a success – London Docklands could be a prime example and there may be other examples in Birmingham or Glasgow. Yet still people talk of homelessness in most of the cities. Are the levels of inequality greater than they need be? Are the cities tending to be dualistic in the sense that you have a managerial and a professionalized city while the unskilled worker has missed out on the opportunities. So, are we moving towards a dualism in the developed countries that, perhaps, did not exist before structural adjustment programmes were undertaken? Now, this is a consequence of the informalization of activity. There is permanent, stable employment with guaranteed security for a minority. For the rest there is a service sector composed of a highly paid professional managerial class and the other poorly paid majority subsisting on part-time and irregular employment.

Judged on many of the criteria that are fairly well accepted, it is difficult to recommend the process to less developed countries. Perhaps I am being unjust to the experiences – partly because of my ignorance, and partly because I have not visited the cities to get a feeling about what is really happening, rather than reading it in papers and books.

The other criterion that is often employed is that of efficiency, and that is the story of structural adjustment and globalization itself. The big difference in the conditions in less developed countries in contrast to the European and even Latin American countries, is that these societies are highly urbanized, whereas in India we are still a rural, agriculture-dominated society.

The kind of problems that structural adjustment addressed in the developed countries were that, in many cities, industries were obsolete and suffered as globalization took place and trade barriers were reduced. This was an experience quite different from the Keynesian kind of depression, and attention focused on the supply-side factors. These Siamese twins of trade and technological development devastated industries. That was the basis of the need for structural adjustment. This was a crisis of the whole urban economy. It affected the common man, an urban dweller, and, wherever there was an urban crisis, it affected the common man in Europe and Latin America. This does not happen in India where the common man is still in the villages, although less so than before. Urban crises, if they can be called that, are a much more limited experience.

In India, we have had over 40 years of import-substitution planning. The crisis we entered was not one that was well debated, nor was the acceptance of structural adjustment well debated. It was a response to a crisis, and a government decision. No-one was consulted. By comparison, globalization – in the sense of the formation of the European Union, or the British debate on whether to join the Common Market – was well debated, as shown in England by the vote on the issues. Such a thing has not happened in India, and the results of such a debate could be quite different. In Europe there was a much greater acceptance of the benefits that would flow from integration in the world economy, and that was felt even at the ordinary person's level, but there is no such perception in South Asia. That may explain why people have such doubts about what good it would bring, because in the developed countries (except for the Asian Tigers or the Cubs) the evidence as far as the unemployment rate is concerned is not conclusive enough for us to follow. In the less developed countries, faced with the challenge of economic decline because of new competition, the alternative was perhaps worse. If Glasgow was to allow industry to die, to allow the textile industry to decline or the metal industries to be eliminated without action on the part of the city, the conditions might have been worse.

The counter factual is important. What is the counter factual against which we are measuring the successes? If there is agreement that conditions would have been worse without structural adjustment, then what structural adjustment has achieved would be regarded as fairly remarkable – and successful. I would consider the success of the programme only on these grounds. On other grounds I would reserve judgement to a later date.

Almost every case study tells us something. Consider Johannesburg, for instance. Of particular interest was the point regarding differences in the perception of people living in the city. It is a quite fragmented society. The perceptions differ substantially. Those Blacks who started small enterprises in structural adjustment programmes benefited substantially or in small ways from the policies followed. Others have had the opposite experience. So perhaps this could be a pointer to the different assessments. The pessimistic views expressed by many intellectuals about structural adjustment programmes and their applicability to less developed countries, and in particular countries such as India, may arise from this difference in perception. There is a chance that employment and incomes of unskilled workers will increase in certain circumstances: if, for example, the developed countries open to import the activities in which they are not efficient, or if they refrain from pursuing policies that restrict the import of goods or, as someone mentioned earlier, the entry of people who go to work there on contracts. So, if some of these obstacles are removed, some of the developing countries will be able to see the benefits that would accrue. But without that, it would be difficult for anyone to see how structural adjustment programmes would contribute much to the welfare of ordinary people.

The earnings and profits of the managerial and professional classes, the business people, perhaps the highly educated, teachers and so on, may increase, but this may not filter down. But that is not going to make much difference in the short or medium term. What will certainly make a big difference is a change in the demand for unskilled labour in urban or rural areas.

One of the points in an earlier discussion on Jamaica was that one should open both rural and urban economies. This issue did not exist in the case of the developed countries. In India, the structural adjustment programme has not touched the rural sector. And therefore the benefits that could accrue in terms of increased employment in rural areas have not materialized, and it is doubtful whether they will materialize in the next few years unless there is a change of plans.

What are the difficulties? If food is exported (and Indian agriculture could claim to be more efficient in the production of some food commodities – for example, certain varieties of rice) surely the domestic prices of food would increase, and the urban economy, which depends on stable prices for food, surely would suffer. Thus, it would be difficult to open up the agricultural trade to international competition because it would reduce domestic supplies in the short term.

One of case studies from a Latin American country mentions that migration to the city dropped, and helped the city. I would love to see that occur in the case of Bombay. Rather than have administrative controls on migration, restrictions that are economically justified would be more effective and leave no hard feelings and no ethnic or constitutional problems about preventing entry. The developed countries did not have these problems, so this made acceptance and implementation of structural adjustment easier. In developed countries the problem was loss of population from the cities, whereas in our cities there is a flooding of the cities by the migration process. But although one could tackle the first issue, the second one is an immediate problem.

Another thing that is important is that, although urban land could be made available through a change in policies – freeing of land use controls, general deregulation – a city such as Bombay has a physical land constraint. There are areas that are not utilized properly, and the release of such land could increase supply to a particular point. But reading the experiences in developed countries, there does not seem to have been a land constraint. The derelict areas were there. People had left those areas, and it was a question of developing them and persuading people to put them to alternative uses.

Here, if you take the textile industry, the space occupied is tiny. The land price is going to be extremely high even in those areas. The problem is not that there are derelict areas, but people are not prepared to leave them. Although it is granted that there are alternative uses possible, there is much opposition to leaving. This is expressed in participation of social groups; of civil society. This problem was not as acute in the developed countries as it is here.

People in the developed countries have experienced a higher standard of living, and the question is of lowering the standard. In our case, it is a question of improving the standard. The possibility of a drop in standard is seen as an immediate danger, and people react. Current levels of poverty and living standards are accepted, and people have not been exposed to change. Making a sacrifice for something they have never experienced is expecting too much. For people at the poverty level, the struggle is over subsistence. The promise of a better future after things have worked out does not persuade anyone to make sacrifices now.

Can we learn something from the developed countries? What has been done in urban renewal and urban restructuring programmes? Concentration on small industries is of interest: training for small industry, with free consultancy services and advice on withstanding shocks; education and training programmes run by industrial associations and geared to small industry – for example the micro-enterprise experience in Johannesburg. The reason I select this is basically a feeling that structural adjustment is for the big capitalist and not for the common man or the poor.

The success in the cities in the case studies is attributable to a change in psychological make-up – there had to be a vision, an effort to find out and seize the opportunities. These are valid things for all cities to imitate. There must be flexibility of administration. Our city management system in India is fragmented, with little coordination. Each issue is looked upon as a separate project, but the whole city project is lost. One has to develop a city region and the multiplicity of agencies could be reduced.

If one were to go through the structural adjustment programme, deregulating the city, and so on, would it affect the informal sector? There is nothing in the deregulation programme that is designed to benefit the informal sector – the illegal hawkers, vendors, occupants of streets and sites that are not permitted and that violate municipal regulations. There is not much that deregulation can offer to the street economy of the city. It can offer something to the middle classes where the supply of flats, owned or rented, would increase substantially.

We have discussed major events such as the Olympic Games and what can be made of that event in the long term. Events are not going to be of much use or relevance to us here. Urban investment programmes would be of more use in relieving the constraints on the production of goods and services, as would improvements in transport (the development of ports and airports). These have a long-term impact on city economies.

One of the salient achievements of Singapore was its housing schemes, and this is something worth emphasizing; housing can increase health and efficiency, the feeling of security, of belonging and so on. This can improve the productivity of poor people and the informal sector. The Singapore scheme operated from the top down. There are doubts about whether this type of infrastructure can be effective. However, with, for example, WCs within the dwelling unit as opposed to having common toilets that no-one looks after, the problems may be eased. Bombay, as Delhi, has a water shortage, so poorly maintained WCs can lead to major water losses. Western cities are well endowed with some of the basic things such as water, so essential for any city's existence, so this problem may not occur.

The top-down approach does not leave room for participation. There is a provision in Indian housing schemes that 70% of a slum population can impose their agreement on the 30% who refuse to join any improvement scheme. But even then the management of the maintenance of infrastructure may lack participation and so suffer. NGOs working in the old textile area say that redevelopment will displace the population and, because of this, there is no participation in anything, even in housing projects. There is no participation by the NGOs who strive to protect people from the developers. The difficulties are not insurmountable, but one has to think of the ways in which participation can be increased.

Reading the studies presented here I did not get a sense of the mechanics involved. At some stage, we need to know how changes were achieved. For instance, in London, I am told, city planning processes involve NGOs and interested citizens; everyone is involved in discussing the proposals, and leaves perhaps with the satisfaction that parts of his or her plan or arguments have been incorporated in the plans for the city. Is this only an example of Western civil society, a long-established phenomenon and founded in a participative democracy? There traditions are yet to be developed here; we have to struggle to get people to participate in civic and political life. Given such a difference, what we learn from experiences elsewhere would have to be tactfully and intelligently adapted to the needs of cities here.

The discussion

Chairman: D. M. Sukhtankar
PARTICIPANTS: Sandy Taylor, Amitabh Kundu, G. Virmani, Nigel Harris, Julio Dávila, G. S. Gill

The doubts concerning some of the social implications of structural adjustment received much attention in the discussion. One participant noted that the negative effects of reform in terms of unemployment had been apparent in India from 1991, and the impression that unemployment was an inevitable product of the economic policy package seemed to be confirmed in the city case studies. In India, employment had been stable since the 1970s, but its nature had changed – it was increasingly casualized, with low productivity and incomes. The growth of output in the 1980s (in manufacturing, some 7–8%) had barely increased employment (and wages had improved very little). There seemed also to have been an increase in child employment, despite all the statutory prohibitions. This created a dual labour market, parallel to the dualism in the provision of basic amenities – a picture replicated in the case study of Johannesburg. This deterioration in the quality of employment was the reason people opposed deregulation, although there was a strong case for the reform of the regulatory regime. Markets needed to be developed in parallel with institutions.

Others disagreed that there was any simple employment implication from structural adjustment programmes. Each city produced a unique output and therefore had a unique relationship to the world economy, so reactions to liberalization would also be unique. For example, in the Santiago de Chile case study, the city was shown to be entering the sixth year of the lowest rate of unemployment in the country's records. In East and Southeast Asia, liberalization had gone with a rapid growth of employment and incomes. Indeed, one vindication of structural adjustment was not that it helped the rich; some large companies would go under or be taken over in an open competitive market (and some very large multinationals had suffered in global competition – IBM and General Motors, for example – or been obliged to emulate smaller companies through downsizing, networking or dividing themselves into a group of companies). The real justification for reform was that it released a country's comparative advantage – in India's case, an abundance of relatively cheap labour. Thus, the aim was a massive increase in employment and the incomes of the mass of the population, such as had occurred in China.

Where successful, as in East and Southeast Asia, the most striking effect was in employment. But the programme was not always successful, as Sub-Saharan Africa showed. It was therefore important to understand what distinguished success from failure. A key element here was the role of government in facilitating thoroughgoing reform at the same time as seeking to protect the most vulnerable sections of the population – and in this last case, targeting the poor for relief was very much more successful in helping them than providing free or subsidized services to all.

A third theme stressed the considerable local obstacles to reform – for example, inefficient public utilities in Maharashtra. Indian ports handled about 130–300 containers per day, compared to the major ports of Southeast Asia, handling 1300–3500. Indian industry had still not made the transition from a closed seller's market to an open buyer's market. Forty years of protection had not been overturned so quickly. Companies still paid too little attention to prices and quality, unlike the fiercely competitive informal sector, which was obliged to pay attention to the consumer.

Participation was another important theme. In Birmingham, it was said, in the past the interests of established institutions dominated policy discussion, whereas now there was a dialogue with business and the citizens, hence the popularity of the word "partnership". City officers now interacted much more closely with community groups, and this included religious committees (for temples, mosques, etc.), a recognition of one of the city's important economic strengths, its cultural diversity. The Council financed an Employment Resources Committee, linked to, among others, the religious committees, to provide those with whom they were in touch with access to work training, job offers and employers. Another speaker noted the extraordinary growth of non-government organizations in Bombay, a recent meeting on Chowpatti beach had brought together all those involved in environmental questions, including some of the poorest (the associations of rag pickers and of fishermen, for example); for the first time, "recognized" and "unrecognized" organizations met.

Increased participation ought to be part of administrative decentralization, and in this connection it was regrettable that the case studies included no eastern European cities. There, central governments had been forced to decentralize responsibilities to relieve the central budget. At the city level, the housing stock had been privatized with the same motive and, similarly, local government had been obliged to assume responsibilities formerly monopolized exclusively by central government. On the other hand, in the case of housing, tenants often resisted reform – they were unwilling to give up subsidized rents, and the banks were unwilling to lend to tenants to buy their housing because of the doubtful value of the assets.

In India, resistance to the transformation of local government into being development agencies was founded in a deep suspicion of local authorities inherited from British colonial rule. They were permitted to do only what was statutorily specified, and that was defined as providing listed services. In

Bombay, the City Corporation was managed on a day-to-day basis by an appointed civil servant, not a city manager drawn from a cadre of local government officers as in Britain. The Municipal Commissioners was ultimately responsible to the state, not the city. This entailed that the Corporation was ill equipped to be a development agency, or even consider broader issues. This was quite unlike the situation in Europe and Latin America. Thus, Barcelona was not a practical model for India; if Bombay won the nomination to hold the Olympic Games, no-one would expect the City Corporation to manage the affair, but rather the national and state governments. On the other hand, as another speaker noted, Bombay was the first city in India to innovate in contracting out service provision to contractors or groups of citizens. It was also recruiting part-time retired people to undertake casual part-time jobs, improving their incomes without vastly inflating the payroll.

Another speaker noted Professor Deshpande's emphasis that Singapore's public housing programme was where India should draw lessons from abroad, not in deregulation. He argued that Singapore's housing programme depended entirely on the city's spectacular rate of growth of manufactured exports for the past 25 years, and hence on macroeconomic policy and steady structural adjustment. India could not achieve that kind of housing programme without a no less robust macroeconomic policy package, and hence structural adjustment.

In reply, Professor Deshpande agreed with the point made on Birmingham, that the strength of a city lay in its mixture of people of different cultures and origins. Such a city was likely to be far more innovative than one with an "homogenous" population.

He qualified his approach to structural adjustment, which he regarded as unavoidable, but reiterated that more needed to be known about its implications for the employment of the poor. The discussion of training schemes abroad to help improve the skills of the poor was one of the more important issues in the discussion. But in the past in India, deregulation had been damaging and unjust, promoting inequality. Changes in pricing policy to reflect geographical distances had favoured some areas, such as the Bombay–Poona axis, and penalized others such as Bihar. On the other hand, free or subsidized goods or services for all, invariably justified in terms of helping the poor, in fact benefited the rich – or at least, those who were better off.

The advantages of structural adjustment – increased trade, technology transfer, and so on – had to be balanced by recognizing the costs. Economists argued that changes were good if there were gains after those who lost were fully compensated. But in practice, the losers were never paid. What was to be done to compensate those laid off? This was the key issue if the policy package was to be sold to the population at large – those who ultimately would vote on whether the policies should be continued.

The Indian export performance was impressive, but it was increasingly constrained by infrastructural deficiencies. How were the required new investments to be financed? Foreign capital might be induced to help, but there had been problems in this approach in the past – and difficulties in bargaining to get the best deal.

Rapporteur summary

Richard Tomlinson

In 1987 I was giving a paper at Yale. The year was one of the worst in South Africa. I was being vigorously questioned, and it was a long session. The woman who was chairing leaned over to me and said: "Just answer the questions you like and ignore the rest". And I was grateful for that advice and proceeded accordingly. The discussion today has been wide-ranging and I hope you will indulge me if I do the same, and draw on local examples to set the tone. It is particularly appropriate on Barcelona, since the 2004 Olympics may be in Cape Town.

Cape Town has the same population as Barcelona, but of course is much poorer. Cape Town is the one city in South Africa that, despite the last decade of recession, has a growing manufacturing sector and the fastest growing financial and business services sector, is the major tourist centre and has three universities, two of which are pretty good. It is fairly well down the road to being favoured for the 2004 Olympics. The Olympics have never been held in Africa and supposedly the International Olympics Committee considered Cape Town in this light. The Rugby World Cup was held in South Africa recently and was viewed as a test run. It has enhanced Cape Town's position.

In the discussion, many stressed the need for infrastructure. It is a theme that has been emphasized almost to the point of equating economic development with infrastructure. In South Africa we have just formulated a municipal infrastructure investment programme, focusing on major services, such as water, roads, electricity, sanitation. Over a ten-year period a US$15 billion investment programme is proposed. There are four components to the study: working out the backlogs in services, trying to work out the cost of those backlogs, what financial instruments are needed to finance the investment, and how the investment and the subsequent operation and maintenance should be managed. It is anticipated that there will be intense private sector involvement, which has hitherto not occurred in the provision of capital. So, public–private partnership is the rage in South Africa. The private sector is a bit confused about this. The banks are keen to lend. But if large engineering companies are asked to manage infrastructure projects, it is problematic. In the meantime French companies entering South Africa are happy to do so. So a rapid learning process has to occur in the country.

There is a kind of reverse investment process. South Africa has good roads, good telecommunications and a surplus of energy, but a disastrous level of services in the townships and settlements. In a sense we are doing what should have come second. What should have come first we're now doing second. Here in Bombay we discussed developing the airport, getting the road to the airport operational. We have that – but not adequate basic services for the majority of the population.

Cities need to change the way they view themselves and to promote economic development. In South Africa the Ministry for Reconstruction and Development in the Office of the President is promoting a change in the way city authorities view themselves – to make them development agencies, not simply service suppliers. It is facing some opposition from the Department of Trade and Industry, which is nervous about cities having a dynamic role.

What about the information deficiency? How many people live in Johannesburg? To admit how many people lived there was to acknowledge the failure of apartheid: the urbanization of Africans had occurred. Therefore, the lie was advanced: you had to under-count, with disastrous implications for the efficiency of the elections, because ballot papers were distributed on the basis of this lie.

It was said earlier that the Spanish government supplied 40% of the infrastructure costs for the Olympic capital programme. In South Africa this would be extraordinary, because Cape Town is controlled by the National Party. Cape Town and its Olympic bid depend upon an ANC controlled national government for 40% of the budget. The point was made earlier that local politics matters.

There was a discussion after the Barcelona presentation about the Asian Games managed as projects of of public works and housing, and not economic development. That is certainly true in South Africa. Perhaps the Reconstruction and Development Ministry will succeed in selling local economic development. Our first local government democratic elections are being held next month. The demands on the politicians are certainly not on how to promote local economic development; they are on how to get elected.

Under what conditions will the private sector get involved with the public in some form of public–private partnership, either in managing service delivery or promoting economic development? Overtly now, although previously it was probably covert, the private sector is collaborating with government. It is no longer an unsafe practice to do so. Did you see Mandela's speech on being released from prison? He said: "We stand by nationalization of the private sector". The government's rhetoric has changed. The government proposed that a portion of the banks' lending would have to go for prescribed purposes: low-income housing or small business. In the face of threats from the government, the private sector managed to accommodate this. It built a consensus around the Reconstruction and Development Programme, and this led to a change in the rhetoric: it became more constructive. Policy was subject to considerable refocus. Not all the provinces recognize it.

One final comment on Barcelona. What are the equity implications of festival-based glitz? What are the employment implications for the mass of the low-income population? That surely is the measure. The point was made that perhaps image has a more long-lasting implication as a basis for subsequent investment. Investment in what? Cape Town is a beautiful city, a tourism centre for the country, but it is also far from Europe and Asia. Barcelona is much closer. Investment in tourism in Barcelona will be much safer. Investment in manufacturing is more sustained in Cape Town and might be sufficient to justify the levels of expenditure. But there are grave doubts here.

On Professor Deshpande's paper, I came to India with much optimism The potential for successful exports is immense. In Bombay, there is so much enterprise going on, a tremendous level of things to be impressed by. When people referred to the informal sector in a negative way, I was not sure I was correct in understanding it. For me there was a major production system operating inside these shacks. I wished that one could see the same degree of enterprise in South Africa. There is a much greater focus at home that a proper job is a formal sector job. An informal sector job is short term and not something to invest in.

There are other questions – for example, urban migration. In South Africa considerable attempts were made to prevent migration. What they led to was a vicious order. Urbanization occurred anyway, but with a very inefficient city form, because people were located in the most dispersed locations. On migration, we changed from trying to stop it to trying to manage it.

The political struggle and the labour movement in South Africa have been based on a very democratic process, extensive focusing backwards and forwards. Prior to the elections, the ANC and the National Party got together to start formulating policies with many other groups, including NGOs and other political parties. For example, they formulated the country's housing policy. These policies brought together conflicting principles and built a kind of consensus without confronting the contradictions in the principles. For example, there will be delivery at scale: a million houses for South Africa. The amount might sound small for India, but for South Africa it is enormous: houses for all, in five years. After the first year, 9000 were delivered. Delivery on the targeted scale depends on social compacts before you start. If the social compacts dissolve in local politics, if they specify the use of local labour or at least the local community, if you must train local, small contractors, the problems become impossible. There is a real disillusion within government about civil society. Public–private partnerships are one thing, but links to community-based organizations have great problems.

CHAPTER THREE
Finance and governance

I Financing city development

Ricardo Samaniego

What I will try to do in this 40 Mexican minutes is to talk about four topics. The first is a general one, but has much to do with the purpose of this symposium and with the role of cities in economic development. Then I shall address general issues concerning the instruments for financing cities that are available to local government. Thirdly, I will talk a little bit about the experience of México City. And lastly, because of the interest of people in concrete solutions to specific problems, I will talk a little bit about what is going on in the water industry in México City.

Much is written in specialized publications about Robert Lucas's work on the use of the hypothesis of rational expectations in macroeconomic models. Basically, that is the contribution for which he was awarded the Nobel Prize. This, as you may know, has many implications for monetary policy. Mr Lucas argues that governments cannot increase employment by using an active monetary policy. He has also written much about the implications for macroeconometric modelling of being careless in using predictions of what might happen if one pursues different policies. He says that all the parameters we employ in econometrics are subject to change once we change policies, so we must be especially careful with those forecasts. But since I was his student in 1981–2, he has become concerned to understand why growth rates among countries differ so much. Why is it that growth in Korea has increased at 6% per year during the past 30 years but in the Philippines at only 2%? If you compare the numbers for 1960, the two countries looked very much alike. The total population, around 27–8 million, is practically the same. The structure of production in terms of how much went to agriculture or manufacturing is almost the same and the percentage of people in the labour force is also very similar. But 30 years later we find that Korea's income per head doubled every 11 years while the Philippines income per head doubled every 34 years.

What makes these differences in development and growth so variable between countries?

One of his hypotheses has to do with the role of cities in economic development (as Nigel Harris mentioned in the Introduction): the high concentration of human intelligence in cities is a major force, a knowledge spill-over externality that generates, through the human capital interactions, growth, stability and sustainability in the sense of continued growth. So, in order to understand the role of macroeconomic reforms, we have to study cities because they are the places where you can see these interactions taking place, and taking more tangible forms. When you change the policy in a city the effects are rapid. For example, good pricing of services shows up quickly, so you can influence – hopefully for the better – the wellbeing of many people by undertaking sound local policies. Lucas also links different performances to the openness of the economy. Why Korea grew and the Philippines did not has much to do with open markets, with learning by doing and by introducing new products to the market. International trade, by bringing new technologies to countries, can really influence the rate of growth.

In the Introduction, Nigel Harris pointed out at least ten points in the agenda of macroeconomic reform. All had to do with public finances. If you consider, for example, the diminishing of protection in most of the countries that have undergone macroeconomic reform, this has meant that the importance of main cities has decreased, and especially capital cities such as México City. That happened in México City very tangibly: ten years ago, when we had a major earthquake that killed at least 8000 people, we also had an economic earthquake, which meant that the opening of the economy and the reform of the government reduced the power of the state to influence development of the city. On the one hand, the size of the public sector decreased and, on the other, activities found other more attractive locations. Since the late 1980s, no large manufacturing enterprise has established itself in México City or expanded its activities significantly.

New locations for production affected the tax bases. When we speak of global competition for capital, we also have to think about the limits of imposing taxes in a certain region or city. When we talk about the decline in services and the prevalence of direct and targeted programmes such as the ones we have in Mexico, that has meant that México City received 16% of its budget from direct transfers for subsidizing transportation. At the moment we receive no transfers from the federal government because of the new policy of targeting programmes.

Rapid growth of exports also means that the size of the internal market becomes less relevant. There is pressure on public finances as a result of the adjustment process. For example, the *Times of India* today cites the Reserve Bank, saying that local and state governments should reduce their deficits in order not to worsen the global deficit in the macroeconomic accounts. So, local finances also suffer from these restrictions in the macroeconomic arena.

Globalization and liberalization of services also mean a different tax base in terms of structure and size.

A concern for the environment is also important. The four largest car manufacturers had plants in México City ten years ago, but now there is only a large General Motors plant 5 miles from the central district, and that is being transferred to Guanajuato. The land is very valuable.

Finally, the influence of informalization and the decentralization of functions also has implications for public finances in cities. In México City there is much street vending, which is in a sense counter-cyclical. Once there is a large increase in formal sector unemployment, there is also an increase in the number of street vendors. But that means also that the tax base is weakened.

In summary, structural adjustment has been very important in México City for ten or twelve years. We have discussed the topics here and in Chapter 9 Gustavo Garza has criticized the neoliberal model in the case of Monterrey. But we must be careful not to throw the baby out with the bathwater in this case.

Let me give an example. In the nineteenth century, when we had a large debt crisis, it took 70 years to allow the government to return to world bond markets for new loans. In 1982, when we had another debt crisis, it took Mexico seven years to return to world bond markets. This time around in the 1994–5 crisis, we have returned in seven months; that is mainly the effect of the recognition by the international community of the effort that Mexico made in terms of economic reforms.

How are we to finance urban services? This is a critical issue. Consider some numbers for India, Brazil, Colombia and Mexico on the average municipality's source of financing. For India, transfers represent 20% of the source, local taxes 70%, and fees and user-charges 10%; for Brazil the numbers are 65% transfers, 25% taxes, and fees and user-charges 10%. These are averages for all the municipalities. For Columbia transfers represent 48%, local taxes (mainly property taxes) 45%, and fees and charges 15%, and for the whole of Mexico, transfers, including revenue-sharing, represent 60%, local taxes 15%, and fees and user-charges the remaining 25%. There is much variation, but user-charges tend to represent about a third of income and transfers and revenue-sharing are of increasing importance.

So, what are the major characteristics of the sources of financing? Governments, both national and local, intervene in cities, by means of first telling us what to do and what not to do, basically through environmental policies or zoning regulations; secondly by taxing and subsidizing some activities, that is, changing the relative prices; and thirdly, by providing urban services. Basically there are five major sources of financing for services:
- user-charges or fees, a price for the delivery of these services
- taxes, and in the majority of countries, property taxes play a major role
- grants, transfers or revenue-sharing
- loans

- a source that is seldom used but could be important in some cases is own-revenues from properties in the city.

What are the major characteristics of these five sources? First of all, user-charges could be good sources of income for the city, but they are not always ideal. Sources of income should be judged on three grounds. First is the amount of revenue they bring, and how that revenue will behave in the future: what is the income elasticity of this source of income? That is important. Secondly, there is efficiency. That is, if there are disruptions in the allocation of resources, is it bad or worse with this source; it can never be totally neutral except for head-taxes, but these have caused some governments to fall. Thirdly, there are income redistribution effects. So, user-charges are good in terms of yield, because they are a direct form of raising income. They provide much information to the supplier of the service about demand and the characteristics of the demand for that service, and they help to plan the provision of future infrastructure to expand the service. They are also not very distorting in terms of efficiency. But the redistributional role depends much on what type of pricing is followed. Governments tend to use average pricing; average cost pricing, which is simple, is useful but it has no redistribution benefits and it can even be regressive. For example, if water is charged on an average cost criteria, then it might be that those that consume more (basically the rich) may get more subsidies from their consumption.

Marginal-cost pricing is a thing that we economists love, but it is impressively terrible to put into practice. There are many different marginal costs depending on the time of day, on the region served and on the type of user. So, it is basically an idea that is very hard to follow, and so is seldom used. In México City, for example, trying to have peak pricing for underground railway transportation would be something like a revolution, or at least be surprising, because there are genuine aspects of redistribution there; the poorest live farthest from their jobs and they would have to pay much more to get to work. There are two other types of pricing that might have a future. One is having two-part pricing, as for telephones: there is an installation charge, and then a rate that varies with use. That can be good in terms of efficiency, but it is not very good in terms of redistribution. Finally, there is cross-subsidization or discriminatory pricing, where, for example, more is charged for commercial or industrial uses of water in order to subsidize the poor in terms of consumption. That might work, but efficiency is lost even though there is a gain in terms of subsidizing the poorest users of the service.

Property tax is the second largest source of revenue. There has long been a debate on property taxes. Usually they are considered regressive, because the income elasticity of the demand for property is less than 1, which means that, in relation to their incomes, the poor spend more on housing or properties than the rich. There are others who say that, true though this is, there are many discounts for the poor and in that sense it will be progressive. The discussion is more empirical than theoretical. It has been found that, for some income brackets, property taxes are regressive, but for others they are progressive.

Grants are the third form of revenue raising. This is very important because they are an instrument for regional development. In Mexico a big discussion on the new fiscal federalism is going to take place. We currently have a formula for redistributing a fund made up of income taxes, value-added taxes, other oil taxes and other specific production taxes. The size of the grants made to the regions is determined by the size of the population (45%) and the states' tax contribution to the federal government (45%) with a further element (10%) related to the relative poverty of the region. There is much discussion about whether more responsibilities should be decentralized to the states, giving them more taxation powers.

Loans are limited in their scope. Basically, local governments, the federal district (México City) especially, cannot enter into debt freely. Debt has to be approved by Congress, because of the macroeconomic considerations. México City is so large that it could not run a large deficit without affecting the general macroeconomic programme. I heard earlier from Joaquim Clusa that the ratio of debt to annual income was about two in Barcelona. In México City, total debt is 1.5 billion pesos and total income for a year is about 20 billion, so there is much room to get indebted. But we do not do so because we are paying a low service charge for current debt, and many of the states in Mexico are having trouble paying the burden of that debt. The experience in the 1980s, when the federal government had to assume our debt, is also important; the government does not want that to happen again. It is comparable to New York City, which went into heavy debt in the 1970s by borrowing to finance current expenditure. Debt must be used to finance infrastructure that will yield revenues for repayment.

Finally, there is income from property. This is a source that can be used if a city is a large owner of real estate. In the case of São Paulo, for example, the city took advantage of increases in the value of property to finance more infrastructure, instead of allowing those capital gains to go to the private sector.

Now the third theme: what has happened in México City since the early 1980s? The case of México City is almost identical to that of São Paulo in terms of population growth – the first million was reached in the 1930s, rising through 3 million in the 1950s, and 9 million in the 1970s to 15 million in the 1990s. Right now there are about 8.5 million people in the federal district plus 8.5 million in municipalities of the State of México. In the same years, the area concerned went from about 80km^2 in 1930, through 115km^2 in 1950, and 360km^2 in 1970, to about $1200–1500 \text{km}^2$ in the 1990s (the figure depends on how it is measured), so population densities first increased, and then have tended to decrease a little bit in terms of the whole area of metropolitan México City.

In the manufacturing sector, employment went from 3 out of 10 workers in 1970 to 2 out of 10 in 1990; the service sector and some commercial activities have been expanding.

From 1983 to 1988, local sources of income, including the revenue from, for example, transportation enterprises and other publicly owned operations, were only 16% of the total budget. In 1988–94, that increased to 56%. Revenue-sharing transfers dropped from 60% to 40% of that total (those are the subsidies mentioned earlier). Subsidies to transport fell from 15% to 2%. Subsidies are currently only used for the solidarity programmes, the poverty alleviation programmes, and that financing also fell from 9% to 2%.

Why did it happen? There has been a large increase in all sources of income through the increase in taxes. Property taxes went up five times in real terms in six years – I have found no other precedent in large cities anywhere. Water fees, which were formerly not charged, went up five times in real terms. It was a large adjustment. There was a big reform by which the values of properties and all the water fees were adjusted, but also the effect had to do with what happened in 1983–88. Then we had hyperinflation: 159% in 1987 and 100% in many other years. This eroded the tax base, so it is a large increase, but from a diminished base.

México City is now receiving less in proportion to the revenues shared with the Federation. It is interesting to note how the funds are distributed. If we make a fund of 100 units, say, out of personal income tax and value-added tax, and so on, the Federation keeps 80 of those and redistributes 20. Out of the 20, México City used to receive 25%, that is, about 5 of the 100 in the total fund. Now we are receiving less than 14%. That means that the old claims that used to be made in Mexico and elsewhere – that México City was being subsidized by the rest of the country – are no longer true. The reverse is true. México City is transferring resources to other regions, and that is a good thing, but it has reached a limit in the lower band.

What we have not studied in México City is the effect of these efforts on the redistribution of income and opportunities. In terms of services, transport and water take about 35% of the whole budget of the city. Within transport, bad price policies (very low prices) operated in the underground system (linked incidentally to the Olympic Games in 1968). When it was designed, the underground system was a matter of pride for the city. When it opened (in 1969, not 1968) it cost 1 peso to ride about 40 km. That peso covered operational costs only. The city (and it was not the city that built the underground, but the Federation) decided not to consider the infrastructure costs, but to recover operating costs only. After 27 years of operation the fare increased from 1 peso to 40 cents in new pesos (which are 1000 times the old because of the monetary reform of 1993). But operating costs have gone up to 1.20 new pesos. Thus, the current price covers only about one-third of operational costs. The user can travel 178 km in the system, so its extent has quadrupled, but the share of the price in operating costs has fallen to one-third. The poor suffer more from not having the metro system as it was designed 26 years ago. We should have by now double the infrastructure of the underground system, but resources are not there to continue building. So, the poor pay much more than users of the underground because they live far away. They have to take 2 or 3 buses and they take longer in their journeys to work. In theory it may be a good thing to have a subsidized metro. In reality it benefits some manufacturing workers and their employers, but the really poor cannot use the metro because it does not reach the poorest regions of the city. The same happens with water.

Pricing policy is tricky in the sense that sometimes we intend to benefit some group, and we end up harming them with our policies – as occurs in Bombay with the freezing of rents. It is the same in México City. Areas where rents were frozen are now really in very bad shape.

Now the issue of water. As you know, privatization has meant in many cities that telephone companies, telecommunications, transport and so on have been largely privatized. In Mexico there were stories of how to promote private sector participation in water. But in the end it was decided not to follow the Buenos Aires model, by which a concession of the infrastructure for water provision was set up. Instead, México City contracted out services to companies. There are four companies providing metering of water services. They will also be handling the building of the water system on behalf of México City government. This is the first stage in the strategy. This is an improvement on the old situation, because then it was an inefficient public monopoly. There was also a fragmentation of functions: one organization installed the meters, another built, and another managed the hydraulic system, and they did not communicate. So a Water Commission was created that tries to coordinate all these activities. There was some indirect competition in some elements of the market, because the contracts are given to the best bids or the lowest-cost providers of these services. The idea of having four companies was to have a little competition, even if there is a local monopoly in the city. If one of the companies is not doing well, at least there is another one that can take its place.

We aim to have universal water metering. The intention is environmental, because 70% of the water consumed in México City comes from the aquifers below the city. More water is being taken out every year than is being replenished, so one day it will be exhausted.[1] But also, there are important risks from earthquakes, because when the ground beneath México City was full of water, it acted as a shock absorber. When it has no water, the risk of major damage during an earthquake is much increased. So the idea is to decrease water demand for environmental reasons. Water is also brought from 140 km away and this is very costly. It takes much energy to bring water up more than 1000 m and then go down again to the valley of Mexico. There is also some unjust distribution of water supply in regional terms. We take water from other parts of the country, and that is not sustainable. So we have to meter and charge water correctly so that people will begin to decrease consumption.

---

1. As a result, buildings have been sinking – anyone who has been in México City may have noticed that the steps are 4 m below the ground in some monuments.

Actually, the daily consumption of water in México City is 300 litres per head. It is almost twice as much as in Paris, and we are many times poorer. Those are the incongruities of this model.

What will happen in the future? The company will buy water wholesale from the government of the city and distribute it to homes. Profits will come from two sources. It has to pay for the water mains, the secondary network of water supply in México City (which, by the way, is losing 30% of the water every year), but if it has good maintenance techniques, and if the company acts correctly, it will increase its profits. Secondly, if it has a reliable register of users and a good building system in the first stage, then in the second stage it will also increase its company profits. So, the idea is to have in some years from now full-market prices for water, together with a subsidization programme for the poor.

The idea might be similar to a scheme in a city in Chile, where the government is charging water at marginal cost and is subsidizing basic water consumption heavily for poor families, but not consumption above a certain level. That is a good scheme because it favours the poor mostly. The paradox of our recent system was that, in theory, poor families could consume all the water they wanted because there were no metered consumption charges (there was only a low fixed charge), but actually there was no water for them, and they had to buy it from private vendors – at a price many times more than that paid by the richest families in México City, both in time and in terms of the price per litre of water.

The discussion

Chairman: Julio D. Dávila
PARTICIPANTS: Zilton Macedo, Lalit Deshpande, Richard Tomlinson, Peter M. Townroe, Diego Carrión

The discussion largely consisted of points of clarification, questions or comparisons. From São Paulo, four separate problems were raised concerning:

- The competition of states and cities to offer financial inducements to inward investment, leading to serious reductions in state or city revenue without any clear effects (the companies that invested may well have invested without the incentives).
- The tying of revenues to specific expenditure, as specified under the Brazilian constitution, was another problem drastically reducing the freedom of manoeuvre of states and cities.
- The anomalies in the method of charging for water and electricity, which allowed large-scale avoidance of paying.
- The large loss of water through leakages. To overcome this, the author-

ities allowed free water supplies in slum and squatter settlements, provided a person was appointed to shut off the water when not being used; and there was an educational programme on saving water.

Another contributor asked about the merits of marginal-cost pricing for services in Mexico, and whether the capital costs of infrastructure were subsidized. With high inflation and wage indexation, costs must rise more rapidly than taxation could be adjusted; how was this situation handled?

In South Africa, the World Bank had recommended both the complete privatization of local public services, and for it to have a direct lending relationship to cities, both of which proposals were rejected by the government. But half infrastructural spending was now private, in various combinations with the public authorities. Was this a good model for other countries?

Finally, a speaker asked how this technical policy discussion related to the real world of corruption and violence in the city, especially where the drug trade was important.

In reply, Ricardo Samaniego made five points:

- Mexican states, like the Brazilian states, pressed hard to raise their revenues by charging for infrastructure use, but competition was traditionally curbed by federal regulations on tax levels. There was pressure to relax these, but so far this had been resisted on the grounds that all states could be worse off in competition. So far as cities were concerned, the impact of local taxes was small – under 3% of starting a new business in México City – so there was not much inducement to offer incentives (but both states and cities competed in offering land on concessional terms). There were in Mexico also mandatory taxes; formerly 15% of the states' budgets had to be devoted to education, although this had now been scrapped. It made some sense to embody national priorities in this way lest states just transfer funds between heads for other purposes.

- The Mexican Constitution listed the public services that municipalities were supposed to provide, but it was not clear why all of these should be publicly provided. In the case of water, for example, its consumption could be individualized for charging purposes, and its marginal cost was not zero (the defining characteristics of private goods). The same was true of transport and garbage collection and disposal. Because there was too much in the public sector, priorities became confused and genuine public goods were neglected. For example, in México City the public authorities spent too much on transport and water, which could be privatized, and too little on the administration of justice and the police services, which could not.

- With the privatization of México City's water supply to four companies, it might have been possible to introduce marginal-cost pricing, but this was likely to have hit the poor very hard. In the short run, it was too complicated to introduce a scheme that fully protected them, so the decision was taken not to employ marginal-cost pricing. A large subsidy element remained in the water system; the cost was 2 billion pesos, but charges raised only 800000 pesos. Over time it would prove possible to move to a more sensible system.

- The shift to much more local revenue-raising had raised costs in the Federal District of México City, and thereby perhaps discouraged inmigration (and encouraged it to move to the large part of México City outside the Federal District). It went with increasing democratization: in 1997, for the first time since 1928, the mayor would be elected, along with 16 city councils at the level of the delegations. They would all demand a right to participate in the raising and spending of moneys, and that would encourage a much wider participation. So, more local revenue raising was part of the process of greater financial accountability and democracy.

- No city issues can be considered in isolation from things such as corruption. In México City, deregulation instructions and administrative simplification proposals were regularly issued, and disappeared in the delegations. All one could say is that one needs, in every decision, to know who is most at risk by the change, so that funds can be established to compensate them. If a project is socially desirable but privately not, then public funds need to be committed to make it possible. So far as corruption was concerned, progress was limited until higher pay was possible; and for that, the city needed to raise more revenue or waste less in expenditure.

II New forms of governance

O. P. Mathur

Why are we talking more and more about issues of governance, of management, particularly as we refer to cities in the developing countries? What has happened over the past five years or so to make this subject as important to us in India as in other countries?

Secondly, who are the actors in managing or governing cities? Who are the stakeholders? What is the role of the state in governing cities, of the market, of NGOs and CBOs? What are the signs that a city is better governed or badly governed? What kind of measures can be used?

Thirdly, what are the new challenges that cities in developing countries face as they relate to governance? What are they likely to face in the course of the next ten years or so? Would these challenges mean that the roles of the various stakeholders will undergo a change?

Fourthly, do we see any light in dealing with these challenges? Are the initiatives taken making a difference to the management of cities? These are the four sets of issues I propose to deal with.

If we look at South Asia, the first reason for governance becoming a key issue is that cities are breaking down. Urban populations have risen at a rapid rate, anywhere between 3.2% and 3.7%. In many countries of Africa, rates have been very high. In some of the South Asian countries, rates have been high. But the cities have not been able to absorb this urban population increase. The relevance of the old system of managing cities, the systems and the instruments that we have had for long periods, are losing their relevance, are becoming obsolete; especially the old systems of governance and management.

The second reason is the overwhelming importance of decentralization, particularly in developing countries as also in the transitional economies of the heirs to the USSR and eastern Europe. There is a tremendous shift from central to local control. Power is being delegated more and more to local and urban governments. The trend towards decentralization is not necessarily a result of demand from the local government. It is also coming from the resource crunch that many governments are facing. There is no money at the central government level to deal with the functions they have been handling for several decades. They are decentralizing their expenditure responsibilities to local governments. This is not necessarily being accompanied by a fiscal revolution, or granting fiscal powers to local government, but simply the expenditure responsibilities, which is causing a major crisis at the local level.

In many countries, even the roles thought not to be appropriate at that level, distributional and economic functions, are being decentralized. Poverty alleviation has been one of them. We were told that income distribution is better achieved at the national level, but now even poverty alleviation and economic development functions are being assigned to local governments. This is causing a different kind of pressure on local governments in terms of managing their affairs, of governing cities.

The third factor is a global emphasis on issues such as democratization at a local level, accountability and transparency. There are pressures for more elected councils at the local level. There should be accountability of local government in functions they are responsible for. We are talking more about civil society at a local level. These are new norms. Councils are being asked that, whatever they do, it should be transparent, accountable, which means that even though a city might be better governed in terms of the provision of services, in terms of accountability and transparency, the city may rate low.

Who governs cities and what role do the various stakeholders play? This is not only a complex question but also a highly elusive one. In New Delhi, this is a standard refrain. If anyone can find out who governs New Delhi, that person should be entitled to one of those prestigious prizes given out every year. No-one has been able to discover who really governs Delhi and how Delhi is governed. Local governments have traditionally played a significant role in managing cities because they have been responsible for performing four major types of function, which relate to public health, safety, public works and public order.

Except in a few countries, municipal governments derive their existence not from constitutions but from legislation or central Acts. This has a major implication: the functional domain of municipal governments remains a matter of joint occupancy between the centre and the locality in the case of unitary states, and in the case of federalist structures, the centre and provinces or estates and local governments. Joint occupancy of function is the rule, rather than municipal governments enjoying exclusive powers. This goes straight into the issue of governance. You can imagine the kind of complicated structures that it can lead to. Their functions can be taken away by higher levels of government as and when they like. That has been happening at least in the case of India, where even services, water supply and sewerage, have been taken away from municipal governments and passed on to statutory agencies. The legislature provides powers to intervene and take away those functions.

Thus, they have very limited autonomy. The fiscal powers of municipalities in the intergovernmental distribution of resources is extremely narrow and inelastic. The sources they have at their disposal are inelastic compared to the central or state governments; they are not buoyant. Property taxes have proved to be the most stable of sources on international evidence. Their economic importance is declining almost uniformly. The way in which the fiscal domain has been decided in most countries is independent of functional responsibilities. The imbalance between expenditure responsibilities and the fiscal domain is a common story: demanding more resources than is permitted by the states and the central government.

It is the same case with tax rates, tax bases, the charges for various services such as user-charge. Municipal governments are not free to fix them and adjust them as the cost of providing services increases; these have to be approved by higher levels of government. This lack of autonomy has affected the functioning of local government in almost every country.

Although city authorities have a major stake in city governance, the limits within which they can operate are narrow, and that is imposing major constraints on both infrastructure and service provision, and the performance of the other functions.

Now the operations and maintenance, and infrastructure provision are rather discrete functions. Hence, the origin of creating different institutions in many countries. The technology that is needed for maintaining a city and operating the services is very different from the technology required for capital works and incremental infrastructure. Rather than leaving the matter to municipal governments, it was vested in separate organizations. As the demand for, say, water increased, and water had to be brought from long distances over which the municipalities had no jurisdiction, it was considered essential that there should be higher-level bodies that should become responsible for infrastructure construction as well as meeting these inter-

67

jurisdictional requirements. They are not representative bodies, and it was considered that this would prevent intervention by elected representatives, as happens to be the case of municipal governments. They would be able to operate on commercial lines more freely. But over a period of time they have remained as much dependent on budgetary resources as municipal governments are. And the story in terms of efficient functioning is no different from the municipal level.

The private sector, the state, the market: what are their roles? We have had a dominant assumption that services – water supply, sanitation, street lighting, road maintenance, primary health, basic preventive medicine, and so forth – are publicly run and publicly provided. They were treated as natural monopolies. But this is being proved by evidence as a misplaced assumption. The market has always played a major role even in the provision of water. If you take into account the proportion of people who have been dependent on, say, a hand pump for drawing water, it is often private enterprise. One can extend the same example to many other services and one would find that the private sector has been pretty active. The market has responded even on those services that are collective in nature, such as street lighting, which could not really be charged. There is at least one example of a town in northern India where the street lighting was privatized; the contract was given on the grounds that if the municipality was spending 100000 rupees on maintaining street light but a private party could maintain it on 80000 rupees, why not?

The story of the NGOs is a very recent one. We still do not have a clear picture of whether they substitute for the public sector or complement it. NGOs and CBOs were essentially welfare-orientated in initial approach, but they are now becoming more development-orientated. NGOs are also playing an important role in initiating public policy debates. A few NGOs now prepare what has come to be known in India as the "report card" on cities. In Bangalore one of the NGOs is preparing a survey of public opinion on how the Bangalore corporation functions. Those report cards are becoming available and it is initiating a kind of forum where debate on public issues develops.

What is the collective impact of this range of agencies? There is a state, a market, CBOs. Yet, cities are collapsing. Which brings me to the third point: how effectively are cities governed? The evidence shows that cities are not being governed well and that services are inadequate. Half the people in Mexico get 300 litres of water, and in Brazil 200 litres. But the differences, even in progressive cities in India, would be that in some areas water per capita is 25 litres to anywhere between 700 to 800 litres of water.

The financial part is also bad. In India local governments get less than 1% of GDP. What municipal governments are able to raise works out to close to 0.8% of the GDP. The rest is raised by either the central government or state. The municipal governments raise, as a proportion of what the central government raises, about 3.2% in India.

Yet cities produce close to 50% of the GDP. The municipal governments are outside the network of economic activities that take place in cities. There is a disjunction; they are not able to connect with the economic activities that continue to take place in cities. Cities are rich, but municipal governments are poor.

What kind of regulations are operated by municipal governments? They are highly constraining. A study recently carried out by the NIUA shows that the share of transaction costs for doing anything with the municipal government would be anywhere between 35% and 40%. Whether you ask for a permit to construct a building, to take a licence for setting up a kiosk, the costs would go up by 35%–40%. This is either speed money or corruption.

In terms of the fourth indicator, how participatory is this governance? The story is dismal. At any given point of time in India, anywhere between 35% and 40% of municipalities remain under suspension or dissolution. The situation may change as a result of the recent constitutional amendment. In the fourth largest city in the country, there have been no elections for the past 22 years. The city has been administered by the state government.

The overall picture is rather dismal and that enhances the importance of the whole subject of governance. What of the new challenges? By the turn of the century 50% of people will be urban. How should this demographic shift be dealt with? It constitutes a major challenge for local government in terms of governance.

The economic composition of output of cities is changing rapidly. Cities are becoming informal. The trend towards informalization of the economy is rapid. Forty years ago every activity could be accounted for. Today and in the years to come, cities are becoming informal, to a large extent even illegal. How does one govern cities where half their activities are illegal or informal? Our instruments of control have not dealt with this.

I am reminded of a story. About 15 years ago there was an oil boom and everyone was travelling to the Middle East. I was going abroad and, at the airport, I ran into a friend who was in aviation. I said "Can't you manage this airport?". He said that formerly all the people who were travelling abroad were educated. Today a majority of people are those who do not know which side of the passport is the right side. The same situation exists in cities where there are informal activities. There are more activities on the roadside than in the multi-storey structures.

Along with the economic composition, the social composition is changing. Poverty is not unique to our countries, but the concentration of the poor in cities is a completely different challenge.

Fourthly, issues of globalization, capital mobility and technological mobility place tremendous pressure on cities. In a recent paper we calculated the proportion of foreign investments (FDIs) approved and their spatial distribution for India over the past four years. Of these FDIs, 55–60% have been approved for cities, not rural areas. Secondly, they have been approved for states that are more progressive: Maharashtra, Delhi, Gujarat and so on. Cities have to deal with this mobility of capital, raising the question of whether cities have the capacity to absorb, say, US$2 billion dollars of investment.

This brings me to the issue of the 74th constitutional amendment and its effect over the past three years. The roots of this go back to 1989 during Rajiv Gandhi's time as Prime Minister. He tried to bring democracy to the local level. He introduced what was the 65th amendment to the constitution: that local and municipal governments, and rural local bodies should be recognized by the constitution, given more powers and be revived. This constitutional amendment could not be passed. It was defeated in the Upper House and the Prime Minister had to resign on that issue. It was defeated by two votes in 1989. This led to elections and a minority government, the present one, which in 1992 somehow was able to push through two amendments, the 73rd and the 74th: the 73rd dealing with rural local bodies, the 74th with the urban government.

The amendments ensure that municipal governments, and similarly rural authorities, cannot be kept under dissolution or suspension, although state government still reserves the right to suspend them – but only for no more than six months at a time. Elections must be held.

Secondly, municipal governments are no longer being viewed as civic bodies only. Functions that are of a distributional or a developmental nature are being assigned to local government. The constitutional amendment gives an indicative list. Poverty alleviation should become a local function, as part of the planning for economic and social development. One has to ask whether this would really lead to the emergence of city-states such as Bombay. Would Bombay become more like Hong Kong and Singapore?

Thirdly, on the ad hoc relationship that has existed between the state and local government over fiscal relationships, the constitutional amendment goes in the direction of removing the discretionary nature of the relationship, by providing for the setting up of a state finance commission to deal with these issues. What tax assignment should take place? What taxes should be shared between the state and local bodies? How should grant aid be devised? We hope that there would be some better coherence between what the functions and fiscal domain would be. This amendment also provides for involvement of the private sector, recognizing explicitly its potential role.

In conclusion, governance is a much larger issue and is not to be reduced to the provision of water supply or garbage disposal facilities. The second concluding point is that this adjustment is making boundaries irrelevant. This changes the role of cities in economic and global structures. We have not yet started a debate, but we should enter into one in the years to come. The final point is that the distinction between public and private is becoming rather fluid and thinning out. As students, we learned that public goods need to be provided by public agencies. Private goods, because they happen to be discrete, can be charged to individuals. That distinction is becoming somewhat irrelevant. Financial innovations and new mechanisms of charging make it possible to charge individuals even for those goods that are completely collective in nature.

The discussion

Chairman: Cheryl Gopaul
PARTICIPANTS: Nigel Harris, Gustavo Garza, G. K. Virmani, Julio D. Dávila, Cho Padamsee, Lalit Deshpande, G. S. Gill

Decentralization, it seemed, was emerging all over the world, apparently related in the minds of government leaders to local issues, but in reality impelled by global problems – which was why it was becoming so uniform. It could not be related to cities collapsing, since that had been the perception for over a century. The issue was not simply central-to-local government, since, at the local level, government was giving way to "governance". The term was deliberately vague since it did not refer to one clear agency, but to a changing coalition of interests, the boundaries of which were blurred. Government did not now "deliver", it "facilitated" – it was only one of several leaders in the city. Bombay First was a good example of an extension of public leadership in the city beyond the boundaries of government. Some of the components were stable, others would enter and leave the coalition. Just as "governance" had blurred the concept of government, so "planning" had now become blurred, mixing perspectives, scenarios, policies; in the former sense of planning, no-one now did it – no-one, in an unstable world, could now pretend to determine the outcome of government action.

Decentralization was part of the search for flexibility in the global economy. This was seen clearly with large companies, multinational corporations, in the rage for "downsizing", networking, subcontracting, and even, as with AT&T, dividing the corporation in three. All this occurred after a century and a half of the drive to state centralization. The reversal of the trend suggested powerful necessities. One speaker asked why the management of Bombay was not subcontracted to private agencies?

Another speaker reiterated that cities had become decisive for the survival of countries – three cities in Mexico produced half the national manufacturing output. Furthermore, "governance" had come to include not just agencies outside the public sector but a multiplicity of experimental organizational forms within the public sector. The State of Nuevo León in Mexico, for example, had set up a private land corporation to handle its land transactions on a private basis.

The diversity forces the number of those participating in governance to be very large. Would it not make effective action impossible? How could one limit the number of people involved?

In Colombia, there had been a radical fiscal, political and administrative decentralization, and all to seek to restore the legitimacy of the state. Years of armed warfare, the drug trade and corruption had all undermined that legitimacy – there were 40000 murders in the country this year. This was a crisis of the political system and the two parties swapping office. It had developed over the past decade. Non-party candidates were now tending to win elections. Bogotá, with a population of 6.5 million, had elected a non-political mayor who refused to spend more than $1000 on his campaign. He fought on a six-point programme: to create a citizen culture, to clean up the environment, to protect public space, to enhance urban productivity and to establish institutional legitimacy. One of the key issues was to establish the communal disciplines for living in a city, to increase traffic and pedestrian discipline, and to mobilize public opinion in support of this.

Another speaker wondered whether decentralization meant more than a temporary redistribution of power within the public sector, a process that could be reversed in due course: why was it seen as a necessary trend? A question was also raised as to why the symposium was treating cities as individual entities, instead of, as in the past, looking at urban policy covering the whole sector?

Professor Mathur replied. People had indeed feared the collapse of cities over the past hundred years, but then it entailed only the collapse of one city; now whole countries were threatened if a city fell. Cities were threatening to the national order; in Latin America, for example, they had undermined macroeconomic stability through their debts. The rearrangement of power taking place under the cover of decentralization represented a struggle for power, and that struggle was likely to intensify in the future, producing even more radical changes of distribution. The fragmentation of government also affected even services provided – water and sewerage were dealt with together in the past as a convenient means of assessing levies, but now they, like manufacturing goods, were being "unbundled" so that each stood alone as a costing item. The same was true in subcontracting – it was a form of unbundling: investment activity was separated from operations and maintenance. In China, landownership was vested in the state, but user rights were available to others.

Rapporteur summary

Sandy Taylor

There are ten key issues from the two presentations, which I think provide important messages from this symposium for the 1996 Istanbul Conference. These issues are particularly important, as it is essential that:

- the wider urban and economic regeneration agenda be clearly identified
- strong civic responsibility be achieved
- the two key stakeholders of cities in the world – citizens and businesses – are fully recognized and supported.

Cities exist and cities are required because:

- They provide shelter for *citizens*. But they also provide an important, essential and continuing source of employment and enterprise. As part of this process, they are also places of fun.
- They are also places where *business activity* can take place.

Therefore, businesses must have the conditions to locate, operate and provide employment for citizens in ways that are supportive of the quality of life of those citizens.

It is the responsibility of cities and the civic and business leadership to ensure that the needs of these two key stakeholders are understood, addressed and met by determination of strategic policies and support infrastructure.

I would now like to turn to the ten points that I wish to raise.

Influence of informality

In his talk on México City, Ricardo Samaniego referred to the potential influence of informality in the economy. It is an evident feature in most cities throughout the world, and perhaps particularly in larger cities, that the informal economy is a substantial part of economic activity. This raises several issues that must be considered and addressed, and perhaps greater attention needs to be paid to them. However, the key issues are:

- the informal economy can weaken the tax base of a city, as not all expenditure is being properly accounted for.
- however, it may also provide a counterbalance in any recession within the formal economy. There appear to be signs that this may have happened in the case of México City, and it is therefore something that must be recognized in the future planning of cities.

Thus, the influence of the informal economy can be seen as an important element in developing the formal enterprise economy and urban policy. City government policy must recognize this in local economic development strategies, and envisage a continuum and a process where the gap between informal and formal is reduced.

Financing of cities

Ricardo Samaniego provided some interesting information about the proportion of income for México City that is raised from fees and user charges, and the lower proportion of income raised through local taxes (at 15% compared with 25% for fees and user charges).

This does appear to raise some fundamental questions of equity regarding the application of fees and user charges. It is a matter that must be addressed by city governments in terms of the differential impact that it may have on those who are in severe poverty. This is an issue that is common to all governments and cities. But because of the numbers of people who live in cities and the concentration of those in poverty (both absolute and relative), it is important that the question of the use of average costs versus marginal costs, cross-subsidization, and two-part pricing be considered.

The experience of providing basic infrastructure (water, sewerage, roads, electricity and gas), and the role of private financing in this and, where appropriate, the privatization of the utilities, is also a crucial factor in appropriate fees and user charges.

Appropriate regulatory regimes need to be put in place. In the UK, the privatization of the utilities for telecommunications, gas, water and electricity was supported by the creation of regulatory authorities to act and protect the needs of consumers. Whether these have supported the rights and needs of citizens and businesses in cities needs further debate.

However, it needs to be recognized that the regulatory authorities can only set the environment for price raising, and the customer and the utility then have to react to the financial pressures that are placed upon them and meet the profit targets set within the investment market-place.

However, the key issue relates to maintaining the ability of city governments' capacity to raise taxes locally. This includes the ability to raise taxes from business, and also covers the issues of the appropriateness and use of local income taxes and other specific taxes related to a cities' economic strengths and capacity (e.g. tourism taxes).

The financial capacity of cities to raise their taxes also fundamentally ties them in more closely to the 2 key stakeholders, namely the citizens and businesses of the city. In the UK, this relationship with business in particular has been fundamentally challenged by the UK government's introduction of the Unified Business Rate, which effectively nationalized the local business taxation system in 1989. There is now increasing pressure for that to be de-nationalized.

Impact of frozen prices

Ricardo Samaniego referred to the question of the impact of regulating pricing mechanisms within urban areas. We also heard about the particular situation in Bombay with regard to property rents.

Prices are an emotive subject because of the impact they have on sections of the population, particularly those in poverty. We have heard the issues with regard to user charges and fees previously, but there are serious issues concerning a social policy that seeks to maintain a level of historic pricing without regard to the real cost of current provision.

The particular examples that have been highlighted relate to:

- The construction of the México Metro, where in 1969 the operating costs were 100% financed by the revenue raised from fares. By 1993/4 the fare revenue covered only 33% of the operating costs. The effects of this were that the extent of the Metro system was restricted because there was no money to cover new investment and, as the city expanded through population growth, the lack of that Metro extension meant that the poor, who generally lived in the extension areas, suffered because they were restricted in their opportunities to access employment in the rest of the city.
- In Bombay, we heard about the considerable period of frozen rents for housing, whereby the rent was held at the price level prevailing when the building was constructed. This led to serious problems of under-investment in the maintenance of the existing housing stock, and therefore deterioration in the housing standards of those who were housed. Therefore it did not encourage re-investment in the housing stock, a major priority in a city such as Bombay.

The financing of cities is a complicated balancing act at any time. However, there needs to be proper consideration given to all the financial variables, including the pricing of basic infrastructure. It may well be that the appropriate political and civic judgement is that there should be some degree of subsidy of some of the basic infrastructure costs. However, this must be considered in a dynamic sense and not necessarily enshrined in a legislative format, which becomes difficult to adjust to suit the economic and financial condition of the city.

Local taxation

Ricardo Samaniego drew out the application of local "over-pricing" or additional local taxation in financing cities. Local taxation clearly must have a place in addition to local property taxes. Consideration needs to be given to a range of issues regarding this, but it can never replace an allocation of national taxation to redistribute resources nationally.

However, local taxation clearly can have an influence when it comes to local income tax, petrol taxation, local consumption taxation, and taxation related to economic strengths of the city (e.g. bed tax or tourism tax).

Confidence and trust

With the management of any city, there is always the risk of financial mismanagement and the potential of reduced confidence through either bad management or corruption. It is important therefore that the political and administrative risk of this occurring must be built into the procedures and accountability of the use of public money. This relates to:

- having a clear view of who bears the financial risks; this relates to a clearer relationship between a national government treasury view of financial risk, and the ability of city governments to assess risk in a local political and financially professional way:
- to ensure that there are effective procedures instituted for the financial management of cities and the awarding of contracts.
- ensuring that there is effective accountability to the stakeholders of cities in respect of those financial management issues.

This is fully recognized in the case of Birmingham, partly because of experience in the 1960s and 1970s with regard to the awarding of certain contracts, and also it has been built up in UK city government over many years. The introduction by the national legislation of compulsory competitive tendering for local authority services has also tended to tighten up this process. In Birmingham's case, there is now a clear separation of the responsibilities for:

- specifying the contracts to be awarded
- the procedures for assessing the tenders received and finally awarding the contract.

This ensures that there is a greater accountability in the use of funds and a minimization and almost guaranteed elimination of the possibility of corruption and failure. It also ensures that there is greater transparency regarding the standards that are being sought and for those whom those standards are set.

City governance

Professor Mathur emphasized the constitutional position of cities. In the provision of local government functions, most cities derive their powers from centralized legislation and not from a constitutional right to exist and provide services. This results in a joint occupancy of functions between national and local levels. This brings into question the issue of city governance and who is responsible for determining the future of cities, working with their stakeholders. This also introduces confusion and imbalance between the expenditure and income-raising components of local government.

The issue of city governance is one that is in constant challenge, and there is constant debate between national government and local city governments.

In the UK, during most of the 1970s but also more stringently during the 1980s, there has been a strong tendency for local authority powers and responsibilities to be taken away from cities, in terms of introducing stricter financial controls on city governments, changing the legislative base on which cities operate, and removing functions altogether into centrally appointed non-governmental organizations. This position appears to be changing in the 1990s and the need to support the civic responsibilities of cities is increasingly recognized. This is partly reflected in the development of the City Pride process in Birmingham. Manchester and London. City Pride in Birmingham is based on the creation of a "city prospectus" looking ahead some 10–20 years. It is overseen by a Board comprising the City Council, business interests, community and utility interests. The initiative has no new funds, but seeks to provide a framework for joint and mutual support. However, much more *trust* and devolution of responsibility is required.

Professor Mathur drew out that, effectively, cities are rich in terms of resources and their capacity to support the national economy, but local civic responsibility tends to be generally poorly supported. He feels that this is linked to the lack of a clear constitutional base for the management of cities.

This is a critical issue in terms of city governance, and it would be an important element of the Istanbul Conference to decide whether it is possible to establish the principle of the role of cities being enshrined within national constitutions, rather than national centralized legislation.

Challenges for cities

Professor Mathur drew attention to what might be regarded as "new" challenges. These relate to the continuing demographic shifts, cities becoming more informal rather than formal, the social composition of cities and in particular the concentration of the poor and poverty. A critical issue is that of globalization in terms of capital mobility and, increasingly, the mobility of information and knowledge.

However, cities have always faced these challenges. It may be in some instances that the scale, but in others the pace of change, is challenging human experience and knowledge. We can anticipate some of the aspects of change and know about these and react to them. The critical issue is how do we address the pace of change where it is not known. This is particularly true of the impact of information technology and communications on cities, and the implications of that for citizens and businesses.

Shared civic responsibility

It is evident from Professor Mathur's contribution that there must be a shared civic responsibility. But what is meant by "civic"? An interpretation that I would like to offer is that it is concerned with:

- the development of the city in ways that meet the needs of the stakeholders of citizens and business
- building and maintaining confidence in the city
- fulfilling the potential of both citizens and businesses.

In recognizing who the stakeholders in the future of the city are, then it is possible to think more clearly about what their needs are and to consider how those can best be met through establishing effective dialogue, involvement with and ownership by these stakeholders.

Therefore, in the case of citizens, they look to have shelter and housing, space, the ability to buy consumer goods, jobs and employment, fun and leisure, and also equity in tendering for local authority services.

In Birmingham's case, there is now a clear separation of the responsibilities for:

- specifying contracts to be awarded.
- the procedures for assessing the tenders received and finally awarding the contract.

This ensures that there is a greater accountability for the use of funds and a minimization – an almost guaranteed elimination – of the possibility of corruption and failure.

In Birmingham, the development of a wider economic understanding of the operation of the city is being developed. The establishment of an Economic Information Centre to analyze trends, raise policy issues for debate, and to work with key parties, is an essential part of *civic* responsibility.

Governance is therefore wider than the straightforward provision of services.

Shifting alliances

In discussion, Nigel Harris referred to

- the city's ability to require accountable political leadership
- improving the performance of officers working within city governments
- and the development of shifting alliances.

These shifting alliances are particularly important, as cities are not islands, as we all know. They need to relate:

- to the two key stakeholders in their areas – citizens and businesses
- horizontally with other sister cities both nationally and internationally; Birmingham, for example, relates to other cities in the UK, and to European cities through a Eurocities network in order to promote the urban agenda at a European level
- with national government and international agencies.

These alliances may well be continually shifting, but they are fundamental to the question of building civic responsibility and pride in the city.

In the case of Birmingham the process of involvement and consultation has developed and will continue to develop. This has been achieved through the creation and establishment of several consultative mechanisms. These include:

- a City Pride Board, which brings together community, civic, business and utility interest, to share, discuss and agree long-term strategic direction for the city
- the establishment of appropriate consultative fora related to, for example, the minority ethnic communities in the city (who comprise 25% of the City's population) through a Standing Consultative Forum (which

includes the Pakistani, Bangladesh, Indian, Afro-Caribbean and Vietnamese communities in the city) and an Environmental Forum (which brings together the wide ranging environmental interests in the city, with civic and business leaders, to address Local Agenda 21 from the UN Environment Conference of Rio de Janiero). These consultative fora are critical in building alliances locally.

In respect of national government relationships, and relationships with international agencies, these are fundamentally important if cities have a diversity of population, and facilities that are of national importance.

In the case of Birmingham, the city does have world-class facilities in the form of the National Exhibition Centre and International Convention Centre, which secures major world conferences and events for the city (including Lions International in 1988, and backing as host for international world medical conferences through the years to 2006).

In the sporting world, in hosting world championships in such events as gymnastics, judo and ice-skating in recent years, effective relationships with national government and with international agencies are paramount.

City business plan

This then brings me to the need for a city business plan, which addresses city governance issues. This should not be seen as strictly a financial document or position statement, but as a statement of the ambitions of the city and what it would wish to achieve working with citizens and businesses. I have mentioned the City Pride Board and the City Prospectus. More remains to be done to develop debates about the future. But any city business plan cannot solely have a "top-down" approach. It must build at all levels of citizen and business involvement in the city. It depends on network, communication and the provision of information.

A city business plan is about openness, involvement and commitment, and it takes a great deal of challenging debate.

CHAPTER FOUR
Bombay and the international experience

Chairman: Cho Padamsee
PARTICIPANTS: Gerson Da Cunha, V. K. Phatak, D. M. Sukhtankar,
Lalit Deshpande, Nigel Harris

Bombay First

Gerson Da Cunha

Bombay City is a place that has internationally known problems. It has grown fast, continues to grow fast and has not been able to deal with its growth. As far as the growth of the population is concerned, it is a city that seems to have turned its face away from migrants who have created an informal city, what S. P. Modi calls the "unintended city". Yet if you look at Bombay, you can say nothing without the opposite being equally true. It is enormously wealthy. It accounts for nearly 40% of the nation's income from excise duty and taxes. It accounts for half the country's import and export trade. "If Bombay fails, India will fail".

At the same time Bombay muddles on. Yesterday someone said that cities change as a result of crisis. The city faces mounting crisis; look at crime rates, for instance, kidnappings for money and so forth. We are on the brink of a major outbreak of crime. This was the city that suffered 13 major explosions, of the kind that, if one or two had occurred elsewhere, make international headlines. Bombay suffered 13 of them. Two days later the Bombay stock exchange was working again. It says something about the kind of city this is.

Bombay as we know it today, the commercial entrepreneurial city, was something that began with business. It was the Bombay Chamber of Commerce, 160 and more years ago, that decided how a natural harbour would become a port. It was the British traders, business people in Bombay, who fought for the cutting of the Suez Canal. The people in Bombay have much weight in political circles, in England as well as India. It was commerce that set up the port. The port is Bombay. It was commerce that caused the railways, two major trans-India railways, to start at the port. The executive counsel of the Viceroy would make his first speech at the Bombay Chamber and then after that at the Calcutta Chamber. Bombay First is an expression of the Bombay Chamber's continuing concern with this city. There is an enormous amount of investment going on here, and there is a very good bottom-line reason for an initiative such as Bombay First. What is this initiative?

It is the first systematic effort by private business in Bombay to do something about the city, to make it a better place to live, work and invest in. That is what Bombay First is concerned with. It is not a mouthpiece for business. It is not a promoter of government programmes, nor is it just another NGO. Figuratively, it is at the midpoint of an equilateral triangle of which the sides are business, government and citizens, as represented in Bombay's extremely active voluntary sector. Bombay has one of the things that probably no other city has and that is an active *vox populi*. The money is private but the agenda is public in the "people" sense: doing something about people's lives, about the quality of life.

It began by taking a look at the potential of cities, at the importance of cities and the potential of Bombay. The fate of cities determines the welfare of national economies. Hence, Bombay First makes sense.

Financial services is an area where Bombay already has a head start. It makes a great deal of sense to look at financial services as one of the priorities of Bombay First, particularly as there has been a decline in Bombay as a source of manufacturing jobs. So, if industry is no longer the powerhouse of Bombay, then services are the alternative. If it is to be services, financial services have a key role.

Now Bombay has every kind of problem. But Bombay First could not be expected to tackle them all. We use three criteria to decide what the priorities should be:

1. What is important?
2. What is do-able?
3. Should Bombay First be doing it?

The application of these principles ended in our choosing five areas for immediate attention: financial services, telecommunications, transport, land use and housing (an issue linked to the Mafia, and the nexus between politician and criminal), and finally education (education seen not as basic or university education, but as the kind of preparation for people who will man the jobs that other sectors of Bombay First will be concerned with).

Bombay First has two wings: a foundation and a society. The foundation will collect money and fund the society. The secretariat and activities of the society will be funded by membership fees. We have some prominent businessmen and citizens in Bombay. They are members of our Trust, so it has a great deal of credibility.

We have set up committees in each of the five areas, and committees in four areas have already started working. It is astonishing how people, whose time is extremely pressured, have agreed not only to figure on these committees, but promised much more.

Planning the city

V. K. Phatak

The first point that I would like to make is that structural adjustment has not touched Bombay in terms of planning and administration. The structural adjustments have remained confined in the Ministry of Finance, commerce and in the government of India. Even within the state government, it has been limited to efforts to attract foreign investment. SICOM (State and Industrial Corporation of Maharashtra) is trying to spearhead that activity. SICOM – for the participants – is an agency of industrial promotion in the State of Maharashtra, and its mandate is to provide incentives for industries to leave the larger cities such as Bombay and Poona. SICOM was providing facilities and physical incentives for industrial dispersal. Now they seem to be in the process of augmenting that role by trying to attract foreign investment as well. But the rest of the state government is still not getting into the fundamentals of structural adjustment in its processes of administration.

To give an example: a firm that wants to set up a unit in the Bombay Metropolitan region cannot do so without the express permission of the Industries Department of the state government. The permission of the local government is not adequate for that purpose. The BMRDA cannot buy a jeep for a project or appoint professional staff without the express permission of the government.

These are the kind of processes that came into existence in the pre-liberalization era, and still continue. In terms of either adopting the basic message of liberalization and the regulatory efficiencies that are required to manage these processes, this has not touched the core of governmental administration as yet. Since it has not touched the state government, it has not yet touched the city government, the municipal corporation. If you talk to senior officers of the municipal corporation, the kind of issues that are coming up, such as how to deal with the potential growth of financial services in Bombay as a result of liberalization, is never on the agenda of the municipal corporation. The BMRDA was fortunate to have some open land, so it came out with at least a response: we have a certain amount of land which could be made available for activities such as the diamond market, the national stock exchange, the new foreign banks that will be coming into Bombay, and so on. But as for the city government, such questions were never on the agenda.

The economic transformation that Bombay has been undergoing during the 1980s started with a famous textile strike, and changes in the economic composition of output (the decline of textiles). What kind of alternative employment opportunities could be made available to the textile workers, what kind of land use changes should be introduced for land that was becoming derelict as a part of the decline of manufacturing activity in the city? These issues were never on the agenda of the city government, and they are still not on the agenda.

If you talk to an ordinary middle-level officer of the municipal corporation, the common excuse for problems that the city faces continues to be what we call the "influx of migration". Influx is a favourite word that is used in Bombay. It implies a kind of physical phenomenon, which has no sense and no direction of its own.

The problem that Bombay has to face is the long delays in granting permission for developments, the costs involved, the cost of transactions in terms of obtaining permission and, apart from the cost, the time. The average time required for an average building permission in Bombay is over three years. An applicant has to obtain something like 20–30 separate permissions within the corporation. But this is the kind of administrative system that is still continuing in the municipal corporation. They do not at all fit with the kind of changes that we are going through or we are likely to go through in the overall process of economic development as a part of globalization.

The question is: what kind of administrative mechanism, what kind of procedures, what kind of approaches should Bombay adopt to meet these kinds of challenge? As Dr Sundaram has said, it is a question of mind set. What kind of professional administrators are going to have to manage the city? In the municipal corporation, there is a top layer of professional administrative leadership that is very transitory, which comes for three years and goes away. Below that is a leadership that comes from the engineering profession. They move from roads, to water, to sewerage, to solid waste. So there is no build-up of experience and professionalization of a particular service. But there is a vacuum in terms of what used to be called "corporate planning" in British towns. There are no economists. I was happy to know people having designations as senior economic adviser to Barcelona, or to Mexico City. But that kind of an animal does not exist in Bombay, and in the Bombay administration.

The question that Bombay will have to address is what kind of expertise, what kind of manpower, are we going to need in city management, and with what kind of procedures? Deregulation and de-bureaucratization were the key words when, in 1991, the first industrial location policy was introduced. Essentially the industrial policy of the government of India assumed that investment decisions are best left to the market; they know where to put in the money and where to invest. This has a locational implication that has not been understood in the city and in general by planners. There is still much concern about controlling the locational decisions or variety of investment programmes without really understanding the whole mechanism of how these things are done.

In that kind of perspective, the Bombay First initiative, particularly in terms of telecommunications, transport and education, is promising. These three areas sound promising, because telecommunications and transport are crucial for the city economy. Telecommunications is institutionally separate from the city government, handled by the government of India. The transport sector institutionally is again very complex: railways are with the government of India; the buses are with the local government; part of the road network is with the state government. So, the initiatives coming from Bombay First in these two sectors are promising.

Governance in Bombay

D. M. Sukhtankar

Bombay is the industrial, commercial and financial capital of the country. It is the citizens of Bombay and the business and industry in Bombay, the people who run the economic activities who have the maximum stake in the city. But both the central and state governments also have high stakes in Bombay, because the total central revenue from income, corporation, excise and customs taxes are the main sources of income of the central government – anywhere between 35% and 40% comes from Bombay. In the case of customs duty, maybe it is much higher. There is an element of exaggeration in that various corporate offices are located in Bombay when physically their activities may be outside, so whatever tax they pay is paid from Bombay City offices, but is not generated in Bombay. The point remains, Bombay is an important city. Similarly for the state government, 80% of the sales tax revenue – and sales tax is the most important and buoyant source of revenue for the state government – comes from the city of Bombay.

These two stakeholders, although they are importantly concerned with Bombay because it produces the revenue, are also responsible for certain kinds of functioning of the city. For example, under the Indian Constitution, the major ports, the entire railway network, the airports, the telecommunications, which are vital items of city infrastructure, are all in what we call the Union list – as also are the national and express highways. That is, it is the central government that has the power to legislate and control these important infrastructural services. It is only now that we are talking in terms of privatizing ports, or certain ports, or opening the telecommunications sector. We know that, for financial services and telecommunications, exchange of information is very important, yet the state and the city governments have no direct influence on policies or investments in infrastructure relating to these. Furthermore, with the judicial system, law and order and security the state government is in charge – even regulating traffic through the police.

Although the city government prepares the development plan, it is in the form of a draft plan, with all the limitations, and, as we heard earlier, with a shift taking place from a land-use physical plan to a more flexible one. Then it has to be approved by the state government. So, the state government has a very important role to play in various land-use decisions, how much can be built in the city, what kind of zoning there should be. Under our constitution, the legal framework relating to land, a scarce and important resource, is entirely regulated by state legislation.

What is left for the city government? It is still important because of some of the remaining important items of infrastructure: it operates water supply, sewerage, stormwater drainage, granting of development permissions and, very importantly, primary healthcare, elementary or primary education and free primary education. There are 800 000 young children studying in municipal schools, run in ten different Indian languages by the city corporation. About 24% of the total expenditure of the city government is on primary education. The city government runs three major hospitals, which have on average 1400–1500 beds, and it runs a premier medical education system.

The city government has always been a democratically elected body. I had the dubious distinction of being the administrator of the city corporation for about six or seven months, when the term of an elected corporation ended. The elections that should have followed immediately were not held for political reasons that need not concern us, and I was installed as the Municipal Commissioner in 1984, the administrator of the city. After a year the elections were held. But barring this aberration, which seems to prove the rule, it has been a democratically governed city.

It is also a city of opportunities and is highly cosmopolitan. Bombay First is to set up a policy research institute to create an information and database about Bombay, which is woefully lacking. It will do relevant research on various problems, so that whatever policy Bombay City wants to advocate, it is not based on simple impressions or anyone's fads and fancies, but is backed by good research, proper information and data. The idea is that Bombay First is a society, broad-based to reflect various shades of public opinion, so that whatever agenda for action we prepare, based on the research information, carries some conviction and is able to elicit popular support.

Bombay's economy

Lalit Deshpande

Some eight years ago, my wife, Sudha, and I started working on a study of the management of Bombay at the instigation of ILO. The conclusion we drew was that this was an absolutely dynamic city. To come to Bombay was to come to a land of opportunity. On the street, ask any man what he thinks of Bombay; he has come from all corners of India, but the answer you are likely to get is that if you are industrious you will make it in Bombay. Not that he is going to be a millionaire, but compared to what life offers in the village, the migrant will be looked up to as someone by his peers. He sends money to his relations, helps them buy a piece of land which provides sustenance, helps them pay the taxes, helps them pay for the repairs to their house and helps them to buy a cow or a bullock to farm his lands.

Bombay City, we are often told, is a city that has acquired an inhuman face. How did Bombay become, along with other cities, a land of inhuman space? Consider travel. Perhaps eight people die daily from falls from the trains, they are so crowded. That is many times more than in Tokyo. On the roads, it is the poor people, the pedestrians, not the car drivers who suffer.

Whether it is the distribution of water or access to certain municipal services, it is the poor who miss everything. Yet they looked up to this city as a land of hope and opportunity.

How does one make this city a human city? There are so many opportunities for the richer people, so that one has to set the prices right and tax the rich – as much as we can without harming industrial or business interests – and then try to subsidize the amenities, primary education, health and so on, as well as the physical facilities such as water, garbage and clearance and all that. This was the task that we set ourselves. However, the City is changing its character. The structure is changing, manufacturing is leaving and there was informalization of the City and its activities. The income that is being generated is not adequate to renew the infrastructure.

There is a need to change the policies, the planning, decentralization and associated policies (e.g. housing controls). The public sector assumed the dominant role in distributing housing, land and everything. One can free the energies of individuals to generate income, and they have given enough proof of what they can do in the informal sectors.

Now the decline of manufacturing raised special problems, especially in the textile industry. But the policy followed in textiles has nothing to do with the structural adjustment of the post-1990s. The decline of textiles dates back to 1960s. It was the wrong policies, perhaps, that were followed at that time, which ruined the textile industry, and the problems have accumulated over the years, and there is a crisis.

What alternative activities can we develop? I was fascinated by the case studies and the similar kinds of problems – without the same intensity – as Bombay. Cities elsewhere have faced similar problems, have thought about them, and tried remedial action. The results are not clear, but at least there is an agenda to look at, to see whether we can learn from them. I did not come across a failure that could be branded as such. There are different degrees of success. Half of the city's population live in slums (although not everyone in slums is poor). But the number of destitutes, the proportion, is much less than what you would find in other cities, let alone in rural India. That is the contribution that Bombay has made. Bombay has the best anti-poverty programme that we have or we can boast of. The people coming to Bombay are able to cross the poverty line and attain a reasonable standard of living, however hard their life may be.

Two things emerged here: there was no group or agency that was thinking or concerned about what is happening or what is going to happen to the city. How should we try to alleviate the problems that everyone knows about. Who was trying to take a total view of the city and what would happen in the future? Now for the first time we have an opportunity to anticipate events. Structural adjustment programmes are alleged to be a programme for the rich. What the developed countries have tried is of little relevance to us. I share some of the doubts but not in their totality and not on every count. Some of the tasks that other cities have undertaken could be adjusted successfully here. Especially those suggestions that relate to how to help the informal sector, the training and education programmes and the rehabilitation programmes. We have to sell the programme to a large mass of poor people, who must think that now there is a chance of an alliance with the captains of industry, where their view will be respected and will be taken into account, that Bombay First is not purely an organization of the rich trying to skim off the milk. This is an organization of the people of Bombay, which includes everyone who has a stake in this city, to manage the city much better and make it more human.

Lessons for Bombay?

Nigel Harris

Several issues emerged during the proceedings. One was the question of deindustrialization. There is a danger that people in Bombay think deindustrialization is inevitable. It is not inevitable. Bombay is not Sheffield, nor Birmingham. It is a unique combination of activities and therefore what happens may not repeat the experience of other cities.

The textile industry, for example, went down almost consistently from the early 1960s. But from 1991, after the collapse of the Soviet market (an uncompetitive market, but one on which a large part of the Bombay textile industry had been able to grow) there was a terrible crunch. Then some mills started expanding. It is not the end of the Bombay industry by any means. As protection declines, we may find that the high-value garment end of the business becomes more deeply entrenched in Bombay. Bombay must sooner or later become specialized in high fashion and styling, whereas the low-quality stuff goes somewhere else. For that we should be grateful if we are interested in Indian development. Sooner or later, Bombay must lose most of its textile industry, and that is a good thing for India, because that can generate employment in other places.

Two high-growth sectors in world trade since the Second World War have been petrochemicals and capital goods (and engineering more generally).

Those are two industries that Bombay specializes in.

What is going to happen as the structure of protection changes in petro-chemicals and engineering? What is going to happen to the taxation level because the Indian capital goods industry is marked by high levels of taxation on the upstream output? What are the ramifications of that for the industry in Bombay? Since we do not know the answers, we cannot know the impli-cations for employment, for housing, for the areas where the engineering workers live, and so on. We have here, in the manufacturing of Bombay, a major area for research, in order to find out what is likely to happen.

Secondly, one of the first effects of structural adjustment is often to pro-duce a high rate of growth of exports. What is Bombay's participation in that high rate of growth of exports? Exports need cheap, fast transport. Bombay's role in the transport system of the world and of India is crucial. What are the problems of moving airfreight from the airport? What are the problems in the containerization of the port? Again, this has ramifications in terms of the labour force. We know there are going to be large-scale lay-offs. Over what time period is not clear, but they will occur in Bombay's port, if it is to become efficient enough to make India competitive in exports. If Bombay's port fails, India's export efforts fail. The whole reform programme becomes jeopardized in terms of the generation of employment. So, you can see the kind of knock-on effects. The decision of the Port Trust, its relationship to the City Council, land communications – all of these are vital for India's export performance, and therefore for the generation of employment throughout the country: another agenda.

We should not become over-preoccupied with finance. It is important, but in the end it will not employ the whole workforce. What will do that is all the other services in Bombay, and there are masses of them: from software pro-gramming to the medical system (if it becomes an export sector); for the uni-versities (if they become an export sector), to the provision of culture for tourists, because it is certain tourism is going to grow rapidly in India over the next 30 or 40 years, and much of it will come through Bombay airport. If Bom-bay is a competitive and attractive city, the tourists will stay in Bombay, lifting the whole economy: manufacturing, agriculture and many other services.

How well is Bombay equipped to deal with that growth, and do so to the benefit of its citizens who are here at the moment, and the citizens who are inevitably going to come in the future? What are the implications in terms of the quality of life in Bombay? The concern with the quality of life is no longer icing on the cake for the citizens. It is vital for the economic future of the city. Whether the streets are clean, whether they are well managed, and so on, becomes economically significant for the Bombay economy.

How will the local authority become a creative agency? There are 130 000 employees in the Bombay municipal corporation. How is the Corporation to be made creative, to become preoccupied with the future of the city, to act as a pressure group on the Maharashtra and the national governments? Who represents the Bombay interest when it comes to setting tariff rates on the cargo going through Bombay port or airport, or on the management of the railway system? Who is to hold the conference on the future of Bombay's local government, to discuss the agenda and timing of reforms? That is: taking a lead for India as a whole, not just leaving it to the central government. What is the national and state government going to do in order to allow Bombay to expand its activities and so contribute even more to the future growth of India?

We had an interesting discussion on the Olympic games. It was to some extent deflected because people were inclined to say sport is not important. We have serious issues – manufacturing – not sports. That was to misunderstand the nature of the discussion, which was how to get the political leverage to improve the whole infrastructure of the city. It does not matter whether it is building pyramids in ancient Cairo, a cathedral in medieval Europe or preparing the Olympic Games in Barcelona: this is the leverage by which investment can be mobilized on a sufficient scale to transform the city and restructure it. The event does not matter provided it allows leverage.

Bombay needs a political coalition that is going to stand for the city. The Chamber of Commerce cannot do it, nor the City Corporation, but some coalition that includes the trade unions and citizen groups needs to speak with a united voice to the state and national governments about what is required to make Bombay's economic future secure, and so the prosperity of India. Deshpande made the point that there is no way in which the contraction of the textile industry can be attributed to structural adjustment. It has been declining for 20 years. Why do the citizens attribute the decline to structural adjustment instead of other key policy questions that need to be changed? It is because there is no forum; because the provision of information, the basic statistics and arguments and the political culture of Bombay are not confronting the central issues. That is something that Bombay First can do something about, changing the political culture so that citizens understand what structural adjustment means and do not automatically assume it is the rich who get richer, the poor poorer – an ancient slogan in every country, but far from the rather messy accidental character in most places.

The last point concerns research and data. Many of the arguments are complex and difficult, and they contradict our conditioned reflexes. The purpose of research is to provide the reasoned basis by which Bombay can become an effective pressure group on the Maharashtra state government and on the national government as to why they should be introducing reforms that affect Bombay. Secondly, it is the arming of citizens to participate in the coalition. If they do not have the information, they will not participate in defining the future of the city. Thirdly, information is the key to flexibility. Rigidities arise, structures crumble and crash in the world economy, often because of the failure of information. Unless the information is fast and accurate, cities are in danger of making grave mistakes. So, a research centre is a key element in this whole package.

The discussion

Chairman: Cho Padamsee
PARTICIPANTS: Peter M. Townroe, William F. Lever, Gerson Da Cunha,
Gustavo Garza, Zilton Macedo, V. K. Phatak, Nigel Harris

The major part of the discussion concerned the question of the governance of cities. One contributor felt India lacked urban governance because both public authorities and the population at large lacked a sense of social responsibility, as shown in the neglect of the environment. Another disagreed, but felt mechanisms were needed to bring people together, to make planning consensual and based upon consultation and a genuine partnership. Providing such a mechanism could be the role of Bombay First, but even then the City Council would need to be encouraged to involve greater participation in its deliberations.

Another speaker asked how the policy preoccupations of the senior officers of the Bombay municipal corporation could be increased; did they meet to discuss the strategic issues facing the city? Bombay First could play an important role in raising these questions and so enhancing the quality of interaction of the city officers around an agenda of strategic questions.

Another speaker observed sadly that the routine operations of the city authorities did not encourage a wider view of the context of Bombay. Indeed, city officers did not meet to look at the future of the city and the role of the corporation. Meetings considered only immediate problems and short-term questions – for example, in the rainy season (between June and September), how are the authorities to respond to possible flooding, where was the road system most subject to deterioration, and so on? Short-term problems were usually so overwhelming and complex that even keeping track of them and responding in time, ensuring appropriate budgets and contracts were in place, took all the time. This state of affairs was partly recognized in the creation of the Bombay Metropolitan Region Development Authority (BMRDA), which was set up as a kind of think-tank for the metropolitan region. It allowed a more speculative overview of the metropolitan region when the development plan or the associated regulations were under review. But it would be wrong to exaggerate the potential here; the BMRDA was not as effective a forum as some people thought.

The forms of governance, another contributor thought, were key means to mobilize the city government and private business. However, decentralization of powers to the city level might also lead to major errors of judgement in expenditure and major losses – as occurred in the London Docklands or Baltimore Harbour projects. In looking at these large projects, one needed additionally to assess who gained; often, it was not the locally resident poor. Coalitions were not always effective in straddling the contradictory interests within the city to ensure the poor did not lose out.

The discussion

City forums embodying a political coalition of city interests attracted much attention. In Europe, the spread of forums and coalitions had been fostered by the development of city networks, funded within the European Union. They acted as means for politicians and civil servants to meet business, unions and social activists, to exchange views and explore alternative strategies for the city. Business associations had often been key forces in launching the initiative, as had occurred in Bombay. But business initiative raised the question of how representative the coalition was, who financed it? Other elements of civil society might well be suspicious of being used by business for undeclared purposes. Hence, it was politically very important that those who organized a forum reached out to involve as many interests as possible in the council of the forum or its network of committees, in the width of concerns in the forum agenda, and through using the media or open public meetings to demonstrate the breadth of interests involved. Thus, Bombay First needed to decide its membership early, so as to be able to exhibit its wider commitment to the citizenry at large, and thus acquire some legitimacy.

An important lesson of the case studies had been that, while all had been affected by the global economy and structural adjustment, the capacity to respond often depended on non-economic factors – the city's social structure, cultural or religious traditions, the political order, and so on. Often these factors related to the "soft infrastructure" – healthcare, education, and so on.

In managing the political coalition, the forms of governance were becoming increasingly complex, with privatization, new forms of partnership and non-government organization initiatives. The need for continuing consultation was enhanced in this context; a private telecommunications company serving the city had to be involved in discussing its future role. The management issues were further complicated by the fact that people often found it initially difficult to lift their attention from the immediate and short term to the medium and long term. A chief executive of a textile company would come to the forum and do nothing but complain about the traffic congestion the day before, which had delayed supplies to his factory. The leaders of the forum needed to develop a style that allowed such questions to be bypassed without giving offence and for attention to be focused on longer-term questions.

The point of the forum was not just discussion, but to act as a focus for power and influence. In time, a forum could build up a considerable reputation, the basis for great influence, as the effective mouthpiece for the city. For this, it needed to establish the confidence of the citizens and business. Then special significance would come to be attached to the pronouncements of the forum, and national governments would be obliged to pay attention. But this status would only be possible if the organization was accountable. In principle, coalitions involved no direct democratic accountability, so it was important that in its constitution, organization and operation, it was transparently accountable.

In Latin America, several comparable initiatives had occurred. In São Paulo, an association of bankers had come together to champion the interests of all who lived and worked in the run-down central business district. Private business proved to be much more flexible than government in this role, much more easily able to collaborate with other interests in the central city – for example, the street hawkers. Out of the discussions, an agenda arose to put to government, to the politicians and trade unions; a focus for changing the behaviour of the municipal authorities. An example of this change of behaviour was the decision of the authorities to exempt from municipal taxes all those who agreed to upgrade their buildings. Indeed, it was the bankers' club that spearheaded the efforts to upgrade the physical fabric of the central city; it arranged the architects and builders for restoration work, and managed the financing.

Another speaker, however, argued that in Latin America genuine participation was rare. Often, key issues remained the exclusive prerogative of senior officers who did not involve others in their deliberations. This lack of participation meant low levels of knowledge and coordination, leading to duplication and confusion among citizens' groups.

City government was restricted by the fact that key elements of infrastructure, vital for the city's economic future – for example, ports and airports – were outside the competence of the municipal authorities. If privatization occurred, perhaps the City Corporation should consider taking a minority shareholding in the enterprises concerned, so it would acquire a stake in the success of their operations.

The possible research programme of the research centre to be established by Bombay First received some attention. Research armed the city authorities and the citizens in their pressure on national government, in promoting the city and securing effective participation. In Mexico, one participant said, the government of the State of Nueve Leon had, in 1993, passed a state law on urban development that established the coordination of the urban sector through a state commission and a council of advisers – and created an institute of urban development studies. In its first year, the institute had published three books and two journals, and these were important exposures of the issues of urban development for government and citizens. The institute had played a key role in the state plan for urban development.

One or two speakers felt the symposium sufficiently important to warrant the formulation of a set of recommendations for the Habitat II conference. However, it has earlier been noted that the symposium was designed to explore experience, not draw conclusions covering all cities or even Bombay. The diversity of cities meant there could never be a single agenda – and deciding that agenda was not the work of the symposium but of the citizens in the city concerned. Too often general agendas were produced with a fanfare, but in relating to everywhere, related to nowhere – and died.

CHAPTER FIVE
Summing up

William F. Lever

Introduction

The 11 city case studies in this book have been brought together to offer, through discussion, a general agenda of policy issues to be pursued by cities whose economies are undergoing structural adjustment. Although seven of the cities are located in the older industrial areas of western Europe, and four are located in more recently developing national economies of Latin America and southern Africa, there is no implied suggestion that cities and their economies follow a predetermined chronological track. Neither is there any intention that a policy profile might be derived from the city case studies that would accurately meet the needs of a city such as Bombay. Although there have been many attempts to identify good practice by city governments, and by public–private partnerships, in confronting the problems that result from economic structural adjustment, the transfer of policies from one context to another is a process with some dangers. Differing resource levels, political and administrative structures and even geographical locations may mean that an approach or a policy successful in one city may be less successful, or just infeasible, elsewhere. Although the problems of cities undergoing structural adjustment may be easy to identify and fairly ubiquitous – a decline in manufacturing, rising unemployment, inner-city decay and dereliction in industrial and port areas, and strong negative social effects – a single policy prescription is unlikely to meet the needs of all, or even most cities.

The objective therefore is to exchange information about the processes of structural adjustment, the problems thrown up by these processes and the variety and effectiveness of the sets of policies devised to confront these problems. Used to inform policy formulation, information about a variety of cities may be classed as knowledge if we take Knight's (1995) definition of knowledge as information that we have the capacity and ability to use effectively. In a context such as this, information about other cities may serve two roles. First, it does provide access to new ideas about good or best practice in urban management, which suitably adapted can be applied in one's own context.

Secondly, data emerge from the case studies, which are so different from one's experience that the very difference forces one to see one's own city in a new light. Often, urban development is incremental: city planners and managers pursue trajectories that do not veer wildly from one course to another; the long-lasting nature of the fixed capital and infrastructure of cities inevitably means that cities evolve slowly and have limited capacity for sudden or dramatic change; and urban politicians are innately conservative and, when seeking re-election, are unlikely to advocate radical changes in policy that they perceive to be risky. Exchanges of information such as that between the case study cities offer new insights. In these case studies there have been some comments on cities that have provoked surprise. For example, there was favourable comment on México City's ability to fund a high proportion of municipal expenditure from local property taxes (the absence of a local democratic process was clearly not a hindrance to local city development, despite the opinion in other cities that accountability is an important part of the development process) and on the role played by culture in French cities, where more than half of the metropolitan authorities were "subsidizing ballet schools", an interesting facet of post-industrial development.

The literature on urban development offers us several general models that provide an overall framework within which the case study cities can be located. Reference was made to the role of urban hierarchies within central place theory. Individual cities may have to be considered as part of a national urban development strategy in which growth pressures for primate cities may have to be deflected into second-ranking cities used as counter-magnets. The fact that both México City and Monterrey are in the sample of case studies, as are London and three other British cities (Birmingham, Sheffield and Glasgow) offers some scope for the discussion of national policies for urban growth and management beyond the consideration of single cities. Secondly, Rostow's model (1967) of economic growth demonstrates how economies move over time from a predominantly primary sector structure, based on agriculture, forestry and mining, to a predominantly manufacturing sector structure and then to a structure dominated by services. Although this model clearly has relevance to cities and their concern with the management of structural change, Rostow was careful to point out that, in cities and economies in the developed world, the process had taken several generations. His account did not offer a model for the processes currently experienced by cities in the developing world, which are growing much more rapidly and where economies may move from primary to service sector dominance without a period of manufacturing in between. Whereas in the developed world, industrialization and urbanization seem to have occurred in parallel, guaranteeing manual employment for workers migrating from rural areas, if not guaranteeing them good housing or a sanitary environment, in the developing world the term over-urbanization is used to indicate that urban populations are growing faster than the capacity of the urban labour market to provide them with employment. For many, the consequences are under-employment or unemployment, inadequate incomes and housing shortages. Thirdly, Williamson (1965) has developed a model that links the processes of urban (and national) economic development to income distribution. His argument is that, as economies grow and GDP per head rises, incomes become increasingly unequally distributed, and the gap between rich and poor increases; at some point, however, the gap begins to narrow as rising GDP per head begins to benefit the lower-income households.

Patterns of similarities between cities

From the city case studies we can identify seven common themes.

The increasing openness of urban economies

As the trend to the globalization of the world economy increases, both national and urban economies are open to the movement of capital flows in ways unanticipated 20 years ago. Thrift (1996) and others have estimated that over US$1 trillion[1] per day crosses international frontiers, of which approximately 70% is pure capital transfer in the form of arbitrage, debt settlement, purchase of shares, options, swaps and derivatives, and only 10% is payment for raw materials, goods and energy. Given the magnitude of these flows and their volatility and speed, it has been argued that national governments have seen their powers to regulate their economies significantly reduced. These powers have been further reduced by the application of the concept of subsidiarity, by which decision-making in government is assumed to be delegated to the lowest level consistent with efficiency in order to achieve greater accountability. If national governments thus lose their economic powers to transnational business and flows of capital and to local democracy, then can city governments hope to retain or acquire powers to manage parts of their constituent economies? National governments have sought to counteract globalization by forming transnational agencies such as the North American Free Trade Association and the Single European Market, and to engage in transnational economic management through GATT and G7. City governments do not have the constitutional powers to engage in transnationality: are they therefore destined to become increasingly powerless at the mercy of international capital movements? A widely held view is that globalization provides a more flexible environment within which cities and city governments have greater freedom to manage economic change. City governments have greater powers to engage in urban marketing, seeking to attract interna-

---

1. One thousand US billions.

tional capital, hallmark events and public agencies. Many more locational decisions are taken on "quality of life" criteria, rather than as in neoclassical economics, in terms of factor costs and comparative advantage. City governments have much more control over many elements in the quality of life, such as housing quality, the level and quality of the provision of public sector services, cultural and recreational attributes, and infrastructures, than they do over factor prices such as wages and interest rates. Regional federations of cities, either inter- or intra-nationally, have enabled cities, certainly within Europe, to share information and good practice in urban development or regeneration. Within the networks created by the European Commission – for instance, Quartiers en Crise – cities can share experience and demonstration projects in urban regeneration. The PHARE and Overture programmes enable west European cities to offer advice to the new market economies of east and central Europe. At a less formal level the cities of the western Mediterranean littoral, from Barcelona to Genoa, have formed a new growth zone to challenge the older urban core, which extends from London to Milan.

It has long been argued (e.g. ERECO 1992) that the most reliable and consistent factor explaining urban growth rates is the performance of the national economy in which they are located. However, the growing economic autonomy of cities is reflected in the increasing tendency for cities to "delink" themselves from their national economies, producing economic growth rates markedly better than those of national averages. In this sense, Berlin and Munich have significantly outperformed German averages since 1989. Paris, Bologna, Birmingham, Madrid and Barcelona have also done significantly better, in terms of gross value added per capita, than their respective national economies. Such delinking however is not without its problems, as the performance of Marseilles, Rome and London shows, for their growth rates are well below their respective national averages.

The public sector to private sector ratio

The degree of intervention in the urban economy by the public sector, particularly local government, is not a linear process but is one that appears to oscillate. Rising public sector expenditure at the urban scale continues to increase up to the point at which the level of taxation threatens the viability of the private sector through increasingly burdensome taxation. At that point, the expansion stops, as a result of electoral change, external intervention (often by central government) or a recognition that further taxation would be unwise. The early 1980s saw several examples of European cities being forced by national governments to reduce local public expenditure as the national governments sought to manage their economies in deep recession. In many cases these cuts were restored in the conditions of rapid growth in the later 1980s, but in some cases, such as Britain, central government sought further restrictions on local government's powers.

The essence of achieving a successful balance between the public and private sectors is further complicated by the contribution of the not-for-profit or voluntary sector in the supply of some urban services. The three sector approach appears most likely to be successful where it acknowledges and utilizes the different but complementary skills of the sectors. In this context, city government needs to be flexible, responding to the changing economic environment of structural adjustment, and adapting to the needs of macroplanning as they evolve. The role of the local government is particularly to take a holistic view of economic development, assessing the impact of structural adjustment on all segments of urban society, for the private sector, the community and voluntary sectors are likely to hold partial views of necessary courses of action. City forums such as Bombay First, London First and Glasgow Action, which bring together all three sectors, need to be aware of the cross-subsidies and benefits between the three sectors. For example, recent analyses of the investment and employment created in Glasgow as a result of Glasgow's designation as European City of Culture in 1990 criticized the "middle-class bias" of the majority of the events sponsored, without taking into account the employment created both during the event and subsequently for low-skill service workers in the city. At the same time Glasgow has seen that it has a major role to play in empowering the communities in the voluntary sector to play a more active and informed role in the city's development by encouraging their involvement in housing management, in credit finance through the formation of credit unions and in retailing through the creation of community shops. These more flexible attitudes on the part of local government have led to the "unbundling" of services and a more realistic allocation of service provision between the public and private sectors.

Central–local government relations

One common trend from the case study cities is the decentralization of power from central government to regional and urban government, although, in this respect, Britain must be regarded as an exception. The trend of "rolling back the state" is a result of governments applying the concept of subsidiarity, by which decisions are taken at the most local level consistent with economic efficiency, in order to achieve the greatest level of accountability and the demands for increased local democracy. Although this delegation of powers can be effective in areas such as the supply of housing, infrastructure and the delivery of services (such as education, health and waste disposal), it is less effective in the area of economic management. This is because many of the processes involved in economic management and development are macroeconomic in nature, as are the policy responses, such as the manipulation of interest rates and exchange rates. These factors lie outside the power of local governments. Nevertheless, local government in cities has come to play an increasing role in the management of the local economy. In the 1970s

97

much of this role took the form of demand-side management through the use of purchasing contracts, local expenditure and income expenditure effects generated by job creation. However, in the 1980s and 1990s more emphasis has been placed on the supply side, with city government as an enabler for the private sector to generate economic growth. This approach has led city councils to engage in training to ensure an effective labour supply, in providing serviced land and premises to house industry and other activities, to provide a quality-of-life that is attractive to inward investment, and to supply business advice to small and start-up enterprises.

The formal and the informal sector mix

Most of the cities covered by the case studies report an increase in the informal sector of the economy. By its very nature the informal sector, which is often set up to avoid taxation and regulation, is difficult to analyze and to measure. A figure often quoted in western European economies is 15–20% of all economic activity lying in the informal sector. In developing world cities, such as Bombay, the figure can be as high as 50%. Where the informal economy does comprise half of all production or employment, it is difficult to maintain the belief that the urban economy can be managed effectively. Attitudes towards the informal sector are ambivalent. The negative aspects of the development of an extensive informal sector are that the avoidance of tax on a major scale must have a deleterious effect on public sector revenues, that the informal sector may inflict negative externalities within the urban economy, which are not policed, and that there may be elements of exploitation and hazard for those employed. On the first point, however, it is probable that income levels in the sector are low and the loss of tax revenues is likely to be small. On the positive side it is argued that the informal sector is counter-cyclical. When the formal sector is in recession, the informal sector grows, although it may do so out of necessity, as more people are without formal work, rather than because it has an absolute or comparative advantage. Some studies have indicated that the informal sector is not counter-cyclical but requires economic growth in the formal sector to fund expenditure in the informal sector. Similarly, in geographical terms, the informal sector seems to do best where the formal sector is most flourishing and generates income for the black economy. Lastly, a further positive aspect of the informal sector is its ability to foster and provide opportunities for entrepreneurial skills, which may transfer into the formal sector over time.

Income distribution and inequality

One definition of "the good city" is the city that has the most equal distribution of income, in which the richest and poorest are closest together (Donnison & Soto 1980). Although American studies have argued (Haworth et al.

1978) that inequality rises with city size, it does seem from European work that the fastest rates of urban economic growth correlate with the greatest equality of income distribution. The debate on factors affecting income distribution has recently become engaged with the definition of an underclass in the American city, where economic, social and political barriers exist to prevent households moving out of poverty. A class of households of multiple deprivation is perpetuated that is reliant on welfare, crime and charity to survive. In Europe the term used most often is social and economic exclusion, a term that refers both to exclusion from the labour market and paid employment, and to exclusion from the mainstream of urban society and life-style through poverty.

An area of further research relating to income distribution is that of the mechanisms of "trickle down". The assumption that the encouragement of investment in high-quality employment is justified by the income expenditure effects, in the form of an increase of low-wage employment, still has to be proved by empirical study. Similarly, the boosts to urban economies, led by property development, in cities such as Baltimore and Glasgow may improve the urban environment and quality of life for high-income households who are able to enjoy the facilities provided, but may offer little to low-income and unemployed households.

Post-industrialism

Most urban economies appear to move through a sequence that takes them from being economies in which manufacturing predominates to economies dominated by services. The development of cities where 80% or more of employment is in services has given rise to the phenomenon of the post-industrial city. To some observers, this represents a natural evolution, to some it represents a conscious choice to specialize in service sectors where a city has a comparative advantage, to others it represents competitive failure in the basic manufacturing sector and a reluctant acceptance of services as suppliers of replacement employment (Lever 1991). To the optimists the positive aspects of post-industrialism are the disappearance of smokestack industries, a cleaner environment, fewer hard manual jobs in unpleasant working conditions, more leisure, and more informed choice of life-style. To the pessimists, the negative aspects of post-industrialism are higher unemployment, more poorly paid and part-time jobs, a wider dispersion of income, and more social polarization. The greater spread between rich and poor is the result of several factors, including growing unemployment among former manual workers unable to find re-employment in the service sectors, the concentration of service employment into a high-wage professional primary labour market (finance, law, health, education) and a low-wage unskilled secondary labour market (personal services, ancillary services) and a changing fiscal and welfare regime, which appears to be regressive. The lesson of post-industrialism for many cities would appear to be that they should seek to retain as large a manufacturing sector as possible for as long as possible.

Urban collaboration

Studies of urban economic development have sought to use models of spatial competition, based upon those models developed to explain international competition through comparative advantage. In the inter-urban model, cities compete with one another for mobile investment, for hallmark events, for the location of public agencies, and for property and infrastructural investment (airports, harbours, high-speed rail, etc.). More recently, however, an alternative model has emerged in which cities collaborate to exploit their mutually complementary attributes. In this way, networks of cities develop, which jointly generate agglomeration economies that separately they would not be able to furnish. Examples of such networks are to be found in "The Third Italy", in Baden–Württemberg and in Jutland.

A further development of urban collaboration has been the creation of information networks in which good practice in one context is passed on to other cities. Examples of such networks within the European Union include Quartiers en Crises, Overture and PHARE, some of which are designed to utilize the experience of western European cities to inform the marketization of the cities of east central Europe. Other examples of transnational urban collaboration include the designation of growth arcs, such as the western Mediterranean littoral and the Alpine axis from Lyons to Turin.

Conclusion

This chapter began by counselling care in the transfer of urban policies deemed successful in managing structural change from one city to another, and concluded by describing networks designed to do just that. On balance, it does seem that cities have much to gain by transferring information about the policies involved in urban management, for two reasons. In some cases, where there are substantial economic, political and cultural similarities between cities, it may be possible to transplant successful policies. In rather more cases, information from other cities may, by providing a contrast, stimulate a new perspective on the management of structural adaptation.

References

Donnison, D. V. & P. Soto 1980. *The good city*. London: Heinemann.

References

Haworth, C. T., J. E. Long, D. W. Rasmussen 1978. Income distribution, city size and urban growth. *Urban Studies* **15**, 1–7.

Knight, R. V. 1995. Knowledge-based development: policy and planning implications for cities. *Urban Studies* **32**(3), 225–61.

Lever, W. F. 1991. Deindustrialization and the reality of the post-industrial city. *Urban Studies* **28**, 983–99.

Rostow, W. W. 1967. *The stages of economic growth*. Cambridge: Cambridge University Press.

Thrift, N. 1996, forthcoming. Globalisation and financial markets. In *The global economy in transition*, P. Daniels & W. F. Lever (eds). Harlow: Longman.

Williamson, J. 1965. Regional inequality and the process of national development: a description of patterns. *Economic Development and Cultural Change* **13**, 84.

CHAPTER SIX
Barcelona:
economic development 1970–95

Joaquim Clusa

An important part of the arguments and the data of this chapter come from a collective work on metropolitan Barcelona, recently published, by the Department of Planning of the Association of Municipalities, entitled "Metropolitan dynamics in the area and region of Barcelona" in which the author worked for the past two years.

From industrial city to service centre:
sharp structural adjustment

Barcelona, second city of Spain and capital of Catalonia region, has, since the nineteenth century, been the main industrial centre of the country. However, in the past 25 years the city has gone through a process of structural adjustment characterized by industrial sector reorganization, the growth of the tertiary sector and the decentralization of residence and employment in the metropolitan region. The process has been fairly successful in both economic and social terms, in part because of the important role played by the public sector in leading the processes of urban renewal, capital inflow and international promotion.

Thus, despite the sharp economic cycles from 1970 and the intensity and social costs of the different adjustments, the GDP of the province of Barcelona grew by about 50%, in real terms, and the income of the region of Catalonia reached approximately the average income level of the European Union (98%), after having improved 15 points in the ranking during the period 1980 to 1993. Among the reasons for this positive balance, the recent Eurostat study of the European regions gives Catalonia the status of a "solid and diversified industrial structure", a "wide range of salaries for a qualified working population", "a majority of medium-size companies" and a "high and increasing disposable income".[1] The unemployment figures, however, exceed by more than four points the European average.

On the other hand, the integration of Spain in the European Union in 1986 reinforced the process of globalization of the Catalan economy. International competitiveness has special consequences in the Barcelona Metropolitan Region because it has 21% of the total industrial employment of Spain. Because of this concentration, the Catalan economy normally grows at a faster rate than Spain in periods of recovery or expansion, but also its crises are deeper.

Additionally, important technological change allowed increases in productivity and tertiarization, as in all Western economies. An important feature of the economic evolution of Catalonia is the share of foreign capital in industry, which reached nearly 40% of all the direct foreign investment in Spain in 1991, as well as tourism, with more than 14 million visitors in 1994.

The so called Metropolitan Region of Barcelona (3236 km^2 and 4.3 million inhabitants) has contributed significantly to this process because, in terms of resident population, it represents 94% of the province and 70% of the Catalonian region, although the municipality of Barcelona, with 96.4 km^2 and 1.6 million inhabitants, represents only 27% of the Catalan population. In terms of European regions, Catalonia, with 31.930 km^2 and nearly 6.1 million inhabitants, is similar to the South East of the UK (27.222 km^2) or the whole State of Belgium (32.517 km^2). In this chapter, we will refer to the "first metropolitan ring" as part of the "metropolitan area", including the central city, and a total area of nearly 600 km^2 and 3 million inhabitants. It is the territory for two metropolitan administrations for transport and environmental services, as it is the "metropolitan region" for the structural and transport planning.

The processes of change or structural adjustment that the metropolitan economy has experienced during the past 25 years will be the main focus of the chapter. They include:

- reorganization of the industrial sector, in terms of employment, type of activities, size of plants, productivity, externalization of services, geographical relocation and participation of foreign capital
- tertiarization, with different consequences in the field of personal services, public administration and advanced services to companies
- decentralization of residence and employment, with the consequent territorial extension of the metropolitan area, an increase in the consumption of urban land and the reduction of population densities in the centre.

As will be explained, some of the operative conclusions emerging from the recent experience of the economic evolution of Barcelona relate to the intensity of the employment cycles, the importance of public leadership in the adjustment processes, the mobilizing power of an event such as the Olympic

---

1. Eurostat, *Portrait of the regions*, vol. 3. (Luxembourg: Eurostat, 1993).

Games as a pretext to produce the necessary partnerships and agreements to finance infrastructure deficits, and the strength of the private sector to generate economic development. The whole process has not been free of an important range of social and economic costs and, in spite of the general improvement, significant economic, infrastructural and administrative shortcomings persist.

The chapter is divided in three main parts, which follow the process of structural adjustment in chronological order:

1. The impact in 1975 to 1985 of economic crisis: globalization, structural adjustment and political transition.
2. 1986–92: economic growth, urban renewal, public policies and the effects of the 1992 Olympic Games.
3. Urban and economic dynamics after structural adjustment: strong points and weaknesses.

The chapter ends with some tentative conclusions.

The impact of 1975–85 economic crisis

The economic crisis of 1975 to 1985 had a severe impact on the Spanish economy and led the city and the metropolitan area into a deep structural adjustment. The most visible consequence of the crisis was the reduction by nearly 20% in employment, according to census figures.

On the other hand, the predominant industrial sector lost some eight percentage points in the employment structure of the metropolitan region. However, the real income per capita had a slight increase during the period, in which the almost non-existent unemployment of the 1960s and the beginning of the 1970s gave way to a 21–5% rate.

During the crisis, the integration of the city with the international economy did not stop. Thus, the index of imports plus exports related to GDP rose from 29% in 1979 to 40% in 1985. Since then, the proportion was stabilized around that figure, but the GDP has grown at an average rate of 11.2% per year at current prices.

Additionally, it must be remembered that the beginning of the economic crisis coincided with the beginning of the political transition to democracy in Spain. The crisis started nearly two years after the beginning of the "oil crisis" in Europe, and 1975 is usually considered the end of the 40-year-long Franco dictatorship; the referendum on the new Spanish Constitution took place in 1978 and the first local elections were held in 1979.

During the political transition there was an increasing demand for better urban conditions, led, especially in peripheral neighbourhoods, by grassroots movements of citizens, as well as through confrontations in the workplace directed by the recently legalized unions. Inflation exceeded 10% per year for almost ten years.

Some additional characteristics of the adjustment process and the general economic situation were as follows:

- Barcelona metropolitan area is ninth in ranking of residential population of EU metropolitan areas and third in population density, after Paris and Athens. In terms of metropolitan regions, when the German Ruhr and the Dutch Randstad are considered, Barcelona is sixth in residential population, eighth in territorial extension, and again third in density.
- The consumption of land for urban uses between 1978 and 1986 nearly doubled on the level of 1972, as a result of the decentralization and improvement of space standards.
- The metropolitan region has approximately 70% of the Catalonian region, and about 11% of Spain's residential population.
- The second ring, with three municipalities of more than 100 000 inhabitants, an industrial tradition and 30.2% of the residential population, now has a great deal of the urban growth of the metropolitan region, with shares of 56% of new housing, 57% of industrial land, 88% of residential population growth and 95% of the net creation of employment in the period 1975–91 – a model of "diffuse city".
- The industrial sector (excluding the construction industry) with 31% of Barcelona province's output lost 16 percentage points from 1971, whereas the service sector gained 21 percentage points in the same period.
- The tertiarization process and the industrial restructuring meant a loss of nearly 500 000 industrial jobs with employment rates of 25% according to a sample census and 20.6% according to registered unemployed statistics. The total employment decreased nearly 20% from 1971 to 1985, although income maintained its real value.

1986–92: growth, renewal, policies and the Olympic Games

The global results: more than 400 000 new jobs in six years
From 1986 to the Olympic Games of 1992, the city and region as a whole experienced fast economic growth; the process was probably less intensive in the rest of Spain. There were increases of 20–25% in the employment figures and around 35% in the real GDP per capita in no more than six years. Rapid economic growth was also associated with an average increase of 98% in the price of new housing in the metropolitan region during that period, within a general "boom" in real estate (land, offices, industrial premises), initiated especially in the office and residential market near the centre of Barcelona.

The creation of employment (more than 470 000 jobs in Catalonia according the Eurostat *Portrait of the regions* and 405 000 according to the official figures of the sample census) continued up to the beginning of the year of the Olympic Games. At the end of the expansion cycle, the income per capita of Catalonia was at 98% of the European average, having been 83% in 1980.

The expansion coincided with the stagnation of population growth, but also with an important increase in mobility; in 1991, nearly 38% of the employed population in the Metropolitan Region worked in a municipality other than where they lived, whereas it was only 32% five years earlier. Nearly 250000 people commuted to Barcelona for work and more than 100000 living in the city worked elsewhere.

The expansion period did not reduce the unemployment figures below 15% of the active population, because the demographic evolution kept pace with employment creation, and surely this is the most important cost of the post-adjustment period. The whole process is parallel with the decentralization of population and economic activity, as will be explained later; this process will probably have negative fiscal consequences for the central city in the future.

All industrial sectors grew in the expansion period, but especially construction, machinery, food and printing.

The Games: management, finance and employment

The organization of an international event in order to promote and renew a city is, today, a well known "trick". "Expos", "Olympics", fairs and even religious celebrations have led to what is aptly named "the festivalization" of many urban policies. Barcelona used such a pretext when it organized the 1992 Olympic Games. The process began in 1986, which was both the year of the nomination of the city as organizer for 1992 Olympic Games and the year of Spanish integration in the EEC. It was also the first year with net creation of employment since 1975.

Works for the Olympic Games had a crucial role as an instrument of urban and economic renewal. The Olympic Villages accounted for 49% of new housing completed in the central city between 1991 and 1992; they accounted for only 26.2% in the metropolitan area and 12.7% in the metropolitan region. New infrastructure gave centrality to the former disorganized metropolitan periphery.

The Olympic Games represented a large-scale agreement to finance new physical infrastructure among the three main administrations (local, regional and central), and the real estate sector of Spain and abroad. The management created a new organizational form separate from the administration: holding companies (HOLSA for the Olympic holding company).

The Olympics were, as we have said, both an "excuse" and a "catalyst" to mobilize the investment needed to overcome the infrastructural deficits of the city. The total investment associated with the Olympic Games (956630 million pesetas, excluding the operational expenses) was equivalent to the cost of nearly 1100 km of motorways, at the current Spanish prices. Only 9% of this was accounted for by proper sports facilities, whereas the construction of new transport infrastructure (with 75 km of new urban motorways, basically a complete circular motorway crossing 13 municipalities around Barcelona) took 42% of total investment.

Other important works were undertaken in telecommunications (with 13%, of total investment), the new housing in the Olympic Villages (15%) and new hotels (13%). At the end of the investment process, Barcelona had gained an important economic infrastructure to compete with other international cities to attract service activities and tourism. Office investment was located in the so-called "new centrality" areas, designed for the reorganization of the tertiary sector and to increase the international attractiveness of Barcelona. Mainly located on the boundaries of the municipality, the new centralities had important effects on the whole metropolitan area or first ring.

The total expenditure associated with the Olympic Games was equivalent to US$9.375 million (1 119 509 million pesetas), only exceeded in Tokyo in 1964 with US$16 826 million. There are several estimates of its impact on employment. According to the first one[2] there had been the "creation of 160 887 jobs from January 1987 to August 1992 or 30 000 annual average", of which "115 366 were in the construction sector" and 28 851 in public administration sector". According to a second estimate[3] the impact was "an annual average employment growth, 1987–92, related to the direct expenditure . . . of 35 309 jobs . . . related to the induced impact of 24 019 jobs . . . (and) . . . an effect of permanent employment (additional jobs from the compound effect and the change of economic structure) . . . of about 20 000 jobs . . . so, the annual average employment growth due to economic impact of the Games was 59 328 jobs for the period 1987–92 in the municipality of Barcelona . . .".

Based on an input–output table, the Municipal Council estimated a total generation of 128 000 jobs.[4] This would mean an impact of 5.8% (nearly 7% in the metropolitan region) in 1992, significant especially if the growth lasted six years. The Keynesian multiplier calculated by the work is 3.3 with respect to consumption and investment associated with the Olympic Games.

The investment associated with the Olympics came both from public and private sources. Consumption expenditure associated strictly with the "sport-

---

2. J. Ll. Raymond, A. Matas, D. Pujolar, "Anàlisi de l'impacte dels Jocs Olímpics sobre la producció i ocupació a Catalunya", a *Nota d'Economia*, Generalitat de Catalunya, no 50, 61–77, 1994.

3. F. Brunet, "Anàlisi econòmica dels Jocs Olímpics de Barcelona '92: recursos, finançament i impactes", in *Les claus de l'exit. Impactes socials, esportius, econòmics i comunicatius de Barcelona '92*, M. I. Moragas & M. Botella (eds), 237 (Centre d'Estudis Olímpics i de l'Esport, Universitat Autònoma de Barcelona, Servei de Publicacions, 1995).

4. Ajuntament de Barcelona, *El impacto económico de los Juegos Olímpicos*, Gabinete de Programación, 1992.

ing events", 162880 million pesetas (US$1368 million), is only 14.5% of total expenditure when the associated infrastructure is included (1 119 510 million pesetas or US$9.376 million). The fiscal resources of the public administrations used in investment accounted for only 40.3% of the total, according to recent estimates by Brunet (1995).

The rest, up to an amount of 668 386. 5 million pesetas (59.7% of the total) was financed from commercial resources by private investors (28%), the public companies of the central administration (12%), especially the railway and telephone companies – RENFE and Telefónica – the Olympic holding investments (HOLSA) and by the services or sponsors associated with the Games (16%). Private investment coming from abroad (one-third of the private total) had an additional mobilizing effect. But the public management of the event and the infrastructure construction was nearly 72% of the total, and only 17% of this was provided by the Olympic Committee.

In terms of the share of the different administrations in the financing of the infrastructure (956 630 million pesetas), the central administration was the principal operator with 50% of the management and 41% of public finance. The regional government accounted for an additional 22% and 32%, whereas local government had a share of around 20%. The total distribution does not correspond exactly to the distribution of total public investment in each fiscal year..

In spite of its importance, the financing of the Olympic Games had a relatively small impact on public budgets and on debt levels for the future in the municipality. The infrastructure associated with the Olympic Games from public budgets during the preparation period (325 586 million pesetas) represented 29% of the total investment. Finance through fiscal resources was completed with a credit of 112 590 for HOLSA and a grant to the Barcelona Olympic Committee of 12 946 million pesetas, up to a total of 451 123 million pesetas.

There is a technical as well as a political discussion as to whether half of the HOLSA credit (nearly 53 000 million pesetas with an annual payment of 8000 million pesetas up to the year 2000) is a "proper" debt of the municipality. If it is not, the share of the Barcelona municipality in the Olympic investments represented 17.4% of the increase in municipal debt of the period and 16% of the total investment made by the municipality in other types of infrastructures or civil works. But if the HOLSA credit is included, then the "Olympic debt" would have been 35% of the total 1987–92 debt increase. The HOLSA credit represents 26% of the interest paid by the municipality in 1995.

For the future, the debt of the City of Barcelona in 1993 was only 1.87 times higher than the 1987 debt. According to municipal forecasts it will have decreased by 17% by 1999. It is also a positive indicator that the 1987 debt represented 1.9 times the current income of the municipality, whereas it represented 1.7 times in 1992, including the HOLSA credit.

If the share of infrastructure and civil works associated with the Olympic

Games was not excessively high for the municipality, the same can be said for the regional and central governments. The estimates made in this chapter from different sources give a share of 17.2% in the investment of the regional

Table 6.1 Public policies: structural adjustment, promotion, development.

Private operators
- multinational companies investment (Nissan, Wolkwagen-SEAT, Sanyo, Sharp, Sony, IBM, Hewlett–Packard, Olivetti . . .), especially around B–30 and the technology park.
- motorways financed by toll (Garraf, Cadi Tunnel, Vallvidrera, and new lanes in the existing ones . . .)
- industrial private investment in small and medium-size companies
- investment in new service activities in the tertiarization process
- office floorspace investment
- renewal of housing in Barcelona, mainly through Olympic operations
- new housing investment and the new suburban and single-house model in the second ring of municipalities (~18000 units year)
- hotel investments in Barcelona, the coast and the snow areas
- telecommunications investment by Telefonica
- new cultural, medical services . . . and football activities.

Municipality of Barcelona
- Olympic Games: city candidate promotion (1982–86): plans and projects
- Olympic Games (1987–92): road and public transport infrastructure / housing and offices / hotels / telecommunications / sports equipment
- Strategic Plan 2000 (1988 and 1994): *the* comprehensive reference
- new centralities in eight locations ("Barcelona New Projects")
- city marketing
- international promotion of a Mediterranean Cities Network (C–6)
- tourism plans (after the Olympic Games)
- promotion of cultural and medical services
- joint ventures in private companies
- "Consortium of Zona Franca": two new industrial estates in the metropolitan region
- sewerage renewal plan.

Metropolitan administration (First Ring municipalities)
- technology park, close to the Third Ring Road (B–30) and the second Barcelona university; participation of the regional government
- industrial axis (industrial real estates of Can Calderó, El Pla, Carretera del Mig)
- territorial redistribution of resources coming from the central administration and from the municipalities, in parks, intermunicipal roads and planning
- management and new investment in environmental infrastructures for water and refuse disposal (metropolitan)
- coastal infrastructure: planning and investment.

Other metropolitan municipalities
- new commercial and service centres: promotion and competition among municipalities (Baricentro, Sabadell Macià Axis)
- small offices for private companies promotion
- financing local infrastructure mainly by debt.

Table 6.1 (cont'd)   Public policies: structural adjustment, promotion, development.

Regional administration
• increase the investment level reached by the central administration
• Olympic Games finance
• priority in transport infrastructure throughout the region, with the metropolitan area locating less than the demographic share
• new industrial estates (about 60 locations in Catalonia, 10 of them in the Metropolitan Region)
• new residential areas for affordable housing especially in the second ring of municipalities
• new university in Barcelona and new university departments or small universities in other medium-size cities
• progressive reduction of deficits in health services and in primary and secondary schools
• territorial plan for Catalonia ("regional planning" for population distribution reference, urban structure plans at two supra-municipal levels and ensemble of sectoral plans)
• "structure plan" for the metropolitan region of Barcelona (in progress).

Central administration
• social security funds to finance unemployment and companies closures
• ZUR: Zone of Urgent Re-industrialization
• Olympic Games finance, through the Olympic Holding (HOLSA)
• RENFE: renewal of the metropolitan railway equipment
• motorways investments (free of toll): Barcelona–Lleida, Mataró–Granollers . . .

European Union
• ZUR (co-finance)
• co-finance of agricultural transformations
• co-finance of social programs

---

government during the period 1987–92. For the central government the total investment allocated to Catalonia during the period was 39.8% of the central government's "investment tendencies". But it must be said at the same time that the Madrid region, with a smaller population than Catalonia, had 1.9 times more investment than Catalonia during the same period.

So, the Olympic investments financed by public budgets of all administrations do not seem too heavy, especially if one takes into account the results of the event in terms of "city marketing". The leadership of the Barcelona municipality managed to produce a particular and unique concentration of public investment in the city, without producing much more increase in public spending than the "normal" tendencies in an expansionary period.

Other counter-crisis policies: industry and infrastructure
The Olympic Games were accompanied by other public policies and especially by the investment of the private sector in new activities. The cycles of employment were too coincident with the nomination in 1986 and the cele-

bration of the Olympic Games in 1992 to minimize its importance and its function as a "lever" to move the whole system.

The main counter-crisis policies of the regional government were investment in new infrastructure and industrial estates, trying to increase the level of public investment before the setting up of new regional governments in Spain, after the approval of the Constitution in 1978. At the local level the construction of a "Technology park", 15 km away from the centre of Barcelona, was one of the most important initiatives by the Metropolitan government before its abolition in 1987, apart from the creation of an "industrial axis" to extend the supply of industrial land. The list of public policies presented on pages 109–10 also points out some of the more relevant private investments that allowed structural adjustments.

The important investments undertaken by the Regional Government Agency on Urban Land Infrastructure (INCASOL) has proved very useful in providing new urban land in a very rigid market with a high prices, making it difficult to built affordable houses with public benefits ("protected housing"), as well as industrial estate premises.

Post structural adjustment dynamics (1992–95)

The expansion period initiated in 1985–86 finished in 1991–92. The 1992–93 crisis represented a loss of about 10% of total employment in metropolitan Barcelona, more than 70% of the employment created during the previous expansion period. In 1994 a period of employment creation started again. During the two-year crisis, the share of service employment increased by nearly 5% points in the economic structure of the metropolitan region.

The strengths of the new situation came mainly from the fact that the city has managed to change its scale, in both economic and spatial terms. Barcelona is now a metropolis of more them four million inhabitants, with a diversified and attractive economy, a good international image and a fairly appropriate network of infrastructures (especially in the central parts of the city).

Nevertheless, important weaknesses persist, mainly associated with an inability to provide employment to the growing active population, the shortage of affordable housing, the deficits in transport and environmental infrastructure and the complexity of the public administration.

Strengths: the change of scale of the city in the second ring
When analyzing the situation of the city after a process of structural adjustment, the first phenomenon to consider is the stagnation of overall demographic growth. This is mainly attributable to low birth rates and the

interruption of inmigration flows from the rest of Spain. The region of Catalonia with 6059000 inhabitants in 1991 had a population growth of only 103000 in ten years, whereas it had had a growth of nearly 1.8 million people in the 15-year period since what is considered the beginning of the modern process of economic development (the Stabilization Plan of 1959) until the beginning of the 1975–85 crisis.

The net migration flows from the rest of Spain were an important consequence of the general development process and the industrial concentration. In the period of the strongest adjustment (approximately between the census dates of 1981 and 1986) the region had a negative net migration of nearly 80000, when many former migrants returned to their regions of origin; they were either long-term unemployed or retired.

At the metropolitan level the loss of resident population started, in census terms, in 1970 in the municipality of Barcelona, in 1981 when the first ring is included (metropolitan area) and in 1986 in the metropolitan region, following a "normal" process of decentralization.

However, population stagnation has been accompanied by another important phenomenon: the increase in residential mobility in the metropolitan region. The direction of these movements is typically from the more dense and consolidated central areas to the small settlements on the metropolitan periphery. Thus, the increasing demand for suburban land has led to a doubling of the extension of urban land since the mid-1970s.

According to Serratosa,[5] land with urban uses in the metropolitan region of Barcelona occupied 21482 ha (6.7% of the total area) in 1972. In 1986 the occupation was 39151 ha, almost doubling the urban area in 14 years. During the period 1986–92, with the level of population almost stabilized since 1981, urban land increased by 15%. The demand for urban land in the form of infrastructures, industrial estates or residential areas reflected a demand for suburban residential location in low-density areas, but also the demand for second homes or holiday residences, which accounted for nearly 15% of the total housing stock.

This process of metropolitan integration has led to the ultimate change of scale of the urban phenomenon, with the second metropolitan ring now attracting most of the urban growth. The consolidation of a second ring at a distance of 20–40 km from the centre of the municipality of Barcelona (1.6 million inhabitants and nearly 100 km^2), added 1.3 million inhabitants to the population within the traditional boundaries of the small metropolitan area.

The second ring, partially organized around five cities with a tradition of endogenous industrial growth (Sabadell, Terrassa and Mataró within the range of 100000 to 200000 inhabitants), received the progressive influence of Barcelona and the first ring of municipalities; the whole territory has been

---

5. A. Serratosa, "Els espais oberts en el planejament metropolità: realitats i propostes". In *Papers: Regió Metropolitana de Barcelona*, no 20, 39–47, 1994.

designated the "Barcelona Metropolitan Region" with 4.3 million inhabitants and 3236 km^2.

With a share of 30.2% of the population of the metropolitan region, the second ring attracted nearly 56% of new housing built during the period 1987–92, 57% of the land for industrial uses, 88% of the residential population growth, 95% of the net creation of new employment during the inter-census period 1975–91 and 67% of net migration leaving the central city. The growth model has been qualified as one of the "diffused city"; the availability of land, its price, and the network of motorways and railways explain the attraction of the second ring.

Weaknesses: unemployment rates, infrastructural deficits and administrative shortcomings

The process of structural adjustment, however successful, has not been free of significant social and economic costs. There are important limitations in information to assess the evolution of social costs; for instance, it is hard to find evidence of whether spatial differences have increased with the personal income improvement. Some of the costs are as follows:

- a structural inability to create enough employment, especially for newcomers to the work market, and therefore maintaining high rates of unemployment, not below 13% of the active population.
- cycles of intense destruction or creation of net employment, with positive and negative rates ranging from 10% to 25%, as in the periods 1975–85 and 1992–93 for the recessions and 1986–91 for the expansions
- high prices and rents in the real estate market of Barcelona municipality and its surroundings, as well as a lack of new residential areas at more affordable prices
- excess of office floorspace supply, after the intense construction phase at the end of the 1980s, without reduction in prices
- rates of annual inflation above 4.3% and mortgage rates of about 11–14%
- deficits of communication infrastructure and public transport, producing, in some cases, social costs associated with daily commuting to work and general urban mobility
- the important debt of the public administrations to finance new infrastructure built since the early 1980s
- lack of competitiveness because of deficits in the economic infrastructure associated with the port, airport, transport junctions and high-speed train lines to France and Madrid.

The difficulties of creating enough employment, especially for young people, is beyond doubt, the most important shortcoming of the economy of Barcelona. The registered unemployment rate at the end of 1994 was 12.6% in the municipality of Barcelona, 15.3% within the first ring and 15.7% within the second ring. Although the rates were decreasing in 1995, they are at least four points below the average rate for Spain, and far from the European average of 10.4% at the end of 1993. The low rate of job creation, the financial deficit and the price of new housing are the most significant costs in social terms for metropolitan Barcelona.

The impact of unemployment rates is reinforced by some urban dynamics. Thus, employment and residence have different decentralization rhythms during the economic cycle. The decentralization of economic activity from the municipality of Barcelona, measured in terms of employment, has overcome the decentralization of residences during the periods of crisis, as happened during 1975–85. However, the decentralization of activity is lower than that of residences during expansion periods (1969–75 and 1986–91). During the period corresponding to a completed economic cycle 1975–91, the metropolitan region roughly maintained its share of Catalonian employment (70–71%), while the municipality of Barcelona lost the equivalent of 5.5% in employment and only 3.8% in residents during the same period. Considering a longer period, such as 1970–91, the population share of the metropolitan centre lost 7%, expressing the fact that the decentralization of residential population is independent of the economic cycles. The municipality had a net loss of residential population of nearly 14300 per year during the period 1987–93; but in 1993 and 1994 the annual net loss was more than 20000.

Planning regulations have prevented the worse potential effects of these dynamics. Metropolitan Barcelona is still congested in terms of population densities, lack of parking facilities and open spaces in the municipalities of Barcelona and the first ring.

The metropolitan master plan for Barcelona and 26 neighbouring municipalities, approved in 1976, established a maximum capacity for the residential areas of 4.5 million inhabitants, on different assumptions on housing and persons per house or flat. The municipal policies of planning, the tendencies of decentralization and the real estate market mechanisms explain the maintenance of the population of Barcelona and the first ring at 3 million, because natural growth compensates for the migration losses.

Another initial weakness for the future of the city and the metropolitan area and region is the persistence of important infrastructural deficits. Even after infrastructural investment for the Olympic Games there are still important deficits in infrastructure for economic activity in the form of main roads, such as the "fourth ring" to link the cities and the growth of the second ring, railways, airport, port, environmental infrastructure for water recycling and refuse disposal or open spaces. All need huge amounts of public and private investment.

These funds will hardly be provided only by central government. This stresses the importance of local policies such as the Strategic Plan Barcelona 2000 and regional investments in infrastructure and industrial estates. It should be remembered that, even during the seven exceptional years before the Olympic Games, the Madrid region had a share of direct investment equivalent to 1.6–3.2 times the investment in Catalonia, despite having a million fewer residents.

In this context the Strategic Plan Barcelona 2000 has been a fairly useful tool to establish a local consensus among public and private agents about the policies to be applied. However, the problem of the lack of a metropolitan authority for the region of Barcelona, with a fair representation of local interests, especially Barcelona Municipality, remains unsolved.

The metropolitan region is now divided into some 200 local administrative units, belonging to seven different administrative tiers (municipality, metropolitan area, country – "comarca", province, region – "autonomous community", state and Europe, in addition to the district level in the municipality of Barcelona). The resulting complexity is a rather heavy burden for the development of the city, especially in order to reach agreements and partnership for the future investments.

Since the 1987 administrative and territorial organization laws passed by the Catalonian government, the ambit for the management of metropolitan services (transport, water and refuse disposal) is the "metropolitan area", whereas for the planning of transport and land use it is the "metropolitan region".

Conclusions

How can a city be managed through a process of structural adjustment? There is a widespread consensus about the goals to be reached:

- On the one hand, taking advantage of the process of change in order to improve the competitiveness, attractiveness and productivity of the city's economy.
- On the other hand, passing through this process without increasing social polarization or compromising the ecological equilibrium. Just the opposite: the economic change should be an opportunity to improve living conditions for the majority of citizens and to reduce environmental risks.

The first goal can be summarized by an increase in the gross domestic product and as a result income per capita. The second goal is more difficult to measure *ex ante* and *ex post*. I understand the concept of "entrepreneurial city" as a particular mixture of "agents or operators", "policies" and "strategies" in order to produce a reasonable result in the processes of globalization and technological change of a metropolitan region.

From the former points of view, three main aspects of the Barcelona experience might be of general interest as a conclusion to be implemented in other urban situations:

- The utilization of a special event, the 1992 Olympic Games, in order to mobilize resources and promote the city and metropolitan area, besides other policies created by the central and the regional governments.

- The key role played by public initiative in order to create the conditions (infrastructure, industrial estates, housing, ...) in which a relatively successful process has taken place.
- The strength of the economic system ("the private sector") of the whole region in terms of investment, consumption and exports ("tourism" being one of the most important sectors, accounting for 10–13% of GDP), which has overcome most of the consequences of the economic crisis 1975–85.

Apart from that, some other specific conclusions can be drawn. The first would relate to the explanation of the intensity of the employment cycles because of the rigidity of salary structures. The second conclusion relates to the importance of public and local leadership in the adjustment processes. And, thirdly, one could wonder whether there is a need for mobilizing events such as the Olympic Games or the strategic plans as excuses to produce the necessary partnerships of public administrations and private operators in order to meet the deficits of infrastructure. Finally, from the metropolitan institutions of Barcelona, as one of their informal representatives, I should also wonder whether "big cities do not need big governments" (*The Economist*, August 1994) or what is the form and territorial ambit to produce strategic agreements and partnerships to improve competitiveness in our world of cities.

CHAPTER SEVEN
Kingston, Jamaica: structural adjustment and policy

Cheryl Gopaul

Introduction

The Jamaican experience with Structural Adjustment Programme (SAP) reform is particularly interesting, because Jamaica was one of the first countries where SAPs by the World Bank were implemented, and in which the loan conditions were somewhat harsh. Jamaica is also distinguished by the fact that, prior to the onset of SAP implementation, the country's economic position was relatively good. In addition, Jamaica had a strong tradition of political participation.

This chapter examines the impact of the SAP reform adopted by the government of Jamaica (GOJ) on its economy, with specific reference to the Kingston Metropolitan Area (KMA). My objective is to examine the performance of the KMA before, during and after the implementation of SAP reform, and to identify the successes and failures of policy measures to mitigate adverse SAP impacts. The chapter comprises four sections. Section I provides a brief background of the macroeconomic reform programme in Jamaica during 1977–90. A description of the KMA at the beginning and end of the SAP reform period is provided in Section II. This includes, to the extent available, primary and secondary data and, through extrapolation, population, role, output of goods and services, and the distribution of employment by sectors. Section III consist of an assessment of the impact of SAP implementation on the economy of KMA. An outline of the success and failures of public and private intervention to mitigate the adverse impacts of SAP in the KMA are discussed. Section IV comprises a discussion of the prospects for the KMA.

I Background of structural adjustment programme in Jamaica, 1977–90

The Structural Adjustment Programme in Jamaica lasted 13 years, from 1977 to 1990. During this period, various fiscal, monetary, and trade policy measures were implemented within an economic liberalization thrust. The macroeconomic environment can best be summarized as one of economic discipline, as the main objectives of the structural adjustment programme included liberalization and privatization of the economy, diversification of the country's economic structure, reorientation of the economy towards the promotion and diversification of exports, increased investment and employment opportunities, improvement of the country's balance of payment's position, reduction of the fiscal deficit and inflation reduction. Exchange controls were imposed, so as to reduce demand for unnecessary imports, to stem capital flight and to direct the flow of foreign exchange into those activities that were high on the government's list.

The first Stand-by Agreement was signed with the IMF in July 1977. A second agreement – a three-year Extended Fund Facility (EFF) came into effect in May 1978, following the breakdown of the first agreement. Between 1978 and 1979 two other loans were signed with the World Bank – one to finance imports and the other an Export Development Fund (EDF) programme. During 1974–80 Jamaica experienced a cumulative decrease of 21% in its growth rate, an increase of 22% each in both inflation and unemployment, an increase in overall public sector deficit of 18% GDP, and an unsustainable balance of payments position (current accounts deficit of 6.2% of GDP in 1980). The consequences of the downward economic performance were amplified by a series of external shocks (increased costs of most of the country's imports, a decline in volume and value of the main export products, and deterioration in the aluminum facilities as a result of high production costs), and internal factors (a slowdown in the major sectors: bauxite, aluminum and tourism). These poor macroeconomic indicators were the *sine qua non* of the economy failing one of the performance "tests" in 1979.

The overall performance of the economy during the 1980s can best be described as mixed. Between 1981 and 1983, the growth rates increased by 2.5%, 1.0% and 2.6% in 1981, 1982 and 1983 respectively. Inflation increased from 3.8% in 1975 to 26.9% in 1984, and unemployment to just under 13% in 1982. The merchandise balance deteriorated from a negative US$208.6 million in 1980 to a negative US$595.2 million in 1983. The current account deficit reached 14.4% of GPD, with a corresponding increase in public sector deficit. External debt increased by 75%, from US$1866.8 million in 1980 to US$3266.9 million in 1983 (Tables 7.1, 7.2).

In 1981, a newly elected government introduced a broader based SAP, prepared in consultation with a joint IMF/World Bank team. This "new" SAP was aimed at correcting the severe internal and external macroeconomic imbal-

118

ances accentuated by the 1977–80 SAP policies, and to lay the long-term foundation for economic restoration, with the private sector playing a leading role. The aim was to address low production and high unemployment by diversifying the economy to attracting foreign investment, especially in manufacturing and tourism.

During 1982 and 1987 the government (GOJ) signed three additional Structural Adjustment Loans (SAL) with the World Bank. The first SAL for US$76.2 million was signed in 1982, the second SAL for US$60.2 million in 1983, and the third SAL for US$55.0 in 1987. Two sector loans were also signed in 1987 for US$40 million, including a Public Enterprise Sector Adjustment Loan (TFSAL IN) and two Standby Agreements with the IMF in 1984 and 1985.

By 1983 the three-year EFF had been suspended. Between 1984 and 1985, monetary and fiscal policies were tightened, in accordance with the conditions of the 1984 and 1985 Standby Agreements. The 1984 Standby was completed only after several waivers were granted, and the 1985 agreement was later abandoned. By 1985, the last of the three SALs was executed, and the majority of the reforms undertaken. Despite these reforms, the economic situation continued to deteriorate. The growth rate declined by –0.95% in 1984 and by –4.6% in 1985; the rate of inflation increased from 26.9% in 1982 to 31.4% in 1984, and the current account deficit as a percentage of GDP increased to a high of 15.7% in 1985. Total debt as a percentage of GDP was –160.7, and –276.3 relative to the exports of goods and services in 1985. In the light of these developments, the GOJ and a tripartite mission from the IMF, World Bank, and USAID carried out a comprehensive review of the economy, and a decision was taken to speed up the pace of reform.

In 1986 and 1987 a favourable external economic environment, reflected in the improvement in trade (arising from the lowering of the price of oil) and increased prices for such major exports as bauxite/aluminum and sugar, as well as a changed macroeconomic framework (the country had no IMF agreement in place), laid the groundwork for an improvement in most of Jamaica's major economic indicators.

Subsequently, growth rates increased by 1.7% in 1986 and 6.2% in 1987, and inflation declined appreciably for the first time in a decade. The major factors responsible for this positive growth trend were the significant growth in tourism and the service sectors, especially construction, as well as increased investment levels in the clothing and apparel manufacturing subsector. In 1987, two Sector Adjustment Loans were implemented, to complement a new IMF agreement that was intended to continue the adjustment process.

The SAP continued with the election of the new government in February 1989. Since then, two new adjustment loans have been negotiated with the World Bank: a Social Sector Adjustment Loan in 1990 and an Investment Sector Adjustment Loan. The latter was co-financed by the IDB and several bilateral donors. A Second Trade and Financial Sector Adjustment Loan (TFSAL II) in addition to several direct and indirect bilateral balance-of-payment sup-

Table 7.1   Distribution of employment by sector in the KMA.

	1975	1980	1985	1991	1994
Agriculture	9.5	9.9	10.4	6	8.8
Mining	2.1	2.1	1.8	2.1	2.4
Manufacturing	6.9	5.3	3.9	4.3	5.6
Utilities	3.1	2.7	2.5	3.8	4.2
Construction	8.2	8.6	6.1	4.9	5.8
Trade & tourism	16.3	14.1	18.2	15.1	13.0
Transportation & communication	5.3	6.8	9.2	8.2	10.4
Finance	14.9	14.7	15.8	15.6	13.1
Social services	21.4	20.8	15.0	12.1	17.4
Industrial	4.1	4.2	3.8	3.1	3.0
Unemployment	8.2	10.8	13.3	24.8	16.1
TOTAL	100.0	100.0	100.0	100.0	100.0
Under-employment	5.0	8.2	11.9	21.1	117.9

Source: Statistical Institute of Jamaica, 1975–94.

port programmes from multilateral agencies and foreign governments were negotiated.

Jamaica also benefited from several programmes and projects, financed by the World Bank, which were designed to support and strengthen its structural adjustment strategy and to achieve specific socio-economic objectives (such as poverty reduction and an increase in real wages), and a greater degree of public sector autonomy.

The arrival of Hurricane Gilbert in 1988, combined with political instability during general elections, interrupted the positive growth trend of the SAL. The agreement was eventually renegotiated when the newly elected government (PNP) took office. Attempts to mitigate the worst effects of the hurricane saw a relaxation of fiscal and monetary policies between 1988 and 1989. This led to considerable deterioration in the macroeconomic framework and, by 1990, the government entered into another agreement with the IMF.

II Kingston Metropolitan Area
before and after SAP implementation

The city of Kingston is the capital of Jamaica and the seat of government. It is the main commercial and service centre and the hub of trading. Kingston Harbour is the eighth largest natural harbour in the world and was a popular cruise-ship port until 1974. During the late 1960s and early 1970s, political unrest resulted in the formation of garrison/ghetto communities within the city of Kingston. These communities, which became political strongholds, were characterized by high crime rates and killings. This in turn had a blight-

Table 7.2 Inflation (%).

	1975	1978	1980	1982	1984	1986	1987	1988	1989	1990	1991	1992	1993	1994
Jamaica	3.8	8.2	12.4	26.9	31.4	10.4	8.4	8.5	17.2	29.8	80.2	40.2	30.1	33.2
KMA	4.1	8.7	13.2	27.8	35.2	10.1	7.3	8.6	16.1	30.9	77.7	39.0	31.4	37.6
Other towns	4.2	8.4	12.8	26.1	34.0	9.5	9.2	7.0	17.1	30.3	81.9	39.3	30.1	32.1
Rural areas	3.9	8.5	12.9	30.3	34.6	11.4	8.6	9.9	18.7	28.1	82.3	42.1	28.5	29.8

Source: Bank of Jamaica Reports, 1975–94.

ing effect on the downtown area, and led to the continued migration of commercial and institutional establishments away from downtown Kingston and the formation of a new corporate centre in the city of New Kingston. The government was therefore simultaneously confronted with the economic costs created through the under-utilization of existing infrastructure and unused building space in the downtown area and the incremental investment necessary to support the rapid pace of development of New Kingston. In order to address the management of the urban landscape and the dual costs of twin cities, the entire urban area was renamed the Kingston Metropolitan Area (KMA) and was managed by one mayor with one city council.

In comparison to other areas in Jamaica, the KMA continued to enjoy a significant amount of government expenditure (recurrent) for the operation and maintenance of infrastructure and social services (Table 7.3). Nonetheless, the output of basic services (Table 7.4) – potable water, number of sewerage connections, and the number of public buses on the roads – was barely adequate for the KMA population at that time. It was within this framework that SAPs were implemented in the KMA.

The impacts of SAP on the Jamaican economy are both long and short term, direct and indirect, and positive and negative. The negative impacts were

Table 7.3   Social services expenditure (J$ million).

	1976	1978	1980	1982	1984	1986	1988	1990	1992	1994
Education	74	31	30	54	76	80	110	157	276	533
Health	40	21	18	22	38	41	53	86	176	216
Social services	33	28	19	16	14	32	48	25	27	50
Housing	21	19	15	11	10	8	6	5	8	23
Water	19	14	11	9	4	4	6	11	21	67
Other	20	22	16	13	15	18	23	38	45	57

Source: Ministry of Finance, 1976–94; Statistical Institute of Jamaica, 1976–94.

Table 7.4   Output of services.

	1975	1980	1985	1990	1994
Potable water	65201	28734	33302	58821	63708
Sewerage	20019	1680	3214	11821	29028
Transportation	305	139	212	609	826
Cruise ships	632	10	2	0	0
Health (graduand nurses)	60	45	49	71	83
Education (total school enrolment)	26840	14982	16284	18409	32584

Source: Economic & Social Survey of Jamaica, 1975–94.

basically short- to medium-term social impacts experienced in the major urban area, that is, the KMA. The positive impacts are long term and were initially experienced within the manufacturing areas located centrally on the island in the Parishes of Clarendon and St Elizabeth, and tourism centres located in smaller urban areas on the entire northern coast of Jamaica.

The impact of SAP on the Kingston metropolitan area

The impact of SAP reform on the KMA may be categorized as:

- urban population pressure
- urban decay
- slums and squatting, and non-conforming land uses
- deterioration of urban infrastructure, social facilities and social services
- collapse of urban transport system
- increasing unemployment, poverty and inequality especially among women.

Urban population pressure   In 1960, out of a total national population of 1.6 million, approximately 550000 or 34% lived in towns and cities. By 1991, more than half of Jamaica's population (50.2%) lived in towns and cities. The KMA is the primate city in Jamaica, accounting for 57.8% of the urban population in 1991. By the year 2020, the estimated projection is that Jamaica's urban population will increase to 2642000. This uncontrollable influx of people to urban centres has led to a situation of severe overcrowding, acute housing shortages, sanitation problems, unemployment, and under-employment and degradation of the environment. Rural–urban migration accounted for more than 50% of the population growth in the KMA, which led to the spiral growth of slums. In some instances, the population in slums increased at a staggering rate of 10–15% of the entire city's population in a year (Table 7.5).

Young people (under 30 years of age) continued to migrate to the KMA because there were no economic reasons to remain in the rural communities. In an effort to find a solution to relieve the migration pressure, the government, in a process of citizens' consultation, identified the lack of assets held by young people and the need for a purpose to stay in the rural area as the root causes for rural–urban migration. The main asset in the rural area is land, which is mostly owned by the government and leased out in small plots to farmers for one- to two-year periods. Further, the small size of plots (less than 2 acres) did not allow the farmers to compete on the export market (a condition of the SAP), since competing meant direct competition with US farmers for the local tourist market (e.g. lettuce was imported from Miami on a daily basis for use in the tourist resorts in Montego Bay). Thus, it was quickly realized that the management of the urban areas could not occur in isolation from rural resource development.

Table 7.5   Urban growth in Jamaica, 1970–91.

	Population ('000s)			Growth per year	
	1970	1982	1991*	1970–82	1982–91
Urban					
KMA	506.2	524.6	587.8	0.85	1.3
Portmore	0.5	73.4	90.1	25.00	2.3
Over 15 000					
Montego Bay	43.5	70.3	83.4	4.10	1.92
Spanish Town	39.2	89.1	92.6	5.70	0.40
May Pen	25.4	41.0	46.7	4.10	1.49
Mandeville	13.7	34.5	39.4	8.00	1.49
Old Harbour**	9.5	18.5	20.8	6.7	1.23
St Ann's Bay**	13.0	16.8	19.3	2.2	1.49
Savanna-la-Mar	11.9	14.9	16.6	1.77	1.10
TOTAL	156.2	285.1	318.8	5.7	1.09
Centres 5–15 000	69.9	117.7	140.0	4.9	1.9
Centres under 5000	28.7	46.2	37.0	4.4	−1.9
TOTAL URBAN	761.5	1047.0	1173.7	2.7	1.2
Rural	1086.9	1143.4	1162.3	0.4	0.16
TOTAL JAMAICA	1848.4	2190.4	2336.0	1.42	0.86

* Preliminary   ** Includes Old Harbour Bay and Ocho Rios.
Source: Calculated from 1991 and 1982 census data. See also McCarthy 1995.

Table 7.6   Population growth in the inner-city communities in the KMA 1982–91.

	1982		1991		
Inner city topology	Number	%	Number	%	Change
Type 1	59810	10.0	60300	8.9	490
Type 2	124118	20.8	141964	20.9	17846
Type 3	35401	5.9	25907	3.8	−9494
Type 4	36603	6.1	42902	6.3	6302
TOTAL POPULATION KMA	598064	100.0	677936	100.0	79872

Source: adapted from the 1982 and 1991 population censuses.
Type 1. Most of Kingston's low-income population live in the slums of the central city and western Kingston.
Type 2. Both areas mentioned above have had increases in population with population change being most rapid in the slums of west Kingston.
Type 3. The transition zone of the city is rapidly losing population. This is probably as a result of individual dwelling units being converted to non-residential uses.
Type 4. Type 4 are units in good conditions within the inner city.

Urban decay   During the 1960s and early 1970s, several major developments were undertaken in the downtown Kingston Waterfront area by the Urban Development Corporation and its subsidiary, the Kingston Waterfront Redevelopment Company. The Kingston docks from Port Royal St to Newport

West were removed to facilitate the demolition of the old inefficient finger piers and to construct a new Ocean Boulevard with waterfront bulkhead, apartment complexes, hotels and financial office towers. The impetus for development provided by this massive redevelopment project led to a natural progression of private improvement to neighbourhood property along parallel and perpendicular roads in the area.

The economic crises of the late 1970s and 1980s brought a halt to all this development as government funds were redirected through SAP cuts to finance capital projects in the manufacturing and tourism sectors. Consequently, some businesses literally ceased operations. The abandoned buildings became prey to scavengers from the nearby depressed areas.

Efforts to reignite the development of downtown Kingston in the mid-1980s were attempted by the siting of the Jamaica Conference Centre (an international conference centre to accommodate 5000 people and to tap the Caribbean's conference activities). The centre was constructed to host the Law of the Sea Conference in Jamaica. Although this facility generated much activity of its own, it failed as the catalyst for the redevelopment process, as its spin-off effects were minimal.

Slums and squatting Another consequence of SAP reform is the accelerated growth of slum areas within the KMA. Although slum areas existed before, poverty and the inability to pay house rent, compounded by the drastic shortage of housing supply, accelerated the spread and intensity of slums. The slum areas within the KMA may be categorized as those in the downtown area, those in the western portion, and slums as holding or transition zone (McCarthy 1995):

- *Slums of downtown Kingston* These areas contain a population of 60 300 persons, according to the 1991 population census, or an absolute increase of about 490 persons compared to 1982. During the intercensal period of 1970–82, the inner-city slums experienced a loss of 8000 persons, attributable in large measure to political violence and the transformation into commercial use of residential land around the central business district.
- *Slums of West Kingston* The number of poor households living in the slums of West Kingston is much greater than the number living in downtown Kingston. According to the 1991 population census there are about 142 000 persons living there.
- *Slums in transition* Immediately to the north of the inner-city slums is a zone where housing is of a better quality than that of the inner-city slums, but where deterioration is beginning to take place. This is an area where 30–40% of housing was built before 1960. Since 1985, about 30–40% of the housing units were converted to commercial and light industrial uses.

Deterioration of urban social facilities and social services   Structural adjustment policies were deliberately designed to shift a greater share of the cost of the social reproduction of labour from the state to the individual and the family, while protecting the position of private capital. This is so despite the fact that the economic recession that prompted these policies made it more difficult for families to assume greater responsibilities. During SAP reform, subsidies were removed and government funds redirected to capital projects in the manufacturing and tourism sectors and subsectors, so as to earn foreign exchange. The contraction in the government's budget, as well as the shift towards privatization and the free play of the market, had immediate consequences for the social goods available to the population. These social goods included education, health, food and nutrition, housing and public transport – all of which were subjected to higher costs, reduced supply and lower quality.

The rate at which adjustment was implemented resulted in chaos in several departments and hence a disruption of service provision, as expenditure levels were often slashed overnight, with no opportunity for any action to be taken to reduce the impact. Hence, health clinics and hospital wards were closed without any warning and even the most basic supplies were unavailable in schools and hospitals.

The reduction of the rate of growth in expenditure levels resulted in the government making thousands of workers redundant. In several instances, these workers were female ancillary staff on the lowest wages, including cleaners in hospitals and schools, and employees in several government departments, which were closed permanently. Employees in local government departments were the hardest hit, as they were the prime target for budget cuts.

On the other hand, where state-owned enterprises were divested, new ownership resulted in an improvement in the quality of service and increased wages. The divestment process was unfortunately very slow and not always transparent.

Collapse of the urban transportation system   The urban public transportation system was also adversely affected. The decision to close the Jamaica Omnibus Service, and to allocate routes to individual mini-bus owners as part of the divestment process, has resulted in chaos during peak hours in certain sections of the urban areas. Although some routes were well serviced, others were neglected for various reasons; operators for some buses refuse to complete entire routes and would only service the short and popular routes, which were most economical. Often passengers had to complete their journeys to work by walking. This resulted in lateness, loss of productivity, or loss of jobs (high job turnover rate). In other instances, bus operators refused to accept school children, especially on the longer routes. School children had to walk to school, were exhausted before they reached school and were unable to learn effectively. Furthermore, in an effort to maximize revenue, mini-bus operators engage in a variety of practices that imply increased danger for their passengers. Buses were overloaded and were kept in operation in a state of disrepair and in violation of traffic regulations.

By 1990 the public transit system was considered non-existent. The absence of regulations and insufficient traffic police and patrol vehicles resulted in complete chaos. This in turn resulted in an astronomical increase in the number of private vehicles. Often, relatives abroad would sent remittances or import vehicles with special concessions given to returning residents. Consequently, during the period 1984–90 the number of private vehicles increased by 500%. This resulted in absolute grid lock during peak hours in the KMA. The traffic deterioration was further compounded by the fact that since 1960 no new roads have been constructed to meet the growing transportation needs of the city of Kingston. More than 80% of all traffic lights in the downtown area did not work. However, since mid-1994, a concerted effort has been made by the government in collaboration with the private sector to finance and rehabilitate most of the traffic lights in the area.

Increasing unemployment, poverty and inequality The economic contraction that was ushered in by 1974, and the export-led growth of the 1980s, were both reflected in the supply of jobs. Structural adjustment imperatives led to the fostering of some industries, the neglect of others and the radical pruning of others.

In 1983, after five years of spiralling unemployment rates, employment creation moved onto an expansionary path. This expansion rivalled the high-growth years of the late 1960s and early 1970s, and was remarkable in that it was accompanied by the shedding of public sector jobs and the relative stagnation of several leading industries.

The major significance of this expansion in job creation is that most of these new jobs were located either in the informal sector or in the secondary sector of the labour market (Anderson & Witter 1991). As such, they were characterized by low wages, low skills, job instability and the virtual absence of worker protection. The trade-off from structural adjustment was that, where employment increased, job adequacy in terms of earnings decreased and under-employment increased in the KMA compared to jobs in export-processing manufacture, in tourism, and small-scale service industries in areas outside the KMA. The sharp increases in the cost of living engendered by SAP policies served to undermine the viability of many employment options across social classes. The responses to the increasing pressure on wages included the search for supplementary sources of income, or additional hours of work, greater reliance on multiple earners within and across households, job abandonment, labour force withdrawal and external migration (Table 7.7).

Although the labour force grew at an annual rate of 1.99% between 1977

Table 7.7   Changes in employment, 1968–90.

Period	Average annual change in employment		
	Both sexes	Female	Male
1968–69	35 100	4800	10 300
1972–74	16 900	8500	8400
1974–77	10 200	6400	3800
1977–80	7600	2000	5600
1980–83	14 600	4100	10 500
1983–86	22 000	12 600	9400
1986–88	32 900	20 700	12 200
1988–89	−2400	−700	−1700
1989–90	24 500	18 700	5800

Source: STATIN, Labour Force Surveys.

and 1985, the rate of annual increase was only 0.5% between 1985 and 1989. The slow growth of the labour force during the second part of the period is related to the increased tempo of external migration as well as to the downward trend in labour force participation rates for both sexes. The urban poor who depend on the state for employment and social services were continuously marginalized as they struggled to meet their subsistence needs. It was therefore not surprising that in the KMA the implementation of SAP resulted in the increased deprivation of more than 70% of the population – the urban poor.

Data for the KMA show that between January 1975 and December 1990 inflation increased by 26%. Most of the increases in the period occurred between 1980 and 1982, when the final effects of the devaluation policy pursued during 1978 and 1979 were being felt. Between January 1990 and December 1991, inflation increased to 80.2%, but decreased to 33.2% in 1994.

In assessing the effects of policies on the poor urban households in the KMA, perhaps the area of greatest concern is their ability to purchase adequate food to meet basic energy and nutrition requirements. In 1989, as a share of the national income, the compensation of employees was 16% lower than it was in 1977. With the elimination of public subsidies on consumption, the capacity of the poor to command resources for consumption has fallen even more than the shift in the distribution of income suggests.

The latest available consumption data for the country are for the year 1993. These data allow for an appreciation of some dimensions of poverty in the KMA. Poverty is widespread. Of the KMA population, 28% fell below the poverty line in 1993. Its magnitude can be appreciated by the fact that, in per capita terms, it would require an income of J$4.4 billion (or US$130 million) to bring the incomes of all those persons below the poverty line up to the poverty line. The significance of this analysis is that it points in the direction of a spa-

128

tial redistribution and an improvement in the position of selected occupational groups over the 1990s. It is possible to speculate that the downward compression in the standard of living under SAP resulted in a change in the class structure, so that there was a narrowing of the peak and a widening of the base. Although the population below the age of 25 constitutes 54% of the population, they make up 61% of the poor. Women comprise 51% of the total number of poor people. They make up 53% of the poor in the KMA and 50% of the rural poor. The preponderance of females in the KMA noted above is related, in part, to their penchant to move from the rural areas in search of work as domestic servants. The majority of poor women in urban areas are involved in street vending. For those in the labour force, poverty is not so much associated with a lack of occupation as with low-paying jobs and under-employment.

Another area of concern in the KMA is healthcare. The Jamaica Survey of Living Conditions, 1993, sought to determine total annual expenditure on secondary healthcare. The report concluded that the poor are paying less at the public hospitals, although they are spending more time there. The mean total secondary healthcare expenditure for the poor was $94.92 (US$3) per visit. Thus, it is obvious that the poor pay for their own medical care – another condition of SAP.

Gender issues under SAP   For women in Jamaica, there has always been a precarious struggle to balance the dual roles of production and reproduction, and this balancing act has become more difficult through the adoption of the structural adjustment programme. Ironically, it may even be true that Jamaica's sociocultural structure may make it an attractive arena to implement those aspects of the adjustment programmes that encourage foreign investment, since the economic vulnerability of urban women and their tradition of economic activity mean that they constitute a readily available supply of low-wage labour. This unfortunately was not the case, as the number of jobs available to women fell drastically in the KMA.

A National Mobility Survey, conducted by the Institute of Social and Economic Research of the University of the West Indies in March 1984, revealed that, seven years after the implementation of SAP, the level of unemployment among female heads of household in the KMA was 24.9%, compared to 13.6% for male heads. Female partners of male heads also recorded a high rate of 40.3%. This represented an increase in the level of female unemployment by 9.2% from 1976. The extent of women's labour market disadvantage becomes most striking when compared to the income levels of male heads of household in the KMA. The survey showed that 72.6% of female heads earned less than J$400 monthly, or the equivalent of US$18 weekly. During that period, the purchasing power of the Jamaican dollar decreased by 75%, while household commodities increased in line with inflation by 28%.

In a general sense, the resolution of the problem of the unemployed urban female worker is dependent on the state of the national economy. However, there are certain characteristics of this unemployed labour force that must be addressed either to find or to create employment opportunities. The most striking of these characteristics is the virtual absence of training for young women during the years of SAP implementation. According to the conditions of SAP, the government was forced to remove all subsidies, including those for training. Thus, for three to five years there were virtually no skills training programmes. This situation was eventually addressed by a collaborative effort of non-governmental organizations and the private sector.

III Policy measures to mediate the adverse impacts of the structural adjustment programme

Paradoxically, the SAPs have had some positive impacts on the KMA by worsening existing problems and thus forcing the implementation of countermeasures to mitigate the negative effects. Several policy measures were implemented; many were generally applicable to the entire island, including the KMA, and some were specific only to the KMA.

Measures that were applicable to the entire island including the KMA were:
*   *Rural resource development – land tenure and land titling* The management of KMA could not be achieved in isolation from the surrounding rural areas. Through a process of up-front citizens' consultation, the needs of the rural poor and young people were incorporated in a policy to empower them, thereby reducing the magnitude of rural–urban migration to the KMA. An island-wide land titling project was financed by the World Bank in the years 1982–86 and another project is under way, financed by the Inter-American Development Bank (IDB). Although the data are not yet available, it may be surmised that very little external population pressure is being exerted on the KMA from the rural areas. This is reflected in the fact that the tourism sector now obtains most of its food supply locally instead of from importing from the USA.
*   *The redirection of capital investment in manufacturing and tourism to other parts of the island* Government-owned manufacturing enterprises, including the sugar estates, were divested and, although employment opportunities within manufacturing have been substantially reduced with improved technology and different management, the output figures for many of these enterprises have increased by more than 100% between 1993 and 1994 (according to the 1994 Budget statement). In addition, various researches undertaken by the University of the West Indies have shown that, between 1990 and 1994, there was an

increase of 60% in jobs in the service sector and other urban/tourism areas on the North Coast of Jamaica. The multiplier effect for each tourist to Jamaica is 4.8 (local jobs created).[1] In addition, Jamaica was rated among the top ten tourist areas by the World Tourism Organization (WTO) during 1992 and 1994; the Sandals Resort was ranked the top tourist resort by WTO in 1994, with an ability to net over US$212 million per year. This resort is only one of many world-class resorts on the North Coast. Tourism revenue accounted for 68% of the GDP in 1994 (Ministry of Finance 1994).

- *Food Security Programme*   The Food Security Programme was aimed at supplementing the food for nearly a half of the Jamaican population, including primary school children, lactating mothers and the indigent.
- *Human Employment and Resource Training Programme (HEART)*   HEART was located in KMA and geared towards addressing the problem of unskilled and unemployed youth. As in the case of the Food Security Programme, despite evident shortcomings, HEART provides the basis for training unemployed young adults.
- *Adolescent health issues and associated social problems*   These are an integral part of the NGO's regular programming activities in the KMA and rural areas. This was achieved through UNFPA-funded consultation with the NGOs, government and the private sector.

Policy measures specific to the KMA

Policy measures specific to the KMA include:

- *Urban upgrading of the city of Kingston*   The objectives of the urban upgrading policy are to:
  - provide infrastructural services such as roads, water, electricity, drainage and sewage disposal system within the central business district of the city of Kingston
  - build social facilities such as schools, health clinics and community centres
  - start a community development and education programme to equip the inner-city communities with the skills to manage their own affairs.
- *Joint Coalition "ASCEND" and "Operation PRIDE"*   As a means of dealing with the problems of access to land and squatting, the government has a "Programme for the Resettlement and Integrated Development Enterprise (PRIDE)". PRIDE and another organization, known as ASCEND, are mandated to publish a set of minimum acceptable planning infrastructure and utility standards that will allow for the official and legal sub-

---

1. See Carl Stone, *Impacts of the tourism industry on the North Coast* (Kingston: University of West Indies, 1992).

division of lands, where the policy would be one of incremental development of infrastructure over time. Operation PRIDE functions as an advisory group to government, to facilitate the acquisition of land for people; it examines areas in which lands have been illegally occupied, with a view to the possibility of regularizing some of these occupations.

- *Restoration of downtown Kingston*   Another major initiative by the government is the restoration of downtown Kingston from late 1988 to the present day. Recognizing that urban renewal could be achieved only by consensus-building and partnership, the government undertook a broad-based advertising and marketing strategy to relocate businesses in the downtown area. Collaboration was sought with various other organizations, such as the Social Action Centre, church groups, service clubs and small enterprises. The formation of the Kingston Restoration Company (KRC) and its association with USAID have provided funding for the restoration of several structures that KRC now rents or leases to small industrial and commercial companies. To date, KRC has been able to influence the redevelopment process only limited to cosmetic improvements and urban landscaping. The project investments made by KRC have been funded solely from grant funds supplied by USAID.

- *Tax incentive to relocate businesses in downtown Kingston*   Although construction costs are the same in New Kingston as they are in downtown Kingston, there is a significant difference in the demand for accommodation. The rental rates between prime and derelict areas of Kingston reflect the preference by a ratio often in excess of two to one. For the proposed entrepreneur to make a choice between the two locations, he must have a major incentive in order for him to choose the less desirable one, and this can only be through a significant saving in his rental. Moreover, for the private developer to make an investment for which his rental is expected to be so much lower, there must be some other opportunity that will allow for his achieving similar internal rates of return on investment as those developers in the choice areas.

Similarly, a company, seeking to construct offices or light industrial facilities where construction costs are the same in the two areas of Kingston, would have to be afforded an incentive in order to locate in the less desirable area.

- *Human settlement forms*   The main thrust of government's objectives and strategies in the human settlements sector are to:
  - consolidate and protect the existing housing stock and infrastructure from further deterioration through the renewal of blighted areas and the rehabilitation of both urban and rural infrastructural facilities
  - increase the housing stock by redirecting the role of public sector from direct construction to the provision of an appropriate policy framework and conditions conducive to greater private sector participation in housing development through joint venture arrangements

132

- encourage private sector participation in urban renewal through the issuance of Urban Renewal Bonds, the bonds being redeemable on the completion of the development
- reduce housing costs and enhance affordability by the provision of infrastructure and certificates of title to upgrade and rationalize informal settlements; the provision of serviced lots with a bias towards low-income earners; and the provision of core, shell and starter homes, encouraging self-help and community assistance
- encourage non-governmental organizations (NGOs) in the construction and management of human settlements by entering into a variety of arrangements with NGOs, e.g. transfer of property to the NGO/community in exchange for a rehabilitation project
- provide financial and fiscal incentives for investment in downtown Kingston by the private sector
- *Development of small-scale enterprises*   Support for the development of small-scale enterprise is accorded high priority, since growth in the sector has the potential to increase employment, reduce poverty, improve incomes for the poor, increase national production levels, encourage social stability, and provide an outlet for local creativity and entrepreneurship.

To date, over 1000 permanent jobs have been created and 180 000 ft^2 of factory space added in downtown Kingston, through rehabilitation of appropriate derelict structures.

- *Commercial Development Programme*   The major objectives of the programme are:
  - to stimulate retail and office investment in downtown Kingston
  - to arrest and reverse the trend towards relocation of offices from the downtown Kingston
  - to demonstrate to the Jamaican private sector that investment in the downtown can be profitable

The programme consisted of the restoration of commercial properties in collaboration with the private sector.

- *Community Development Programme*   The objectives of the programme are:
  - to provide educational and recreational opportunities for community youth
  - to improve community access to healthcare
  - to market the skills of the community.

The Community Development Programme consists of the following main components: Summer Programmes for community youth; the operation of a Teen Centre and Youth for Education on Sexuality (YES); the operation of a health centre; and the creation of an Artisans Directory.

In addition, the programme has had an indirect impact, in that it has strengthened community support for Kingston Restoration Company and has also contributed to the diffusion of political tension in downtown Kingston.

- *Public improvement programme*   Under this programme the physical appearance of King Street and Duke Street were improved through the following:
  - street repairing
  - sidewalk repairs
  - removal of redundant telephone and power lines
  - installation of concrete planters.
- *Restoration Grants Programme*   Under this programme, grants are given to property owners to enable them to restore their derelict commercial properties. As against a target of $100000\,\text{ft}^2$, nearly $250000\,\text{ft}^2$ have been restored through this programme.

IV Prospects for the KMA

The future prospect for the KMA is good. Given the strong tourism and manufacturing base created through the SAP policies, the government can now concentrate on revitalizing Kingston as the commerce centre for the Caribbean. With the incentives in place that will facilitate economic rates of return on investments in real estate at a significantly reduced retail income, companies will be forced to contemplate seriously the economic benefit to be gained by relocating their operations to the downtown Kingston area. Inevitably many will still choose the uptown area, but there ought to be many who will overcome their preferences and fears of the downtown area and move there. Thus will begin the redevelopment and revitalization of the capital city of Kingston and the Kingston Metropolitan Area.

In addition, a feasibility study was recently completed by the private sector to examine the viability of Kingston as a tourist area and the return of Kingston Harbour as a cruise-ship port. The tourist product to be offered by Kingston would be different from that offered on the North Coast, in that Kingston can offer eco-tours of its many surrounding marine areas – coral reefs and mangrove tours, and archaeological tours to the historic Port Royal. In the seventeenth century, Port Royal was considered the richest and most notorious port in the world because of its pirate and buccaneering activities. Although much of the landscape has changed because of several devastating earthquakes over the centuries, many historic remains still exist today. The importance of the Port of Kingston to the KMA, Jamaica, and the Caribbean region can only continue to expand given its locational importance and current development pattern. Herein lies the future of the KMA.

References

Anderson & Witter 1991. *Crisis, adjustment and social change: the case of Jamaica.* Kingston: University of the West Indies.

Government of Jamaica 1993. *Survey of living conditions.* Kinston: Government of Jamaica.

McCarthy, P. 1995. *Country paper on urbanization and growth patterns in Jamaica,* Kingston: UMP.

Ministry of Finance 1994. *Annual statistical reports.* Kingston.

Statistical Institute of Jamaica 1991a. *Population census, 1970–1991.* Kingston.

—1991b. *Labour Force Statistics, 1970–1991.* Kingston.

Further reading

Anderson, T. & N. Davies 1989. The impact of recession and structural adjustment policies on poor urban women in Jamaica. Paper presented at the Caribbean Studies Association Annual Conference, Barbados.

Brown, H. 1993. *The Jamaican economy in a changing world: the way forward 1993/94 and beyond.* Kingston: Headley Brown & Co, Economic Analyst & International Consultants.

Government of Jamaica 1993. *Structural adjustment of the Jamaican economy 1982–1987.* Prepared by the National Planning Agency, Kingston.

IICA 1994. *Notes on the structural adjustment process in Jamaica.* Kingston IICA.

Khan, S. 1987. *Macroeconomic adjustment in developing countries: a policy perspective The World Bank Observer* **2**(1), 32–7.

LeFranc, E. 1994. *Consequences of structural adjustment: a review of the Jamaican experience,* Canoe Press, Kingston.

Mayo, Malpezzi, & Gross 1986. *Shelter strategies for the urban poor in developing countries. The World Bank Observer,* **1**(2).

Planning Institute of Jamaica 1990. *Structural adjustment in Jamaica: 1981–1990.* Planning Institute of Jamaica, Department of Economics, University of the West Indies.

—1994a. *A framework for the development of poverty alleviation in Jamaica.* Planning Institute of Jamaica, Department of Economics, University of the West Indies.

—1994b. *Economic and social survey, Jamaica, 1975–1994.* Planning Institute of Jamaica, Department of Economics, University of the West Indies.

—1994c. *Jamaica survey of living conditions, 1990–1994.* Planning Institute of Jamaica, Department of Economics, University of the West Indies.

Urban Development Corporation 1992. *Downtown Kingston redevelopment tax incentives.* Kingston.

Witter, M. 1989. *Analysis of the Food Assistance Programme in Jamaica.* Jamaica Poverty Line Project Working Paper 1, Planning Institute of Jamaica, Department of Economics, University of the West Indies.

CHAPTER EIGHT
Bogotá, Colombia: restructuring with continued growth

Julio D. Dávila

I Introduction

Large urban agglomerations in Latin America are increasingly faced with challenges similar to those of their counterparts in the richer nations of the developed world. The need to cater for a growing tertiary sector, declining manufacturing activities, the dispersal of population and industries to peripheral locations, and the inflow of international investment and cheap imports, are some of the current themes in metropolitan studies of the region. Although an ageing population and wholesale renewal of central areas are not on the immediate agenda of metropolitan governments, issues that will also be familiar to a New Yorker or a Londoner, such as air pollution and the pressing needs of the poor, are.

In Latin America, a decline in the pace of large-city growth has been the norm in recent decades (Dávila et al. 1991, Gilbert 1994). The rapid rates at which populations of capital cities and large industrial centres grew in the 1960s and 1970s are now the exception rather than the norm. One notable exception is Bogotá, Colombia's capital city,[1] which has continued growing at a markedly faster and more sustained pace than most large cities in the country, while exhibiting a growing concentration of national productive activities, particularly services. Not satisfied with being the largest single market in a country that for decades relied almost exclusively on domestic demand for its industrial products, Bogotá has also played a key national role in the export of manufactured and agro-industrial products, notably cut flowers, books, textiles and leather goods.

Since the late 1980s, furthermore, Bogotá's economic and physical fabrics have been recast as the city is called upon to play a significant part in Colombia's drive to liberalization, opening up its markets to world trade and a mass repatriation of capitals. Like the patience of its inhabitants, the city's infra-structure and its management capacity have been rapidly stretching to their limits, a factor that lies behind the landslide election at the end of 1994 of an outsider to traditional partisan politics as the city's new mayor.

This chapter explores the reasons behind the success of Bogotá in consol-idating and advancing its leadership position in Colombia, particularly in the years leading up to the liberalization reforms of the Gaviria government (1990–94). Following this introduction, the second section examines Colom-bia's unusually dispersed pattern of urban growth, a stark contrast with most of Latin America. However, Bogotá's consistently high population growth and the increased concentration there of national population and production, which marked the second half of this century, could be pointing to changes in this respect, a theme assessed in section III. The fourth section examines the foundations of Bogotá's economic success, notably the competitiveness of its manufacturing and service activities. The fifth section briefly outlines the main components of the liberalization programme launched by the Gaviria government. The concluding section discusses the metropolitan management issues arising from the case study and some of the challenges brought to bear by liberalization.

II Colombia: a dispersed pattern of urbanization

The origins of Bogotá's present political and demographic importance within Colombia may be traced to the pre-Hispanic period. Before the arrival of the Spanish *conquistadores* in the sixteenth century, the "Sabana de Bogotá" – the fertile plateau on which the city sits – was the site of two of the largest kingdoms of what is today Colombia, both Muisca communities of the Chibcha language. Although occupation of the territory by the Muiscas took the form of dispersed settlements, the area was chosen by the Spanish colo-nizers as the site of government, largely because it offered a potentially very rich source of tributes and income for the European invaders, given the area's

---

1. The 1991 National Constitution reverted the city's official name to Santafé de Bogotá, the name that the Spanish conquistadores gave the city upon its foundation in 1538. The administrative area that in the 1950s incorporated a few neighbouring municipalities, also changed its name from Distrito Especial to Distrito Capital (DC). Despite calls dating back to the 1950s, the new Constitution failed to designate a larger "metropolitan area" that would include the municipalities where the city's physical expansion is expected to take place in the following decades. It did, however, leave open the possibility of creating one, although this involves a cumbersome legal and juridical process. The term "metro-politan area" as used in this context is therefore not administrative but functional (Hall & Hay 1980), as explained in more detail in the appendix. Facts and figures in this chapter sometimes refer to Bogotá DC and sometimes to the Bogotá metropolitan area, a distinction that has been clearly indicated in the text.

high population density and its concentration of wealth, notably gold and agriculture.

In recent decades, and more specifically since the second half of the twentieth century, the relative importance of what we have termed here the "Bogotá metropolitan area" (see *n.* 1) has increased even further, particularly in relation to other large urban centres in the country. Given the comparatively small differences in population size between Bogotá and the next largest urban centres, Colombia would not appear to be a case of what the specialized literature calls "urban primacy". For several decades it has been regarded as somewhat of an exception in Latin America, where in countries such as Argentina, Chile, Mexico and Venezuela, population, output and, more contentiously, government investments in the largest city exceed by many times those found in other cities in the urban hierarchy.

In Colombia, on the contrary, other large urban centres – notably Medellín, Cali and Barranquilla – developed almost at the same time and nearly as fast as Bogotá, with the result that the spatial distribution of population and central government investment has generally not been as skewed as in other countries with similar population and average income levels. For some authors, however, this situation of comparative "equilibrium" in the spatial distribution of urban centres may be coming to an end, largely as a result of Bogota's success in concentrating a disproportionate and growing share of the country's population and output. Thus, one author has hypothesized that soon Colombia may cease to be a case of "quadricephaly" to become a case of "macrocephaly" much along the lines of its neighbouring countries (Goueset 1991). Drawing on earlier data from the 1964–73 period, Linn (1979: 64–5) reached a similar inference and concluded that not only is Colombia not an example of what authors such as Harry Richardson have defined as "polarization reversal" but it might even be a case of increased urban polarization in a few urban areas.[2] Table 8.1 provides support for the view that Colombia has not been a case of marked "urban primacy". The table shows that the size differences between Bogotá and the other cities have not been dramatic in recent years. Nor have they been so historically. In the mid-1800s, for example, the combined population of the three largest towns after Bogotá (Medellín, Socorro and Cali) was 1.37 times larger than Bogotá's. Over a century later, in 1985, the gap had narrowed to 1.14 times (although by then the next three largest urban centres were Medellín, Cali and Barranquilla). This was in marked contrast with Latin American countries with national populations similar to that of Colombia. In Argentina, for example, in 1980 the population of Greater Buenos Aires was 3.5 times larger than that of the combined pop-

---

2. "Polarization reversal" is defined as the stagnation of demographic growth in a country's central region (or its largest metropolitan area) accompanied by a rapid growth in peripheral areas. Writing in the mid-1970s, Richardson (1977) cited Colombia, South Korea and Brazil as countries where polarization reversal may have already started.

Table 8.1   Colombia: population of largest urban agglomerations, 1951–93.

Urban agglomeration[a]	1951	1964	1973	1985[b]	1993[c]
1 Bogotá metropolitan area	764933	1768712	2994103	4501337	6701292
2 Metropolitan Medellín	499756	1084660	1614450	2121174	2552078
3 Metropolitan Cali	292694	659648	1028528	1484197	1850130
4 Metropolitan Barranquilla	313222	554626	799011	1151900	1348535
5 Metropolitan Bucaramanga	148896	284339	423132	607134	804618
6 Cartagena	111291	229193	311664	563949	661830
7 Metropolitan Cúcuta	102187	187149	283702	409882	648973
8 Metropolitan Pereira	115342	203060	276272	401632	506605[d]
9 Metropolitan Manizales	141425	238995	257231	338981	420848
10 Ibagué	54347	125233	202850	314954	386423

Notes:
a. With the exception of the "Bogotá metropolitan area", population figures for all metropolitan areas refer to the officially designated areas. Figures include a fixed number of municipalities throughout the period, and include the rural component of municipal population.
b. Census figures adjusted for coverage.
c. Preliminary census figures adjusted for coverage.
d. Not adjusted for coverage.
Source: For 1985: de Llinás (1990, table IV-2); for other years: DANE, national population censuses.

ulation of the next three largest metropolitan areas, and in the case of Lima (Peru) the ratio was 4.3 in 1981 (Dávila et al. 1991).

Colombia's largest cities are spread around the national territory. The earliest reasons for such an unusual pattern must be sought in Colombia's colonial history, when administrative centres, mining towns and ports flourished, but also in the more recent past, when activities linked to intensive agriculture, commerce, manufacturing and, more recently, services have provided a sustained boost to urban growth. Bogotá and Cartagena owe their colonial predominance to their functions as administrative centres and, in the case of the latter, to its pre-eminence as one of the Caribbean's busiest ports under Spanish domination in the seventeenth and eighteenth centuries. Although initially sustained by mining, Medellín was the largest manufacturing centre in the first half of the twentieth century, after which Bogotá took over as the largest concentration of manufacturing jobs and output. Finally, much of the twentieth-century growth of Cali and Barranquilla may be attributed to their location near seaports and close to often prosperous agricultural areas.[3]

---

3. A more detailed historical analysis of this pattern lies beyond the confines of this chapter. Useful sources include Jiménez & Sideri (1985) and Flórez & González Muñoz (1983).

III Concentration of population and production in Bogotá, 1951–94

Bogotá may not be said to have had a "disproportionate" demographic weight in Colombia's urban system in recent decades, although plenty of evidence confirms its growing economic role. In population terms, the national significance of the metropolitan area, which includes Bogotá's Distrito Especial and eight surrounding municipalities, has no doubt increased (Table 8.2). According to national population census data, between 1951 and 1993 its share of national population more than trebled from 5.8% to 18.4%. In a context where the country as a whole was rapidly urbanizing (at an annual rate of 4.3% between 1951 and 1993), Bogotá's relative weight also grew, to reach a quarter of the country's urban population by 1993.[4]

Table 8.2 Population in Colombia and Bogotá metropolitan area (BMA) 1951–93.

	Colombia		Bogotá metropolitan area			Growth rates (% per year)		
Year	Population	Urban (%)	Urban population	National share (%)[c]	Urban share (%)[d]	Colombia	Urban Colombia	Urban BMA
1951	11 548 172	38.7	672 937	5.8	15.1			
						3.2	5.6	7.4
1954	17 484 508	52.0	1 700 487	9.7	18.7			
						3.0	4.5	6.2
1973	22 862 118	59.3	2 922 485	12.8	21.6			
						2.3	3.1	3.5
1985[e]	30 062 200	65.3	4 424 684	14.7	22.5			
						2.2	3.7	5.2
1993[f]	35 886 280	72.9	6 613 308	18.4	25.3			

Notes:
a. BMA comprises Bogota DE and eight municipalities. Figures refer to urban BMA. See Appendix.
b. Population living in "cabeceras" (seats of municipal government); these are generally settlements with 1500 inhabitants or more.
c. Share of BMA's urban population in national population.
d. Share of BMA's urban population in national urban population.
e. Census return figures adjusted for coverage.
f. Provisional census return figures adjusted for coverage.
Sources: For 1993: de Llinás 1990, table V-1; for other years: DANE, national population censuses.

4. The 1993 population census information used in this chapter comes from provisional information made available on diskette by DANE (1994), Colombia's official census and statistical agency. Some of the figures in this initial release, including the population of the country and of the capital cities of departamentos, have been adjusted for coverage. Objections have already been raised by members of the local scientific community about the reliability of figures from remote rural areas and areas affected by political and social conflict as well as about the use of inadequate criteria in adjusting urban figures (ACIUR 1994).

Population growth and migration

When measured in terms of population growth, Bogotá has been one of the most dynamic Colombian urban centres in the second half of the twentieth century. During this period it not only maintained its position as the largest urban agglomeration but it also sustained a rate of population growth that was rarely surpassed by any other large city in the country (Table 8.3). Moreover, during most of this period, its population grew faster than the rate at which the country was urbanizing (Table 8.2).

Table 8.3 Colombia: growth of largest urban agglomerations, 1951–93 (% per year, data from Table 8.1).

Urban agglomeration	Inter-censal period			
	1951/64	1964/73	1973/85	1985/93[a]
Bogotá metropolitan area	6.7	6.0	3.5	5.1
Metropolitan Medellín	6.1	4.5	2.3	2.3
Metropolitan Cali	6.5	5.1	3.1	2.8
Metropolitan Barranquilla	4.5	4.1	3.1	2.0
Metropolitan Bucaramanga	5.1	4.5	3.1	3.6
Cartagena	5.7	3.5	5.1	2.0
Metropolitan Cúcuta	4.8	4.7	3.1	5.9
Metropolitan Pereira	4.5	3.5	3.2	2.9[b]
Metropolitan Manizales	4.1	0.8	2.3	2.7
Ibagué	6.6	5.5	3.7	2.6

Notes:
a. Figures for 1993 are provisional
b. Based on unadjusted 1993 figure

As has been the norm in rapidly urbanizing countries, internal migratory population movements (inmigration) were a key contributor to urbanization in the period after the Second World War. Inmigration was the main contributor to Bogotá's demographic expansion in the 1950s and 1960s, and a substantial part of this migration was rural in origin. In recent decades Bogotá has attracted a larger number of female than male migrants from most regions of the country. In 1973, for example, among the migrants born in the nearby province (*departamento*) of Boyacá there were a third more females than males in the city. Even by 1993, there were 93 males for each 100 females living in the city (DANE 1994). These figures are partly a reflection of economic and cultural factors. Social change and widespread poverty in rural districts have compelled a disproportionate number of young women to seek employment in large cities, notably in domestic service but also in other services, as well as in manufacturing. Since the late 1960s, the cut-flower export industry has grown considerably in importance as a source of employment for young female labour, particularly in municipalities close to Bogotá (it has also made Colombia the second largest exporter of cut-flowers in the world, after Holland).

141

Even in the 1980s and 1990s, and somewhat unusually in Latin America for a city of its size, inmigration still represents a very important factor in Bogotá's growth, as suggested by the difference in growth rates between Colombia and the Bogotá metropolitan area (see Table 8.2). Even allowing for possible errors in the provisionally adjusted 1993 census figures, migrants make up a substantial share of annual growth, with perhaps as many as 200000 inmigrants arriving every year in Bogotá, or over half all new inhabitants.[5] However, in the next two decades or so a high rate of population growth such as that of the recent past may largely be sustained through a high influx of inmigrants, rather than natural growth; this is because Bogotá will have then an older population than Colombia, with proportionately fewer inhabitants of child-bearing age.[6] Whether this is actually the case will depend not only on Bogotá's success in providing jobs and services for its fast-expanding population, but also in the social and economic conditions prevailing in other parts of the country, where increased agricultural productivity and, to a lesser extent, violence have underpinned outmigration.[7]

Economic growth and increased national concentration

A visitor to Bogotá in the early to mid-1990s could be forgiven for thinking that the city was undergoing a complete reconstruction. Building sites provide a highly visible testimony to the vitality of those parts of the city's economy, which in the 1990s benefited most from the liberalization measures introduced by the Gaviria government (1990–94) and from the repatriation of capitals, including, although by no means exclusively, some from the drug trade:[8] the construction industry[9] and commerce, particularly trade geared to the mid- to higher-income sectors.[10] Further evidence comes from an unpar-

5. Assuming that net international migration makes a negligible contribution to national population growth rates (de Llinás 1990: table II–10), Bogotá's natural growth could be assumed to be similar to the country's for the period 1985–93, i.e. 2.2% per annum (Table 8.2). Migration would, therefore, account for the 3.0% growth differential in the metropolitan area, or an estimated 198000 new inhabitants in 1993. If this figure appears unexpectedly high, it must be remembered that so was Bogotá's population growth rate in 1985–93, which seems to have exceeded demographers' forecasts (cf. de Llinás 1990, Granados & Ulises 1992).

6. In 1993, 28.7% of the city's population were aged under 15, compared to 33.8% in Colombia. Given the evidence that inmigrants tend to be individuals of reproductive age, by the time today's children reach a reproductive age around 2010, Bogotá will have a smaller share of child-bearing age-groups than Colombia.

7. Violence, political and otherwise, has been a trademark of rural life in Colombia for the past four decades. In the past, this has fuelled outmigration from many regions, and probably continues to be an important factor, as victims of the indiscriminate actions of the paramilitary, guerrilla groups and drug traffickers flee to the relative safety of large cities. Between July 1990 and June 1994, for example, it is estimated that political violence (including presumed political killings, "social cleansing", disappearances, and deaths in military action) claimed nearly 15000 lives in Colombia (Colombia Bulletin 1994).

alleled expansion in new vehicle stock, particularly private cars, which has led to a traffic congestion never before witnessed by its inhabitants.

And although the recent economic boom appears to have placed unprecedented strain on the city's resources, it is by no means a new phenomenon. The city has enjoyed rapid economic growth in the recent past, notably in the 1970s. Its economic weight in the country has paralleled its demographic significance and, particularly in the second half of the twentieth century, the city's economic importance has outstripped its population weight on several accounts. This was a time when the country's economy expanded at a faster rate than at any other period in its history, with per capita output levels growing at an annual average of 2.2% between 1945 and 1986, a similar rate to the average for Latin American countries (Ocampo et al. 1987: 243–4).

During this period, Bogotá's economy also grew at a sustained and generally higher pace than the national economy, as may be seen from Table 8.4.[11] These higher rates were reflected in a gradual increase in the city's share of gross domestic product, from around a seventh in 1950 to over a fifth in the mid- to late-1980s. But the city's population tended to grow at a faster pace than its output, so while Bogotá's per capita output was more than twice that of the country as a whole in 1950, 39 years later the city's per capita output was 30% higher. In fact, lower average incomes, at least in some key areas, may be one of the factors behind the city's economic success, as will be discussed later.

The sustained growth rates in output for the whole city conceal marked

---

8. It is estimated that since the mid-1980s some us$1.5–2.5 billion from the drug business is repatriated every year, compared to an average private investment of US$2.8 billion a year in the 1980s (*The Economist* 1994).

9. Nationally, construction grew between 9 and 12% in 1994, and thus became a substantial contributor to overall economic growth. In Bogotá, investment in apartment and office buildings reached profit rates of over 40% (once inflation is accounted for). This is estimated to fall to about 15–25% in 1995, as markets reach their saturation point (*Semana* 1995).

10. Apart from construction, laundering of drug money inside the country has involved three main activities (*The Economist* 1994): purchase of agricultural land (up to a third of all agricultural land may be in the hands of drug entrepreneurs), agro-industry (even in loss-making businesses) and subsidized imports of electrical appliances, including computer equipment. Vast warehouses selling a range of imported consumer goods have sprung up in Bogotá, with the some established shopping centres (known as "Sanandresitos", after the first one set up in Bogotá several decades back) where contraband goods were traditionally found, have also expanded.

11. Spatially disaggregated data on economic growth is generally collected and published using a provincial (*departamento*) classification. Information on some government and community services (such as banks, educational and health facilities, judicial courts, and so on) is regularly published by the Central Statistical Office (DANE) for the municipal level. What we call here the Bogotá metropolitan area does not officially exist, so most of the figures quoted in this chapter refer to productive activities within the boundaries of what up to the new national Constitution of 1991 was the Distrito Especial de Bogotá and since then is known as Santafé de Bogotá, Distrito Capital (see *n*. 1).

Table 8.4   Economic growth in Bogotá DE[a] and Colombia, 1950–89.

Year	Bogotá's share of national GDP (%)	Bogotá's relative wealth index[b]	Average annual growth of GDP[c] (%) Colombia	Bogotá
1950	13.9	2.3		
			5.4	6.9
1955	15.0	2.1		
			3.9	4.5
1960	15.4	1.8		
			4.7	7.5
1965	17.6	1.8		
			5.9	8.5
1970	19.9	1.7		
			6.2	7.8
1975	21.3	1.6		
			5.4	na
1980	20.8	1.6		
			2.2	2.4
1985	22.0	1.6		
			4.6	4.6
1989	20.4	1.3		

Notes:
GDP: gross domestic product   na: not available
a. Figures refer only to Bogotá Distrito Especial. See Appendix.
b. Bogotá's per capita GDP/Colombia's per capita GDP
c. Constant 1970 pesos for 1950–75; 1975 pesos for other years.
Sources: For 1950–75, Svenson (1977); 1970–85 GDP growth taken from DANE (1991b: 117); other years, calculations based on Cuervo (1992: tables 5, 6) and national population census data.

changes in the structure of production. The ten-sector classification used in Table 8.5 shows that, between 1960 and 1989, for example, the joint contribution of housing rentals and commerce dropped significantly from 31% to 19.3%; this was compensated for by an increase in the joint weight of finance and insurance, personal and domestic services, and government services (from 27.9% to 39.3%); whereas, with variations in the intervening years, other sectors such as manufacturing, construction and transport generally maintained – or even marginally increased – their overall contribution.

Structural change was also a feature of national economic growth during this period, although the transformation there was considerably less marked than Bogotá's. No doubt the most salient aspect of national economic change was a sharp drop in the participation of the primary sector from nearly a third of total output in the early 1960s to just under a quarter in 1989, a fall for which agriculture was mostly responsible. This drop was compensated for by the growth of other sectors, notably construction, utilities, commerce and services. The contribution of manufacturing, finally, appeared stable throughout

Table 8.5 The structure of production in Bogotá DE[a] and Colombia, 1960–89 (%).

Sector	Bogotá DE				Colombia	
	1960	1970	1980	1989	1960–64[d]	1989
Agriculture, fishery, mining	1.0	1.2	0.3	0.4	32.0	23.7
Manufacturing	24.1	21.6	23.8	24.6	20.6	20.6
Utilities	1.4	1.5	1.1	2.1	0.6	2.4
Construction & public works	5.8	7.4	4.2	6.6	2.9	6.6
Commerce	18.1	21.5	9.3	11.2	9.8	10.7
Transport and communications	8.8	8.5	8.8	9.4	7.4	8.3
Finance and insurance	5.8	6.6	10.3	11.8	5.0	6.9
Housing	12.9	11.8	11.5	8.1	7.3	4.5
Services[b]	10.8	10.3	14.9	13.7	7.3	8.4
Government services	11.3	9.6	14.6	13.8	7.1	8.2
Other[c]	–	–	1.2	−1.7	–	−0.3
TOTAL	100.0	100.0	100.0	100.0	100.0	100.0

na: not available
a. Figures refer to Bogotá Distrito Especial only. See Appendix.
b. Includes personal and domestic services.
c. Difference between income from banking services and import taxes.
d. Annual average.
Sources: For Bogotá: 1960–70, Mohan (1986: 32); 1980–89, Cuervo (1992: table 7).
          For Colombia: 1960–64, Ocampo et al. (1987: 245); 1989: Cuervo (1992: table 7).

the period (Table 8.5).

Another measure of the city's success in maintaining growth is provided by employment figures. As Table 8.6 shows, unemployment in the national capital has been kept below that of other large urban centres, even at a time of poor economic performance in the mid-1980s and a parallel increase in the participation rate of both sexes (although particularly women) in the labour market. The marked increases in overall labour participation rates have been partly attributed to rapid rises in the number of people of working age (Gilbert 1995), and to the increased incorporation of women into the labour market resulting from changing social practices such as pregnancies at an older age and a growing acceptance of female labour in formerly men-dominated formal employment, especially services.

Recent decades have seen Bogotá attain an unchallenged lead over other large Colombian cities in several respects. This is further exemplified by the contribution that the capital city makes to some sectors of the national economy, as shown by the figures in Table 8.7. Some sectors clearly stand out as providing Bogotá with a much larger share of national activity than either its population or its total output would warrant. Notable examples are communications, finance and insurance, house rentals, personal services and government services: at some point in the period 1960–89, at least one-third of national activity in all these sectors was located there.

Table 8.6 Bogotá DE and seven Colombian cities: labour participation rates and unemployment, 1983–94 (%, March of each year).

	Bogotá DE			
	Global participation rate[a]		Total unemployment rate[b]	Unemployment rate in seven cities
	Female	Male		
1976	35.6	68.1	9.5	11.2
1985	46.0	75.9	13.7	14.1
1987	48.1	76.1	13.0	13.5
1989	46.5	75.0	9.7	11.0
1991	50.2	75.2	9.2	NA
1995	49.7	NA	6.3	NA

Notes:
NA: not available
a. Economically active population/population of working age.
b. Unemployed/economically active population; refers to women and men.
c. These are not necessarily the seven largest cities: Bogotá, Medellín, Cali, Barranquilla, Bucaramanga, Manizales and Pasto.
Sources: For Bogotá: 1976–91, Gómez & Pérez (1992); 1995: Gilbert (1995)
For seven cities: 1976: de Gómez et al. (1988); 1985–89: Gómez & Pérez (1992).

Table 8.7 Contribution of Bogotá DE[a] to the Colombian economy in selected sectors, 1960–89 (% of national total).

Sector	1960	1965	1970	1975	1980	1985	1989
Agriculture	NA	NA	NA	NA	0.4	0.1	0.2
Mining	NA	NA	NA	NA	0.1	NA	0.5
Manufacturing	21.5	22.2	23.1	24.2	21.2	23.1	24.4
Electricity and water	21.3	20.2	21.3	21.0	16.8	17.6	17.1
Construction & public works	23.3	27.1	30.9	33.6	18.3	14.8	20.4
Commerce	16.8	19.8	23.5	22.1	20.0	20.7	21.4
Transport and storage	20.5	20.7	22.6	23.8	17.6	18.5	19.4
Communications	37.1	35.6	43.1	45.5	46.9	50.4	40.9
Finance and insurance	37.6	34.9	38.1	40.0	31.6	32.2	35.2
House rentals	39.6	39.3	41.5	43.5	34.1	37.0	37.0
Personal services	21.6	23.8	28.0	31.2	36.2	35.1	33.5
Government services	27.8	34.0	30.0	33.3	39.3	35.9	34.4
Domestic services	NA	NA	NA	NA	17.2	NA	19.0
Value added	NA	NA	NA	NA	20.1	21.3	19.8
Gross domestic product	15.4	17.6	19.9	21.4	20.8	22.0	20.4

Notes:
NA: not available
a. Figures refer only to Bogotá Distrito Especial. See appendix
Sources: For 1960–75, Thoumí (1983: 177), using official regional accounts.
For 1980–89: Cuervo (1992: 6).

IV **The foundations of a resilient urban economy**

By now there should be little doubt in the reader's mind about Bogotá's capacity to sustain growth, even during the 1980s, the years known as the "lost decade" in Latin America because of the slow or negative rates of economic growth, economic restructuring (and consequent unemployment) and increased urban poverty that gripped much of the region. The reasons behind the resilience of Bogotá's economy during the 1980s are complex, but may be found in three complementary factors: first, the command attained by the city in some manufacturing and service sector activities; secondly, the competitiveness and flexibility of several of these sectors, as well as the skills and comparatively lower wages of its labour force; and, thirdly, the city's size, which makes it the largest market in the country.

Since the mid-1950s, when it overtook Medellín, Bogotá has been the leading concentration of manufacturing in Colombia, contributing between a fifth and a quarter of the national output in establishments surveyed annually by DANE, the national statistical agency (cf. Table 8.7). In employment terms, however, there was a marked rise in its contribution, from 25.3% in 1958 to 36.2% in 1989 (Dávila 1994). These parallel trends signal a decrease in the overall productivity of Bogotá's manufacturing industry, but they also point to a set of factors that, combined, may have helped underpin the sustained growth rates of the sector and the city as a whole:[12] smaller establishment sizes, skilled but low-waged labour, and a more diversified manufacturing industry.

During a rapid restructuring process, smaller, leaner production units generally fare better than larger ones, as they are able to adapt more rapidly to changing conditions. This may help explain why, during the recession of the early 1980s, Medellín lost nearly 20% of its manufacturing employment while Bogotá lost less than 4%. The 1990 national census of productive units has provided a detailed breakdown of manufacturing establishments in terms of, among other factors, number of workers (this serves as a useful complement to DANE's annual manufacturing surveys, which cover only those establishments with ten workers or more). Table 8.8 shows that Bogotá has a smaller proportion of small-scale establishments than the country as a whole; the corresponding proportion is, however, even smaller in Antioquia, the *department* of which Medellín is the capital city and main industrial centre. Overall, Bogotá's average size of establishment is smaller than in the country as a whole, but Antioquia's is larger. The size differential is particularly marked in the large-scale category (in fact, it is not unlikely that the figures in Table 8.8 already show lower average sizes for the 100+ category, as Medellín's large textile factories suffered most lay-offs in the early 1980s).

A combination of comparatively low wages and skilled labour may also

---

12. This section has benefited from the comments of Luis Mauricio Cuervo.

Table 8.8 Colombia and Bogotá DC: manufacturing employment by establishment size, 1990.

	Colombia		Bogotá DE		Antioquia[c]	
	Employment	Average size[a]	Employment	Average size[a]	Employment	Average size[a]
1–10	208363	2.6	62317	2.9	26830	2.8
10–49	181363	19.7	67726	19.7	41590	20.7
50–99	83514	67.7	30742	67.9	21071	67.8
100+	372511	295.6	135041	288.5	80644	311.4
TOTAL[b]	845751	8.9	295826	11.0	170135	13.7

Notes:
a. Average establishment size in number of workers.
b. Enumerated establishments.
c. No disaggregated data are published for Medellín, capital of the departamento of Antioquia, of which the city has approximately half the total population and most industrial and commercial activities.
Source: DANE (1991a).

Table 8.9 Bogotá DE: Structure of exports, 1974–89 (% by export value).

Export product	1974	1980	1985	1989
Agricultural products	12.0	16.4	17.4	14.7
Printing & publishing	–	9.3	13.1	14.3
Textiles	0.6	3.4	3.4	12.4
Leather goods (excl. footwear)	3.6	4.5	6.8	11.3
Garments	5.5	5.5	3.9	7.3
Metal products	0.0	1.3	0.4	3.0
Footwear	0.4	2.7	1.0	2.6
Industrial chemicals	3.1	2.3	1.4	1.9
Foodstuffs (excl. beverages)	5.7	2.7	1.9	0.0
Other exports	69.1	51.9	50.7	32.5
Total	100.0	100.0	100.0	100.0

Source: Cuervo (1992).

contribute to Bogotá's manufacturing lead. Table 8.9 shows the changing structure of Bogotá's exports over 15 years after 1974. Excluding agricultural products (most of which consist of cut flowers), the city's main export products are manufactures. These industries were among the fastest-growing sectors during the second half of the 1980s (see Table 8.10), with growth ranging from a modest 2.9% per year in the case of foodstuffs, to an astonishing 38% for footwear production. Thus, these sectors represent a useful entry point to examine Bogotá's manufacturing competitiveness.

Bogotá had a central national role in most of these sectors, in terms of its contribution to both national exports (Table 8.10) and national employment (Table 8.11), with its participation in the latter ranging from a tenth of Colombia's workers, in the case of industrial chemicals, to a hefty 53.4% in the

Table 8.10 Bogotá DE and Cundinamarca:[a] structure and growth of exports, 1985–90 (US$ millions).

Export product	1989 value	1989 share of national exports (%)	Average annual growth (% per year)
Agricultural products	217.7	10.4	9.5
Printing & publishing	29.5	61.3	4.4
Textiles	63.7	42.2	25.1
Leather goods	46.8	51.2	23.0
Garments	18.5	6.3	17.4
Metal products	NA	NA	NA
Footwear	23.0	49.3	38.0
Industrial chemicals	13.6	8.0	15.7
Foodstuffs (excl. beverages)	3.3	3.3	2.9
Other exports	120.0	NA	NA
TOTAL	555.8	9.7	10.1

Notes:
a. By the mid-1980s, over 60% of manufacturing value added produced outside Bogotá but in a radius of 243 km around the city was produced within a circle of 55 km, all of which is located in the departamento of Cundinamarca (cf. Dávila 1994).
NA: not available
Sources: For Bogotá and Cundinamarca: Pineda & Trejos (1992); for national figures: DANE (1991b) and own calculations.

Table 8.11 Bogotá DE: employment and wages in selected manufacturing sectors,[a] 1989

Industry	Employment	Share of national employment (%)	Average wage[b] ('000s of pesos)	Wage/c
Printing & publishing	11600	53.4	842.9	99.8
Textiles	17744	33.3	688.9	82.0
Leather goods	3468	49.4	639.7	91.3
Garments	12075	26.0	576.0	106.7
Metal products	11605	41.3	826.0	96.5
Footwear	5463	36.9	705.5	113.6
Industrial chemicals	1668	10.4	1121.5	72.9
Foodstuffs	16685	25.3	878.9	102.9

Notes:
a. Establishments with ten or more workers.
b. Wages and salaries paid in the year/number of paid workers.
c. Average wage in Bogotá DE (including Soacha)/average wage nationally.
Sources: own calculations based on DANE (1991c).

printing and publishing industry. Despite their export success and rapid expansion, Bogotá's wages in the majority of these sectors were on average lower than their national counterparts, in one case almost a third lower (industrial chemicals), in others almost identical (in the case of printing and publishing, for example, this may be the result of the large weight Bogotá has on national exports, coupled with the highly standardized nature of a comparatively small industry catering for international standards).

Bogotá's inhabitants are also on average more educated and have better access to services and infrastructure than do most Colombians. For example, in 1993, 94% of those aged five or more in Bogotá were literate, 43% had completed secondary education and 16% were tertiary graduates.[13] By contrast, the literacy rate in Colombia was 86%, and 34% and 8% of all Colombians over five years of age had completed secondary and tertiary education, respectively. This is the result of continued improvements in the qualifications of Bogotá's labour force. Gómez & Pérez (1992) note that, whereas in 1976 52% of Bogotá's workers had at least primary education, this share had risen to 70.6% in 1991. They also show that the economic sector with the highest average qualifications was that of services, where over half of those employed were "highly skilled" (i.e. professionals, technical personnel, directors and high-ranking officials). Much lower levels of skill may be found in manufacturing, where a mere 12.3% of those employed in 1991 could be classified as "highly skilled".

Another, by no means insignificant, advantage of the national capital over other urban centres is found in its unusual concentration of tertiary activities. On average, *bogotanos* are more spoilt for choice, when it comes to specialized retail and service outlets, than the inhabitants of any other large Colombian city. As Table 8.12 shows, in 1990 the city had over twice the proportion of car dealers, finance outlets, estate agents and establishments providing services to firms than its share of national population would appear to suggest. With twice the population of Medellín and three times that of Cali, Bogotá had three times more educational establishments and two-and-a-half times more health establishments than Medellín; in terms of numbers of hotels and restaurants and of retail outlets it outstripped Cali's by factors of six and four respectively.

Unlike manufacturing plants, the average number of workers in commercial establishments with fewer than 100 employees tends to be higher in Bogotá than in either Antioquia or Colombia (Table 8.13). This may be a reflection of the fact that the city has a larger concentration of population (and therefore markets) than any other city, so the establishments will tend to be

---

13. All 1993 population data in this section comes from provisional census figures; in the case of Bogotá they refer to the Distrito Capital, the old Distrito Especial, which excludes the eight municipalities within what we have called here the Bogotá metropolitan area (see *n*. 1 and Appendix).

larger. Somewhat puzzling, however, is the much higher national average size of all commercial establishments.

On average, Bogotá's population also enjoys better living conditions than the majority of Colombians. According to provisional 1993 census figures summarized in Figure 8.1, whereas in terms of access to electricity and water supply *bogotanos* were only slightly better off than the rest (with close to 90% of coverage), there were noticeable differences in the numbers who had access to sewerage and those with no access to services whatsoever.[14] Similarly, with a smaller average household size of 4.1 compared to a national average of 4.4, in 1993 Bogotá's households tended to live in dwellings built with more durable building materials, while a higher proportion than the national average used either gas or electricity for cooking.

Several decades of virtually uninterrupted growth in real average incomes notwithstanding, and Bogotá's unequalled pre-eminence among Colombian cities, poverty is still a striking feature of everyday life in the capital. Using an examination of the degree to which a set of five "basic needs" were met or unmet in the Colombian population, a recent study (DANE 1989) concluded that in 1985 Bogotá had a comparatively smaller incidence of poverty than all provincial subdivisions (*departamentos*). Unfortunately, however, the study also found that, for an estimated 17.3 of the city's inhabitants, one of these needs remained unmet in 1985, and there were 6.2% for whom two or more basic needs were unmet – and were therefore regarded as living in abso-

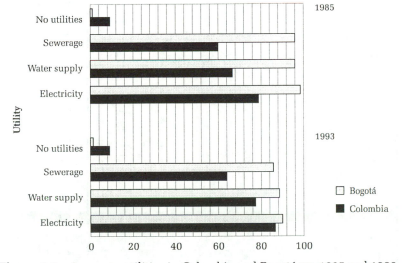

Figure 8.1 Access to utilities in Colombia and Bogotá DC, 1985 and 1993.

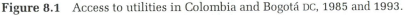

14. As was said earlier, national census figures may be over-estimates resulting from adjustment errors and from inadequate coverage of remote rural areas and areas affected by social and political conflict.

Table 8.12 Tertiary activities in four largest metropolitan areas and Colombia 1990 (no. of establishments by sector).

Activity	Bogotá DE[a]		Medellín		Cali		Barranquilla		Four metropolitan areas total		Total Colombia	
	No.	(%)	No.	(%)	No.	(%)	No.	(%)	No.	(%)	No.	(%)
Car dealers	13145	30.3	3618	8.3	3216	7.4	1994	4.6	21973	50.7	43377	100.0
Wholesale outlets	10170	28.2	3999	11.1	2148	6.0	1696	4.7	18013	50.0	36051	100.0
Retail outlets	86705	24.5	26495	7.5	22153	6.3	12594	3.6	147947	41.7	354390	100.0
Hotels, restaurants	23715	23.5	8357	8.3	4049	4.0	2635	2.6	38756	38.4	100908	100.0
Finance	2588	30.0	967	11.2	628	7.3	422	4.9	4605	53.4	8625	100.0
Transport and communications	4318	25.2	1530	8.9	1297	7.6	823	4.8	7968	46.5	17131	100.0
Estate agents	1201	39.8	558	18.5	318	10.6	102	3.4	2179	72.3	3014	100.0
Services to firms	10874	33.9	3519	11.0	3203	10.0	1667	5.2	19263	60.0	32090	100.0
Education	4676	22.8	1481	7.2	1378	6.7	1491	7.3	9026	44.0	20521	100.0
Health	7611	25.5	3151	10.6	2194	7.3	1878	6.3	14834	49.7	29864	100.0
Other services	12469	28.0	2774	6.2	3587	8.1	1759	4.0	20589	46.3	44464	100.0
Total:	177472	25.7	56449	8.2	44171	6.4	27061	3.9	305153	44.2	690435	100.0

a. Figures refer to Bogotá DE only. See Appendix
Source: Vincent Goueset, *La concentration urbaine en Colombie: de la quadricephalie à la primatie de Bogotá: 1930–90* (draft PhD dissertation, Université de Bordeaux) quoted in Cuervo (1992: table 15).

The foundations of a resilient urban economy

Table 8.13 Colombia and Bogotá DC: employment in commerce by establishment size, 1990.

	Colombia		Bogotá DE		Antioquia[c]	
	Employment	Average size[a]	Employment	Average size[a]	Employment	Average size[a]
1–10	954143	1.8	228828	2.9	113130	1.8
10–49	204291	17.2	63785	19.7	27589	17.3
50–99	53778	66.3	18690	67.9	5922	65.1
100+	112854	313.5	54144	288.5	9035	273.8
TOTAL[b]	1325066	10.4	365447	2.9	155676	2.3

Notes:
a. Average establishment size in number of workers.
b. Enumerated establishments.
c. No disaggregated data are published for Medellín, capital of the *departamento* of Antioquia, of which the city has approximately half the total population and most industrial and commercial activities.
Source: DANE (1991a).

lute poverty.[15] And although the existence of such high levels of poverty stands in the way of the future development of the city, there is perhaps an even more pronounced obstacle in its highly skewed distribution of personal incomes. In 1990, the top 20% of the population earned 55% of the city's income, and the bottom 40% earned a mere 11.3% (Misión Siglo XXI 1993). Similarly, the ratio between the income of the highest 20% and the lowest 20% was 14.1 in the same year, a figure that shows a more pronounced concentration of income than in countries such as Canada (with 7.1 in 1980–91), Sweden (4.6), Singapore (9.6) and Thailand (8.3) (cf. UNDP 1994).

A final factor mentioned at the beginning of this section as one further element in sustaining and fostering the success of the city may be found in its undisputed lead as a single affluent market. The city's disproportionate lead in areas such as communications, finance and government services (see Table 8.7) is not surprising in the case of government services; for example, this pre-eminence is explained by the fact that Bogotá is not only the seat of an historically highly centralized national government but also of the provincial government of the Cundinamarca *departamento* and of the largest local authorities in the country. This, coupled with a rapidly expanding national government throughout the second half of the twentieth century, has been seen as a factor behind the city's lead in other sectors (Gilbert 1981: 68). The concentration of specialized services such as communications and finance & insurance may no doubt be partly explained by the advantages of physical proximity to the government and to ancillary services normally associated

15. The research included a household survey that looked at five indicators: housing quality, basic services in the dwelling, overcrowding, economic dependency ratios within the household and number of children without access to formal education. Households living in absolute poverty (the word used in the Spanish original is *miseria*) were those where two of these basic needs were unmet.

with these activities, but also in terms of a workforce that demands sophisticated amenities usually found only in large cities.

There are other well documented indicators of the city's sustained and even increased pre-eminence in the nation, particularly in the service sector (see for example Jaramillo & Cuervo 1987, Goueset 1991). For example, Bogotá's share in the total volume of loans and deposits in banks and other financial institutions rose from around 40% in 1975 to 50% in 1990, with deposits in the city's banks outstripping loans (Goueset 1991: 13). Throughout the 1980s, the capital city provided the headquarters for two-thirds of the 500 companies with the largest annual turnover (Cuervo 1992: 37). It is also becoming a centre for the export of medical services, particularly eye surgery, in which it has built an international reputation. In all this, the sheer size of the city, and its unparalleled array of international-standard hotels and other services, along with the purchasing capacity of its population, makes it a magnet for local and international capital, as well as for a growing labour force.

V The impact of liberalization

No doubt a further test of the city's resilience is its capacity to withstand and adapt to the wide-ranging changes introduced during the liberalization reforms, initiated in the late 1980s and continued, although somewhat moderately, by the incumbent Samper government (1994–8).

In line with most Latin American countries, up to the 1980s Colombia's growth strategy was largely supported on import-substitution industrialization, with some elements of export promotion. It was not until 1990 that the government of César Gaviria (1990–4) introduced an unprecedented series of changes that structurally transformed the Colombian economy and its institutional landscape, including the country's trade orientation, the national labour market, the financial sector and the public sector. The Gaviria administration also spearheaded other significant reforms, particularly to the justice system, but also wider and very significant changes, which were given form in a new national Constitution approved by an elected Constitutional Assembly in 1991.

Following a World Bank study of the Colombian economy in 1989, which advocated the use of the exchange rate as a lever to promote exports and substitute imports, to reform the existing import licensing system and to eliminate export subsidies, the Barco government (1986–90) introduced some changes in the trade regime and prepared a gradual five-year plan for liberalizing trade. In broad terms, these reforms went along with the Bank's suggestions.

The Gaviria government, by contrast, made liberalization the focus of its administration and provided the basis for a much accelerated "apertura" (liberalization) programme, to be completed by 1993. Liberalization was closely linked to the goal of internationalizing the Colombian economy (Cámara de Comercio de Bogotá 1993), to make it more outward-looking. The most significant reforms introduced in this programme were in the areas of international trade, the financial sector, labour laws, foreign investment, ports and taxation (ibid.).

The import regime was subject to major institutional and operational reforms. Between 1990 and 1993, the share of imports subject to import licensing dropped from 61.1% to 3%. Tariffs were lowered, especially for capital goods and production inputs, from an average of 26.8% to 11.8%, and the effective rate of protection[16] dropped dramatically for most products (see Table 8.14). This was accompanied by an effective liberalization of the exchange market, flotation of the peso and ease in the repatriation of capital.

Table 8.14   Effective rate of protection[a] for selected import categories in Colombia, 1990 and 1992 (December).

Import	1990	1992
Consumer goods	108.6	37.4
Raw materials and intermediate goods	58.6	17.7
Capital goods	38.3	15.0
Sundry	42.3	13.4
National economy	65.2	21.6

Notes:

a. $\mathrm{ERP} = \dfrac{\text{value added (domestic prices)} - \text{value added (world prices)}}{\text{value added (world prices)}}$

Source: Zerda (1994).

In the financial sector, reforms included the creation of a new legal framework to strengthen the financial system, increase competition in the market, and attract foreign investment by eliminating barriers. The labour market was also profoundly changed through a series of reforms that promoted a more flexible labour regime (ease of hire and fire of staff). The country's maritime ports were also beneficiaries of a major reform aimed at stimulating private sector investment in what was traditionally a public sector business, although heavily dominated by trade unions.

Unfortunately, not enough information on the effects that these measures and the accompanying restructuring may have had upon the city's economy was available at the time of writing. Given the nature of the reforms, however, most of these effects will probably not be felt for a few years. However, the few available signs would seem to suggest that Bogotá has profited from them: after reaching a peak in the mid-1980s, unemployment fell continuously through the mid-1990s, to reach 6.3% in March 1995. The construction

16. See note to Table 8.14 for calculation of ERP.

Table 8.15 Colombia and Bogotá DE: value of exports, 1980–90 (millions of US$ FOB).

Year	Colombia	Bogotá Value	Bogotá National share (%)
1980	3945.1	240.6	6.1
1985	3551.9	174.8	4.9
1988	5026.2	196.0	3.9
1989	5739.4	151.5	2.6
1990	6765.0	185.6	2.7

Sources: For 1980–89, Cámara de Comercio de Bogotá (1991); for 1990, DANE (1992).

industry, particularly in the middle- to upper-income markets, and much of it linked to the repatriation of capital made possible by reforms of the financial sectors, had a healthy performance during the same period. Manufactured exports and cut flowers would appear to have maintained their trend, although in the context of a downward trend in the city's contribution to national exports (see Table 8.15).

VI Conclusions

Along with the surrounding municipalities, Bogotá has established itself as the foremost economic region in the country, particularly in terms of the sheer concentration of jobs, productive activities, capital and a vast array of services. Despite the continued demographic and economic expansion of Colombia's unusually high number of large cities, Bogotá's pre-eminence will not be challenged in the near future. At the same time, it continues expanding towards surrounding municipalities, fuelled by capital flowing not only from other parts of the country but also by significant overseas earnings – legal and illegal.

Only a few of Bogotá's export industries have been able to consolidate their national position. More crucial, however, will be their ability to remain competitive in terms of product quality and price, as has been stressed recently by the US-based Monitor consultancy firm (Cámara de Comercio de Bogotá 1994). Many industries already face obstacles for further expansion: inadequate knowledge of the international markets and lack of skilled labour are important bottlenecks for the publishing industry, for example. Cheap labour producing cheap products is not a recommended route in a competitive international market, as has been shown in the case of exports of leather goods, where Colombia can no longer compete with cheaper Chinese products. Rising labour costs, increased prices of public services and a re-evaluating peso have combined to reduce the profitability and competitiveness of the cut-flower industry, which has prompted calls for greater coordination between the government and the private sector (ibid.).

Already some steps have been taken in that direction, with the recent launch of Bogotá's first free trade zone ("zona franca"). One of the main concerns of incumbent mayor Mockus – a former academic and a highly charismatic figure elected against all odds in a political environment dominated by two old-established political parties[17] – include an improvement of a much deteriorated and congested road system, although the issue of who will pay for a rapid mass transit system is still under discussion with the national government. Other issues of current and urgent concern for the mayor and his team include improved quality of life and increased urban productivity (Alcaldía Mayor de Bogotá 1995). The 30-odd volumes of research commissioned to a think-tank (Misión Bogotá Siglo XXI) by a former mayor in 1991–2 should help lay out the basis for such a plan, although few researchers anticipated the effects of the liberalization reforms on the city.

Thus, it is possible that Bogotá may have benefited more than any other city from the recent reforms, although much remains to be analyzed. One thing is clear, nonetheless: as the twenty-first century approaches, Bogotá appears to have taken over from Medellín, Cali and Barranquilla as Colombia's most promising city, with its relative anonymity providing a haven for a vast and growing number of people and activities. But it is precisely this anonymity, the feeling that no one belongs there, that may prove the city's undoing. As has been suggested by the Mr Mockus, there is an urgent need to instil in the city's inhabitants a sense of belonging and the belief that individual and collective efforts can only be made more productive by protecting the city and its environment, which are their common heritage (*Eco-lógica* 1994).

Appendix

Defining the "Bogota Metropolitan Area"
In this chapter the expression *Bogotá metropolitan area* is taken to mean a functional area as proposed by, among others, Hall & Hay (1980), rather than an administrative one. This is could be defined as an invisible physical boundary, where the volume and frequency of exchanges of goods, people and information is similar to that which happens within a much more neatly

---

17. Antanas Mockus, who has no affiliation to any political party and made headlines as a controversial vice-chancellor of the National University, won a landslide election in October 1994, against the machinery of the two more established political parties, which found themselves unable to counteract his simple yet highly philosophical message to the voters. It is claimed that he spent less than US$20000 in his political campaign, a fraction of the sums spent by his rivals.

defined space such as a city centre. Administrative boundaries often artificially leave out such exchanges, simply because of the form in which statistics are collected, published and used in policy and planning.

Thus, the "Bogotá metropolitan area" (BMA) encompasses Bogotá and eight neighbouring municipalities with which the city exchanges a substantial volume of goods, people and information on a daily basis. In most cases, these municipalities are also part of a conurbation, a physical extension of the built-up area of Bogotá, such that it becomes difficult to identify any visible separation between the two in the form of large tracts of rural land, for example.

The core of the BMA is, of course, the Distrito Especial de Bogotá, defined by presidential decree in 1954 as comprising the old municipality (*municipio*) of Bogotá and six neighbouring municipalities. The name "Distrito Especial" was changed to "Distrito Capital" (DC) in the new Constitution of 1991, but its boundaries and functions remained virtually unchanged. Beyond the core lies the "built-up fringe", an area comprising the municipality of Soacha and extending to the southwest of the DC; this has become a seamless extension of the city and one of the fastest growing parts of the functional area, with a large concentration of manufacturing and extractive industries. Finally, the BMA includes an area more removed from the core, called here the "Outer Suburbs" comprising by seven municipalities located towards the southwest, west, north and northwest of the core.

References

ACIUR 1994. *Notas ACIUR No. 2*, Asociación Colombiana de Investigadores Urbano-Regionales (November).

Alcaldía Mayor de Bogotá 1995. *Plan de desarrollo económico, social y de obras públicas para Santa Fe de Bogotá, DC, 1995–1997*. Bogotá: Kaklía Mayor de Bogotá.

Cámara de Comercio de Bogotá 1991. *Bogotá en la Década de los 80*, Bogotá: Cámara de Cornegio de Bogotá.

—1993. *La apertura en Colombia: agenda de un proceso*. Bogotá: Tercer Mundo.

—1994. *Creación de la ventaja competitiva para Colombia*, CCB, Bogotá.

Colombia Bulletin 1994. *A look back at the Gaviria years: 1990–1994*. Intercongregational Commission on Justice and Peace.

Cuervo, L. M. 1992. El futuro de la capital: un estudio de prospectiva urbana: desarrollo económico. , Bogotá: Misión Bogotá Siglo XXI.

DANE 1981. *XIV censo nacional de población y III de vivienda. Octubre 24 de 1973*. Bogotá: DANE.

—1986. *Colombia Censo 85*. Bogotá: DANE

—1988. *Colombia Estadística 1987, Vol. II: municipal*. Bogotá: DANE.

—1989. *La pobreza en Bogotá: descripción cuantitativa*. Bogotá: DANE-UNDP-UNICEF-DNP.

—1991a. *Censo económico 1990: resultados preliminares*. Bogotá: DANE.

—1991b. *Colombia Estadística 1990*. Bogotá: DANE.

References

—1991c. *Anuario de industria manufacturera 1989*. Bogotá: DANE.

—1992. *Estadísticas Municipales de Colombia 1990*. Bogotá: DANE.

—1994. *Información censo 93* [computer diskette].

Dávila, J., J. E. Harday, V. Jimenez-Díaz, S. Drrossi, M. Gutman 1991. *Population and urban change in Latin America, 1850–1989*. London and Buenos Aires: International Institute for Environment and Development & IIED–América Latina.

Dávila, J. 1994. *Colombia's industrial structure and the development of the Bogotá metropolitan area, 1958–1990*. (mimeo).

de Gómez, M. I., C. Ramírez, A. Reyes 1988. Employment and labour incomes in Colombia, 1976–85. In *Trends in employment and labour incomes*, W. van Ginneken (ed.), 33–59. Geneva: ILO.

de Llinás, H. (ed.) 1990. *La población en Colombia en 1985: estudios de evaluación de la calidad y cobertura del XV censo nacional de población y IV de vivienda*, DANE, Bogotá.

Eco-lógica 1994. En Bogotá: sálvese quien pueda [an interview with Antanas Mockus]. December.

The Economist 1994. Colombia's drug business. (24 December).

Flórez, L. B. & C. González Muñoz 1983. *Industria, regiones y urbanización en Colombia*. Bogotá: Fines-Editorial Oveja Negra.

Gilbert, A. 1981. Bogotá. In *Problems and planning in Third World cities*, M. Pacione (ed.), 65–93. London: Croom Helm.

—1994. *The Latin American city*. London: Latin American Bureau.

—1995. Globalisation, employment and poverty: the experience of Bogotá. Colombia (mimeo).

Gómez, A. & M. A. Pérez 1992. El futuro de la capital. Un estudio de prospectiva urbana: El mercado laboral, Misión Bogotá Siglo XXI, Bogotá.

Goueset, V. 1991. La metropolización en Colombia: una falsa excepción al esquema latinoamericano de concentración primacial. Bogotá (mimeo).

Granados, M. del Pilar, R. Ulises 1992. *El futuro de la capital: un estudio de prospectiva urbana: Desarrollo poblacional*. Misión Bogotá Siglo XXI, Bogotá (mimeo).

Hall, P. & D. Hay 1980. *Growth centres in the European urban system*. London: Heinemann Educational.

Jaramillo, S. & L. M. Cuervo 1987. *La configuración del espacio regional en Colombia. Tres ensayos*, Bogotá: CEDE-Universidad de los Andes.

Jiménez, M. & S. Sideri 1985. *Historia del desarrollo regional en Colombia*. Bogotá: CEREC–CIDER.

Linn, J. F. 1979. Tendencias de la urbanización, inversión de la polarización y política espacial en Colombia. *Revista Cámara de Comercio de Bogotá*, 9(36), 33–87.

Misión Bogotá Siglo XXI 1993. *El futuro de la capital: estudio prospectivo de educación*. Bogotá.

Mohan, R. 1986. *Work, wages and welfare in a developing metropolis. Consequences of growth in Bogotá, Colombia* [A World Bank Research Publication]. New York: Oxford University Press.

Ocampo, J. A., J. Bernal, M. Avella, M. Errázuriz 1987. La consolidación del capitalismo moderno. In *Historia económica de Colombia*, J. A. Ocampo (ed.). Bogotá: Siglo XXI.

Pineda, S. & A. Trejos 1992. Bogotá frente a la apertura. *Revista Cámara de Comercio de Bogotá*.

Richardson, H. 1977. *City size and national spatial strategies in developing countries*. World Bank Staff Working Paper 252, The World Bank, Washington DC.

Semana 1995. ¿Los últimos ladrillos? (31 January).

Svenson, G. 1977. *Bogotá DE: el de sarrollo economico deparamental 1960–75*. Bogotá: INANDES.

Thoumí, F. E. 1983. La estructura del crecimiento económico regional y urbano en Colombia (1960–1975). *Desarrollo y Sociedad* No. 10 (January), 151–81.

UNDP 1994. *Human development report 1994*. New York: United Nations.

CHAPTER NINE
Mexican neoliberalism and urban management in Monterrey

Gustavo Garza

The world expansion of capital, the technological revolution that has made the productive process more flexible, the emergence of economic unions between nations, the collapse of the former Soviet bloc with the dissolution of the USSR and the long-term cycle of recession in the world economy – these are some of the factors that explain the growing implementation in the majority of countries of a model that establishes the openness to international trade, deregulation of economic activity, privatization of state firms and the decentralization of public management.

The expiry of the import substitution model, which made possible the Mexican "economic miracle" between 1950 and 1980 and the eruption of an untimely economic crisis in 1982, determined Mexico's incorporation in this neoliberal trend. The principal measure consolidating this process was Mexico's entry into the GATT in 1986, by means of which a new model of economic openness to international trade was institutionalized.

From 1988 to 1994, Mexico implemented a series of policy reforms that contributed to the country's entry in the economic trade area formed by the USA and Canada, culminating in the signing of the North American Free Trade Agreement (NAFTA) between the three countries in December 1992 (coming into force in January 1994). At the same time, Mexico participated in bilateral negotiations to expand its trade with other agreements with Chile (1991), Costa Rica (1994), Colombia and Venezuela (1994). It also signed a trade agreement with the European Union and joined APEC (Asian Pacific Economic Cooperation) and the Pacific Basin Economic Council. These important strategic measures for stimulating development culminated in the formalization of Mexico's entry into the Organization for Economic Cooperation and Development (OECD) on 18 March 1994. Mexico became the 25th member of this organization, which comprises the world's most highly developed countries, its gross domestic product of US$360 billion making it the country with the ninth largest GDP in the organization and the 13th largest in the world.

In so far as the Mexican economy adjusts to the neoliberal model of growth and manages to solve the recent crisis, which erupted in December 1994 and has led to a deep recession in 1995, manufacturing and service firms are expected to concentrate in the cities along the Mexican border with the USA, as well as in the principal metropolises and localities in their hinterlands. This circumstance requires cities to modernize their management policies and organizations in order to adapt their infrastructure and urban regulations to meet the demands of expanding economic activities and enable them to compete with American and Canadian cities.

In 1990, Mexico had a system of 309 cities, that is localities with over 15 000 inhabitants. The main class in the urban hierarchy comprises metropolitan areas with over a million inhabitants: México City, Guadalajara, Monterrey and Puebla. These four metropolises account for 45.1% of the 49.4 million urban inhabitants and 41.8% of the total national gross domestic product (GDP) in 1990 (Garza & Rivera 1995: 60).

Mexico's neoliberal strategy lacks any functional territorial paradigm, since it was decided to let market forces determine the spatial organization of economic and population activities. However, at the local level, significant actions have begun to be undertaken to adapt cities to the new economic strategy, a prominent example of which is the Metropolitan Area of Monterrey (MAM).

The State of Nuevo León, the capital of which is Monterrey, is the most highly urbanized in Mexico, with 91% of the 1994 population in urban areas. The central feature of its urban development is its extreme concentration in the MAM, which in 1990 accounted for 83.1% and 89.7% of the state's total and urban population, respectively.

The following will analyze the macroeconomic changes experienced by MAM and how modifications carried out in the city administration and large infrastructure projects were promoted to fit to the demands of the economic model of openness to international trade and the NAFTA.

Structure and macroeconomic dynamics

Mexico experienced significant economic development between 1960 and 1980, virtually quadrupling its GDP of an annual rate of 6.9%. The oil crisis and external debt led to severe economic recession in the 1980s, with the GDP rising a mere 0.9% annually from 1980 to 1988. The period from 1988 to 1993, during the intensification of neoliberal policies, saw a significant improvement, with the GDP increasing at an annual rate of 4.2%. For these three periods of boom, crisis and relative economic recovery, it is interesting to note Mexico's development in the eight branches in which the economic structure is divided, and contrast this with the nine municipalities of the Metropolitan Area of Monterrey (MAM).

Between 1960 and 1980, the agricultural sector significantly reduced its share of the Mexican economy, from 16.5% to 8.4%. Commerce and services, the main branches of the economy, remained virtually constant, their economic importance falling by only a few tenths of a point (Table 9.1).

Agriculture's fall in relative importance was offset by the most dynamic sectors, including the manufacturing sector and transport. Mining, construction and electricity, although far less significant, also showed advances, given their limited share of GDP (Table 9.1). Services, commerce and manufacturing were the main branches of industry, with their combined share of the GDP rising from 67.1% in 1960 to 70.8% in 1980.

Table 8.1 Mexico: gross domestic product, 1960–93 ('000s of new pesos, 1980 = 100).

Activity	1960	1970	1980	1988	1993
TOTAL	1131131.4	2227175.8	4276490.0	4595495.8	5644659.0
Agriculture	186934.4	254175.6	357131.0	393178.8	419882.0
Mining	62531.2	109847.2	291374.0	371023.1	218242.0
Manufacturing	211233.4	519568.2	985013.0	1047516.6	1261748.0
Construction	63008.7	140125.1	276193.0	239214.1	304740.0
Electricity	4838.4	17178.3	42035.0	1188.4	86482.0
Commerce	265603.3	533057.0	999556.0	937271.3	1278157.0
Transportation	54856.5	100038.9	279112.0	310019.7	404219.0
Services	282125.5	553185.5	1046076.0	1226083.7	1671189.0
(Vertical %)					
TOTAL	100.0	100.0	100.0	100.0	100.0
Agriculture	16.5	11.4	8.4	8.6	7.4
Mining	5.5	4.9	6.8	8.1	3.9
Manufacturing	18.7	23.3	23.0	22.8	22.4
Construction	5.6	6.3	6.5	5.2	5.4
Electricity	0.4	0.8	1.0	1.5	1.5
Commerce	23.5	24.0	23.3	20.4	22.6
Transportation	4.9	4.5	6.5	6.7	7.2
Services	24.9	24.8	24.5	26.7	29.6

Source: Calculations based on INEGI (1985), Sistema de cuentas naciones de México. Estructura económica regional, producto interno bruto por entidad federativa, 1970, 1975 y 1980, México (System of National Accounts of Mexico. Regional Economic Structure, Gross Domestic Products by State, 1970, 1975); INEGI (1988), Sistema de cuentas nacionales, de México, 1985–88 (System of National Accounts of Mexico); Garza & Sobrino (1989), Industrialización periférica en el sistema de ciudades de Sinaloa (Peripheral Industrialization in Sinaloa's City System), El Colegio de México, México; INEGI (1993) Sistemas de Cuentas Nacionales de México (1994) (System of National Accounts of Mexico); INEGI Banco de Datos del INEGI (INEGI Data Bank).

During the crisis years (1980–88), the percentage of commerce and construction fell considerably, actually declining in absolute terms. Manufacturing industry also experienced a slight contraction compared with previous decades. Losses in these sectors were taken up by services, and mining, with the former becoming the strongest sector in Mexico's economy (Table 9.1).

During the period of economic recovery that took place between 1988 and 1993, the agricultural sector continued to contract, accounting for a mere 7.4% of GDP in 1993, while mining experienced an even greater decline. Manufacturing industry remained in virtually the same position, while commerce and services became more important, together accounting for 52.5% of the national GDP in 1993 (see Table 9.1).

Between 1960 and 1980, MAM experienced an annual GDP growth rate of 7.8%, significantly higher than the national rate. By virtue of being a metropolitan area, its economic structure had two main differences vis-à-vis the national structure. First, primary activities were practically insignificant and, in 1980, agriculture and mining accounted for only 0.8% of the GDP. Secondly, this difference was covered by the manufacturing industry, which accounted for 37.4% of Monterrey's economic activities in 1960, as opposed to 18.7% at the national level (see Tables 9.1 and 9.2).

Table 8.2 Metropolitan area of Monterrey: gross domestic product, 1960–93 ('000s of new pesos, 1980 = 100).

Activity	1960	1970	1980	1988	1993
TOTAL	56634.7	114865.2	256280.5	258321.5	305722.0
Agriculture	842.5	616.0	569.7	364.3	270.8
Mining	893.8	969.4	1326.6	1521.4	263.5
Manufacturing	21186.7	54242.9	99978.8	91790.0	106544.3
Construction	1138.1	4162.4	14713.4	12757.7	13936.2
Electricity	383.5	713.0	1879.2	2765.4	3634.7
Commerce	16999.5	23128.1	56924.5	57219.9	66547.3
Transportation	1288.9	4274.1	17529.3	21635.4	22245.3
Services	13901.7	26759.3	63359.0	70267.4	92279.9
(Vertical %)					
TOTAL	100.0	100.0	100.0	100.0	100.0
Agriculture	1.5	0.5	0.2	0.1	0.1
Mining	1.6	0.8	0.6	0.6	0.1
Manufacturing	37.4	47.3	39.0	35.5	34.8
Construction	2.0	3.6	5.7	4.9	4.5
Electricity	0.7	0.6	0.7	1.1	1.2
Commerce	30.0	20.2	22.2	22.2	21.8
Transportation	2.3	3.7	6.9	8.4	7.3
Services	24.5	23.3	24.7	27.2	30.2

Source: Calculations based on INEGI (1985), Sistema de cuentas nacionales de México, estructura económica regional. Producto interno bruto por entidad federativa, 1970, 1975 y 1980, (System of National Accounts of Mexico. Regional Economic Structure, Gross Domestic Products by State 1970, 1975 and 1980), México; INEGI (1990), Anuario de estadísticas estatales (Yearbook of State Statistics), 1987, México; INEGI (1992), Resulados oportunos del estado de Nuevo León (Timely results from the State of Nuevo León); Unikel, Garza y Ruíz (1978), El desarrollo urbano de México (Mexico's Urban Development), El Colegio de México; Garza and Sobrino (1989), Indus- trialización periférica en el sistema de ciudades de Sinaloa (Peripheral Industrialization in Sinaloa's City System), El Colegio de México; 1993 is an estimation based on INEGI (1994), Banco de datos de INEGI (INEGI Data Bank), and government of the State of Nuevo León, Información estadística del estado de Nuevo León (Statistical Information from the State of Nuevo León).

These two differences continued until 1980, while MAM's remaining sectoral shares were very similar to national ones: with commerce accounting for 22.2% and 23.3%; services 24.7% and 24.5%, construction 5.7% and 6.5%, and transport 6.9% and 6.0% (see Tables 4.1 and 4.2). This situation persisted until 1988, although manufacturing declined to 35.5% and services rose to 27.2%, which somewhat lessened the city's overwhelming industrial importance.

Monterrey's macroeconomic peculiarities persisted throughout the relative boom period between 1988 and 1993. At the same time, however, services become increasingly important, reaching 30.2% in 1993 (see Table 9.2). Despite the fact that manufacturing continued to be the most important economic activity in the city, the tertiary sector (commerce, transport and services) was the leading one, accounting for 59.3% of MAM's economy in 1993. The predominance of services required a different urban strategy from the one traditionally orientated towards manufacturing.

The MAM's importance in the national economy underwent significant changes in the three periods considered. In 1960, MAM accounted for 5.0% of the national GDP, despite containing only 2.0% of the country's total population. The México City Metropolitan Area produced 36.2% of the country's GDP, meaning that these two cities alone were responsible for 41.2% of Mexico's economic activity. Monterrey's share of the primary sector was obviously very small, accounting for a mere 0.5% and 1.4% of the nation's agricultural and mining activities respectively. Even in essentially urban branches such as construction and transport, Monterrey's share was small, 1.8% and 2.4%, respectively. Its greatest share was in manufacturing, where it accounted for a tenth of the country's total, making it Mexico's second largest industrial city. Electricity and commerce also became more important, since they represented 7.9% and 6.4% of the national total (see Table 9.3).

In 1970, MAM's economic significance rose slightly to 5.2% of the Mexican GDP, as a result of the increase in manufacturing, construction and transport, which more than compensated for the reduction in mining, agriculture, electricity and commerce. In 1970, Monterrey's manufacturing reached its peak, accounting for 10.4% of Mexico's total in this branch (see Table 9.3). However, the city achieved its greatest economic importance to date in 1980, when it produced 6.0% of the country's total GDP. That year it housed 3.0% of the Mexican population, consolidating its position as the third largest city by number of inhabitants.

Its increased importance was not attributable to manufacturing, since this fell to 10.2% in 1980. Agricultural and mining activities continued to contract until they represented an insignificant fraction of their national counterparts. This decline was offset by construction, which rose to 5.3%, commerce, which increased to 5.7%, and services, which totalled 6% (see Table 9.3).

In 1980, México City produced 38.2% of the national GDP, meaning that, together with Monterrey, they constituted 45% of the Mexican economy (Puente 1987: 94). If one adds the cities of Guadalajara, Puebla, León, Torreón,

Table 8.3 Metropolitan area of Monterrey: gross internal product, 1960–93 (national participation, %).

Activity	1960	1970	1980	1988	1993
Total	5.01	5.16	5.99	5.62	5.42
Agriculture	0.45	0.24	0.16	0.09	0.06
Mining	1.43	0.88	0.46	0.41	0.12
Manufacturing	10.03	10.44	10.15	8.76	8.44
Construction	1.81	2.97	5.33	5.33	4.57
Electricy	7.93	4.15	4.47	3.88	4.20
Commerce	6.40	4.34	5.69	6.10	5.21
Transportation	2.35	4.37	6.28	6.98	5.50
Services	4.93	4.84	6.06	5.73	5.52

Source: Calculations based on Tables 9.1 & 9.2.

Toluca, Ciudad Juárez and San Luis Potosí to these two metropolises, they account for 65–70% of the gross national product. It is therefore essential to coordinate macroeconomic planning with the urban and regional actions of the Mexican state, since they are currently being undertaken independently.

From 1980 to 1988, the years of economic crisis, MAM reduced its share of the country's economy to 5.6%, with manufacturing declining to 8.8% and services to 5.7% of the national total. The same was true of other branches, with only transport and commerce increasing their share (see Table 9.3). The national economic recovery between 1988 and 1993 was slightly less in MAM, whose share of the national economy fell to 5.4% and, with the exception of electricity, all branches became relatively less important, underscoring the problems faced by this industrial metropolis during the process of structural adjustment.

In short, during the decades when the import substitution model was in force, both the national GDP and that of MAM experienced extremely high rates of growth: 7.0% and 7.3% from 1960 to 1970, and 6.7% and 8.4% from 1970 to 1980 (see Table 9.4). During the crisis period from 1980 to 1988, when the neoliberal policy began to be implemented, total GDP rates were 0.9% for the country as a whole and 0.1% in MAM, whose relative importance in the national economy was severely reduced.

However, the city's decline continued during the five-year period from 1988 to 1993, when government deregulation and the sale of state firms intensified and there was a relative economic recovery, since the national annual GDP increase rose to 4.2% and that of MAM to 3.4% (see Table 9.4). MAM's lower rate meant that it became less important in the national economy, although it experienced a significant economic recovery.

Certain peculiarities can be observed at the branch level. MAM's share of agricultural activity declined during the three periods while mining expanded far less than the national rate. This is entirely logical, since these are activities from the rural sector in which cities' participation lessens as

Table 8.4 Mexico and Monterrey: rates of annual growth of the sectorial GDP, 1960–93.

	1960–70	1970–80	1980–8	1988–93
TOTAL				
Mexico	7.00	6.70	0.90	4.20
Monterrey	7.32	8.35	0.10	3.40
Agriculture				
Mexico	3.12	3.45	1.20	1.30
Monterrey	−3.08	−0.78	−5.43	−5.70
Mining				
Mexico	5.79	10.24	3.06	−10.10
Monterrey	0.81	3.18	1.72	−29.50
Manufacturing				
Mexico	9.42	6.60	0.77	3.80
Monterrey	9.85	6.30	−1.06	3.00
Construction				
Mexico	8.32	7.02	−1.78	5.00
Monterrey	13.84	13.45	−1.76	1.80
Electricity				
Mexico	13.51	9.36	6.80	4.00
Monterrey	6.39	10.17	4.94	5.60
Commerce				
Mexico	7.21	6.48	−0.80	6.40
Monterrey	3.12	9.42	0.05	3.10
Transportation				
Mexico	6.19	10.80	1.32	5.40
Monterrey	12.73	15.15	2.66	0.60
Services				
Mexico	6.96	6.58	2.00	6.40
Monterrey	6.76	9.00	1.30	5.60

Source: Calculations based on Tables 9.1 & 9.2.

they become metropolises.

Manufacturing industries are the symbol of Monterrey. The city's share of this branch showed a relative decline from the 1970s onwards, when it grew at an annual rate of 6.3% as opposed to the national rate of 6.6%. During the 1980s recession, the city actually experienced negative growth rates of −1.1%, while national rates rose to 0.8%, although rates did increase to 3.0% between 1988 and 1993 (Table 9.4). The neoliberal model particularly affected the manufacturing industry in MAM and the capital, Mexico's two most industrialized centres.[1] Within the secondary sector, construction grew more rapidly

---

1. México City's industry experienced a far greater decline than that of Monterrey. Between 1980 and 1988, its share of national industry fell from 43.5% to 32.1%, owing to the drastic reduction in the national GDP from 95 810 billion pesos (1988 = 100) to 74 277 billion, in other words a contraction of 29% (Garza 1991: 211).

in MAM than in the country as a whole until 1980, but during the 1980s crisis, it contracted in both areas, recovering between 1988 and 1993 (see Table 9.4). The activities that expanded most in Monterrey were those in the tertiary sector, apparently marking a significant shift in its traditional industrial specialization. From 1970 to 1980, the leading sector, commerce, grew more than in the country as a whole, and was relatively less affected by the 1980s recession, although it expanded less later. The second most important sector, transport activities, essential for the distribution of merchandise, inputs and labour, was the most dynamic sector until 1980, expanding even during the crisis period, although growth rates for the city declined significantly during the period from 1988 to 1993. Rates for services, in third place, were higher than for the country as a whole from 1970 to 1980, decreasing considerably in the 1980s, but experiencing the greatest recovery from 1988 to 1993 (see Table 9.4).

Monterrey is apparently at a stage of transition from a highly specialized manufacturing metropolis towards greater economic diversification focusing on the predominance of services. This process was exemplified by the closure in 1986 of the Monterrey Iron and Steel Foundry, a firm established in 1903, which exhausted its long-term cycle of expansion, becoming technologically displaced. Symptomatically, as we shall see in the following section, a modern complex of services, including hotels, museums, auditoriums, theatres and the International Business Centre (Cintermex) is nearing completion in the 113.7 ha that once housed the firm.

Developed countries are experiencing a "service revolution" in which services for producers are expanding rapidly while the tertiary sector is becoming the basis of is economic and urban development (see Daniels 1982, Noyelle & Stanbak 1984, Howells 1988). In the USA, for example, in 1992, services accounted for 72% of its GDP and in recent years have created nine out of ten jobs. Moreover, it has been estimated that by the year 2010 just 10% of the American GDP will involve primary and secondary activities, crystallizing into a service millennium (Royssen 1987).

Mexico is not experiencing an equivalent "tertiary revolution" and is currently structuring a new development model that will enable it to resume the process of industrialization that was interrupted by the 1980s crisis. Thus, Monterrey should consolidate its traditional manufacturing specialization by stimulating the development of advanced technology firms while stimulating the development of services to the producer, which are essential to the efficient realization of modern productive processes. Its urban development should be orientated in this direction, meaning that there is a need for the appropriate modernization and technical upgrading of the administrative bodies in the metropolitan area.

Metropolitan administration, regulation and policies

In 1994, Nuevo León's urban population represented 91% of the total, meaning that it had virtually completed its process of urbanization and become an entirely urbanized state.[2] Monterrey's metropolitan hegemony is practically complete, since in 1990 it housed an impressive 94.2% of the state urban population, proving that the state's most important economic and social issues are restricted to the Metropolitan Area of Monterrey. This fact, combined with the limited functions of Mexican municipalities, explains why the state government is responsible for metropolitan planning and the management of large infrastructure works.

MAM's laws, plans and management organizations have always been run by the state. In 1927, the first Law of Planning and New Construction in the city of Monterrey was passed, undergoing a series of modifications in 1944, 1952, 1967 and 1976 until it became the Law of Urban Development of the State of Nuevo León in 1980 (see Valadez & Alejandro 1995: 435).

In 1980, MAM comprised eight municipalities and the Law of Urban Development for that year established three new organizations for the formulation and supervision of urban plans: the Planning Commission for the State of Nuevo León, the Consultative Council for Urban Planning, and the Conurbation Commission. The Planning Commission was by far the most important executive body, since it depended on the governor and was presided over by the Ministry of Human Settlements and Planning. It was responsible for the important task of establishing general guidelines concerning land use, authorizing real estate development, land urbanization and the location of infrastructure works, as well as assessing urban development plans and projects. MAM's overwhelming importance within the structure of cities in Nuevo León meant that this commission was essentially for the metropolis. The Consultative Council was an organization for consulting civil society, and the Conurbation Commission combined the metropolitan municipalities to sanction the Urban Development Master Plan for the Metropolitan Area of Monterrey, 1988–2020.

The early 1990s saw the continued implementation in Mexico of the neoliberal actions required to negotiate the NAFTA with the USA and Canada. Federal policies concerning urban and regional planning virtually disappeared, fostering greater participation by state governments in this area. Nuevo León was probably one of the states with most initiatives in this respect, approving a Law of Urban Development in 1991, which was significantly modified in 1993. This new law established a State System of Urban Coordination (SECU) comprising: the Urban Development Commission, the Consultative Council

---

2. This figure of 91% is calculated by defining localities with 15000 or more inhabitants as urban. If localities with 2500 or more inhabitants are regarded as cities, then the percentage of urban population in Nuevo León in 1994 would be 94.6%.

for Urban Planning and the Nuevo León Institute for Urban Studies. Adopting an administrative approach of "total quality", SECU's main aim was to promote the decentralization of urban development administration to the municipalities, establish the administrative base and create a normative framework for the coordination of metropolitan municipalities among themselves and with the state government, and promote the training of specialized technical personnel and rigorous research on the most important issues on the urban agenda (see Garza et al. 1995: 407). By July 1995, seven agreements had been signed between the state government and the same number of metropolitan municipalities, in keeping with the decentralizing scheme of the State Urban Coordination System.[3] The process of restructuring Monterrey's administration extends, as the next section shows, to mechanisms for the financing, management and achievement of political consensus for the metropolis's large infrastructure works.

In 1991, Mexican municipalities accounted for 5.2% of total public expenditure, meaning that their functions have usually been restricted to guaranteeing public safety and traffic control; provision of street lighting; garbage collection; supervision and regulation of markets, hotels and restaurants; and the maintenance and conservation of streets, squares and gardens. Since the reform of Article 115 of the Constitution in 1983, municipalities have been authorized to formulate, approve and execute urban development plans in their localities, as well as acquiring and administering territorial reserves.

Of the nine municipalities currently comprising the metropolitan areas of Monterrey, six had drawn up urban development plans by July 1995.[4] In addition to the municipal functions mentioned above, the Nuevo León government undertakes the majority of metropolitan actions: providing water services and drainage; the public transport system; road services and construction of the underground railway; public housing and regulation of land tenure; and economic promotion through the system of industrial parks and large urban renewal projects.

In short, MAM planning and the implementation of large-scale projects that defined the structuring of metropolitan space are undertaken by the state government, although decentralization of the processing of building permits and land use has been encouraged, together with the implementation of partial plans for the areas of each municipality.

---

3. The state government has signed urban coordination agreements with the metropolitan municipalities of General Escobedo, Apodaca, Santa Catarina, San Pedro Garza García, San Nicolás de los Garza and Monterrey. Linares is the only non-metropolitan municipality to have signed an agreement of this kind.
4. Municipalities that have drawn up a municipal or partial urban development plan include: Garza García, General Escobedo, Santa Catarina, Monterrey, San Nicholás and Guadalupe. Apodaca, García and Juárez have yet to do so.

New administrative approaches to promote large infrastructure projects

National economic adjustments were established within a framework of budgetary restrictions owing to the heavy burden of Mexico's external debt and the economic crisis of the 1980s, which required a reduction of the federal government and state apparatus.

The governor of Nuevo León, Socrates Rizzo García, began his period of government in 1991 by proposing the modernization of the state on the basis of seven premises:

- the internationalization of Nuevo León
- decentralization and regional development
- orderly growth
- improved quality of life
- safety and justice
- modernization of finances and public administration
- democracy and solidarity.

MAM's great economic and demographic predominance implied that these efforts would primarily be implemented in the city, as in fact has occurred.

In 1995, ten large metropolitan projects are currently at different stages of development:

- the Metrorrey underground railway system
- the Monterrey Peripheral toll way
- Valle Oriente Urban Development Project
- Solidarity City
- the Santa Lucía Project
- Fundidora Park
- sewage treatment plans
- the metropolitan ring road
- new areas of integral urban development
- metropolitan industrial parks.

These ten large-scale projects, whose completion requires one or two decades, constitute the most ambitious attempt at metropolitan renovation in the city's history, and their simultaneous implementation is attributable to an innovatory form of partnership between state government and private agents.

Conclusions: new schemes for developing large infrastructure projects

The Metropolitan Area of Monterrey (MAM) increased its GDP growth rate to 7.8% annually from 1960 to 1980, increasing its share of national GDP from 5.0% in 1960 to 6.0% in 1980. During this period, it also experienced a slight increase in its manufacturing importance, which rose from 10.0% to 10.2% of the national total. From 1980 to 1988, a period of severe economic crisis, MAM reduced its share of the national economy to 5.6%, while the manufacturing industry's share fell to 8.8% and services to 5.7% (see Table 9.3). The national economic recovery from 1988–93 was somewhat lower in Monterrey, whose share of the national GDP fell to 5.4% in 1993. With the exception of electricity, the relative importance of all branches fell, with manufacturing declining to 8.4% and services to 5.5% of the national totals.

However, during the five-year period of intense economic deregulation and privatization, lasting from 1988 to 1993, MAM's GDP rose by 3.4% annually, while a clear restructuring of its economy was observed as it began a stage of transition from a metropolis with high manufacturing specialization towards a greater economic diversification focused on the service sector. Considering that Mexico is still not experiencing a "tertiary revolution" of the sort occurring in developed countries, MAM should consolidate its traditional manufacturing vocation by encouraging the location of advanced technology firms while promoting the development of modern financial services, informatics, marketing, communications, and professional services, essential to the running of this type of firms.

National GDP rose by 3.5% in 1994, but at the end of the year another crisis erupted, triggered by a flight of large volumes of financial capital from the stock market and the abrupt devaluation of the peso against the dollar of approximately 90%. During the first half of 1995, GDP experienced a sharp contraction of –5.8%, casting doubt on the advantages of an adjustment policy designed to confront the crisis.[5] Even before this sharp recession, neoliberal policy had produced extremely negative social effects resulting from the increase in unemployment, poverty, marginalization, crime rates, and drug addiction, as has occurred in many countries where this policy has been applied (UNRISD 1995). In Mexico, however, the situation was aggravated by the armed uprising in the state of Chiapas in January 1994.

Whatever the future of neoliberal strategy may be in Mexico, the recurrent crisis and severe social deterioration will force it to be adjusted sooner or later, making it possible to generate higher endogenous levels of accumulation of capital, stimulate technological development, enhance training for the workforce and modernize cities in terms of their administration and infrastructure needed for the location of key economic activities.

Nuevo León is the most highly urbanized state in Mexico, as a result of

---

5. In view of the closure of hundreds of firms, mainly medium and small, and the remaining firms' inability to meet debt payments, the only profitable firms are export ones. However, the export sector as a whole has also been affected and the chairman of the National Association of Mexican Importers and Exporters (ANIERM) pointed out that "The emergency plan has not been successful nor have the causes of the crisis been addressed". In this respect, he points to the "non-existence of a program for the integrated development of foreign trade" (*La Jornada*, 17 August 1995: 1, 44)

which the efficiency of MAM and the rest of its cities is crucial to its development. As regards city administration, 1993 saw the establishment of the State Urban Coordination System, comprising the Urban Development Commission, the Consultative Council for Urban Development and the Nuevo León Institute for Urban Studies. The Commission's functions have followed a certain bureaucratic–administrative routine and have been improved by the implementation of an electronic system for obtaining building permits, changes in land use, and so on. The Council and the institute have enjoyed modest development in relation to their ambitious objectives, the first entailing the promotion of civic participation in decision-making, the second involving the training of specialized personnel and undertaking rigorous research of top-priority issues on the urban agenda.

The government of the State of Nuevo León acts as a *de facto* metropolitan government of MAM, planning, promoting and building infrastructure, as well as designing plans for the city. However, it has encouraged a significant decentralization of urban management by signing agreements with metropolitan municipalities, enabling them to handle approximately 80% of the population's requests on urban issues.

Since 1991, the most innovative part of the state government's urban actions has been the devising of various types of partnership between different urban actors to undertake the construction of the ten large infrastructure works enumerated earlier. An analysis of their features produces the following typology of the management and financing schemes: public federal–state, public state, private, and joint state and private.

The public federal–state scheme includes planned works, financed and administered by the state government, but executed with the financial support of the federal government: the light underground railway system (Metrorrey), the Santa Lucía projects, and sewage treatment plants and collectors. The public state scheme includes the metropolitan ring road alone.

The private scheme includes projects implemented by trusts in which the state government takes part but whose financing and administration is basically private: Monterrey Peripheral Toll way; the Valle Oriente Project, Fundidora Park; new areas of integrated urban development; a combination of the last two is represented by the state–private joint venture, in which various urban agents participate more or less equally with the state government, as in the Solidarity City project.

The implementation of these management and financing schemes for MAM's large infrastructure works has enabled the state government to use its financial resources to encourage new private investment several fold, so that instead of undertaking five projects, according to the classic form of public investment, it has been able to promote twice that number.

The acute recession in 1995 has led to the suspension of some of these projects (Metrorrey, the third stage of the Monterrey peripheral toll way, Solidarity City and Santa Lucia) while the rest have continued more slowly. The future of induced private investment schemes for the execution of large urban development projects will depend partly on overcoming the economic recession and partly on their profitability for private investors.

References

Daniels, P. 1982. *Service industries: growth and location*. Cambridge: Cambridge University Press.

Garza, G. (coord.) 1995. *Atlas de Monterrey*. Gobierno del Estado de Nuevo Leóm. Universidad Autónoma de Nuevo León, Instituto de Estudio Urbanos de Nuevo León, El Colegio de México.

Garza, G. 1991. Dinámica industrial de la ciudad de México, 1940–1988. *Estudios Demográficos y Urbanos* **6**(1).

Garza, G., C. Paniagua, F. Rodríguez 1995. Organos de gestión metropolitana. In G. Garza (coord.), 405–14.

Garza, G. & S. Rivera 1995. *Dinámica macroeconómica de las ciudades en México*. Instituto Nacional de Estadistiea Geografica e Informaties. El Colegio de México, Mexico.

Howells, J. 1988. *Economic, technological and locational trends in European services*, Avebury: Aldershot

Noyelle, T. & T. Stanback 1984. *The economic transformation of American cities*. Newark, New Jersey: Rowman & Allanheld.

Puente, S. 1987. Estructura industrial y participación de la zona metropolitana de las ciudad de México en el producto interno bruto. In *Atlas de la Ciudad de México*, G. Garza et al. (compilers), 000–000. Departamento del Distrito Federal, El Colegio de México, México City.

Royssen, J. B. 1987. The new deal in services: challenger for Europe. In *The economics of services*, G. Akehourst & J. Gadrey (eds), 49–56. London: Frank Cass.

Sistema de Transporte Colectivo Metrorrey 1995. Inicios de la transportación masiva: Metrorrey. In G. Garza (coord.), 246–52

UNRISD 1995. *states of disarray: the social effects of globalization*. Geneva: United Nations Research Institute for Social Development, Geneva.

Valadez F. & J. Alejandro 1995. Evolución de la planeación urbana en Monterrey in G. Garza (coord.), 433–8.

Further reading

Barragan, J. 1991. *Cintermex, centro internacional de negocios*. Monterrey, Mexico: Urbis International SA de CV.

Chávez Gutiérrez, J. 1995. El sistema hidráulico. In G. Garza (coord.), 215–22.

García Ortega, Roberto y Sergio Ortíz Nava 1995. Esquema metropolitano de usos del suelo. In G. Garza (coord.), 311–18.

Garza, G. 1995. Crisis industrial, 1980–1988. In G. Garza (coord.), 139–45.

Gobierno del Estado de Nuevo León 1995. *Plan multidimensional de desarrollo urbano de Nuevo León, 1995–2020*. Secretaría de Desarrollo Urbano y Obras Públicas, Monterrey, NL [document for public consultation].

CHAPTER TEN
The changing structure of Johannesburg's economy

Richard Tomlinson

Johannesburg and the inner city

Based on the research the author and others (Tomlinson 1995) recently completed on Johannesburg and the inner city,[1] six topics are of particular interest in the context of to this book:

- manufacturing
- business and financial services, including the head-office function
- government
- (a quick scan of) commerce, catering and accommodation
- the beginnings of physical decay
- "emerging" enterprise.

The relevance of the first four topics/sectors to Johannesburg's economy is demonstrated in Table 10.1, where they are seen to be the largest sectors. In particular, it is evident that manufacturing's role is declining rapidly, commerce is static, and that the other sectors are increasing their share of the economy. Perhaps inevitably, the financial sector's contribution to gross geographical product (GGP) is about double its contribution to employment, and that of government is the reverse.[2]

---

1. The inner city is defined more loosely than the CBD to include immediately adjacent office areas such as Brammfontein, as well as industrial areas such as Selby.
2. Herman Piennar, who in 1994 was working for the Johannesburg City Council and was supervising the consulting project, provided this data on the basis of his access to unpublished census data.

Table 10.1 Johannesburg: output and employment[2].

	Employment		GGP (R '000)	
	1980	1991	1980	1991
Agriculture	0.32	0.24	0.15	0.03
Mining	0.80	1.19	0.12	0.37
Manufacturing	26.29	20.58	25.48	18.91
Electricity	1.25	1.49	1.51	2.13
Construction	3.97	5.09	5.80	3.53
Commerce	20.78	18.86	26.18	26.12
Transport	6.25	5.82	7.81	7.64
Finance	9.77	12.76	21.86	24.92
Government	30.56	33.97	11.09	16.35
TOTAL (%)	100.00	100.00	100.00	100.00
TOTAL (actual)	576 709	497 620	R29.0 billion	R28.2 billion

Manufacturing[3]

In 1994 the inner city contained nearly 800 manufacturing enterprises and these contributed approximately 40 000 jobs. The largest manufacturing sectors, measured in terms of the proportion of manufacturing employment, were clothing (23%), printing and publishing (23%), textiles (8%), other manufacturing (jewellery and diamond cutting in particular – 7%), food (6%) and fabricated metals (6%). The inner city represents a particular manufacturing niche in comparison to manufacturing in all of Johannesburg. This is because clothing, printing and publishing, and textiles are "over-represented" in the inner city, and fabricated metals, machinery and electrical machinery, food and furniture are "under-represented" in the inner city. Related to this relative specialization is that manufacturing activity is primarily the province of small and medium enterprises.

The 1979 and 1988 census figures show a net loss of 7294 manufacturing jobs in Johannesburg, and the Development Bank of Southern Africa suggests that this loss has accelerated sharply since then. Rogerson & Rogerson (1995) found that between 1980 and 1989 the CBD lost between 6000 and 9000 jobs, which would account for the entire downturn in manufacturing employment in Johannesburg. They further suggest that between 1980 and 1994 the inner city in fact lost between 16 000 and 20 000 jobs, the implication being that the decline of manufacturing employment in Johannesburg can to a large degree be explained by events in the inner city. The major sectors in which these losses were occurring were clothing, food, printing and other manufacturing, thereby indicating that the inner city was losing its competitive edge in precisely those industries in which it previously had an advantage.

However, comparative experience causes one to expect the decline of man-

---

3. Rogerson & Rogerson (1995) have since published separately on the topic.

ufacturing in the inner city. Changes in the manner in which production is organized – for example, the shift from multi-storey to single-storey plant, reliance on trucks rather than rail, and improved telecommunications – all render decentralized locations more desirable. Our surveys reveal that theft and violence (not unique to South Africa, but much discussed) also play a part in decisions to move from the inner city (Tomlinson 1995).

The analysis of the components of inner-city manufacturing change disclose that 45–50% of the overall downturn can be explained in terms of the relatively high death rates of existing establishments as compared to the correspondingly low birth rate of new inner-city enterprises. A further 40% of change is seemingly accounted for by short-distance plant relocations from the inner city, either to other parts of Johannesburg or adjacent industrial areas of the Witwatersrand.

Government[4]

The decision of the Gauteng provincial legislature to locate its capital in Johannesburg is arguably the most important single development for the inner city of the past two decades. There is almost uniform optimism that the decision is good for the inner city. The purpose of this section is to consider the economic implications of the Gauteng legislature's decision for the inner city. This will be done in two stages. First, the statistical structure and performance of the community, social and personal services sector is outlined, into which falls the government contribution to local economic product. Secondly, the potential impact of provincial government activities in the inner city is considered.

The community, social and personal services sector contributed 15.2% of South Africa's GDP in 1991, 15.7% in Gauteng, but in Johannesburg the sector accounts for only 12.3% of GGP. Moreover, although in the province and nationally the trend has been for the government contribution to increase, Figure 10.1 shows that the reverse is true in Johannesburg.

The community, social and personal services sector is crucially important to Johannesburg. In 1991 it accounted for as much as a third of Johannesburg's formal-sector employment, up from 31% in 1980. The sector has two main components:

- *general government activities*: including the legislative, executive, and judicial activities of central, provincial and local governments, as well as the educational, health, police, and other   second- and third-tier government services
- *social and personal services:* including services and activities such as commercial schools and colleges, medical and dental practices, welfare

---

4. This section is based on the contribution of Roland Hunter to Tomlinson (1995).

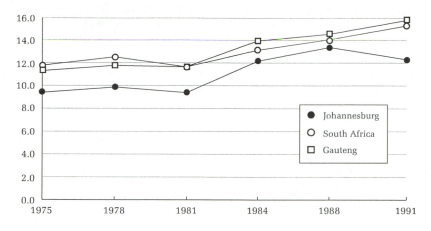

Figure 10.1 Share of community, social and personal services in GGP: Johannesburg, Gauteng and South Africa (%).

organizations, business, professional and labour organizations, religious organizations, political organizations and cultural societies, motion picture and other entertainment services, amusement and recreational services, and personal and household services.

General government is dominant: on a national basis, general government makes up 87% of community, social and personal services, and in Gauteng the average is over 90%. In Johannesburg, however, only about two-thirds of the sector consists of general government. It is possible to interpret this as indicating that in Johannesburg the social and personal services component is unusually large: and indeed, it comprises fully a quarter of the national subsector. This no doubt has much to do with the Central Witwatersrand's economic dominance. It could also be surmised that government activities that might otherwise have been located in Johannesburg by virtue of its centrality were located in Pretoria by administrative fiat. Johannesburg's share of the national general government subsector is relatively small at approximately 7%.

Johannesburg's government social and personal services sector has substantially underperformed when compared with the nation. Over the period between 1975 and 1991, for example, the national social and personal services subsector doubled in size, while in general government the increase was around 75%. The same increases were apparent in the magisterial districts, which now comprise Gauteng. In Johannesburg, on the other hand, GGP arising from social and personal services increased by only 38% over the same period, and the increase in general government was 41%.

In this light, the decision to establish Johannesburg as the seat of provincial government, and the economic implications that may flow from this, therefore appear decidedly significant. Sceptics might, of course, suspect much "hoopla". A substantial government centre is no guarantee of general prosperity. In Washington DC, for example, the capital is surrounded by poverty. How then should the potential impact on the inner-city economy be assessed? In the following discussion, distinctions are drawn between immediate material effects and indirect "spin-off" and "confidence" effects.

Potential immediate benefits are as follows.

- *Office rentals*: private sector property-owners in the mid-town district, in particular, stand to benefit from the prospective government precinct.
- *Employment*: may be generated in the formal and informal commercial and catering sectors, as well as in construction.
- *Local commercial and catering market*: an influx of new provincial staff constitutes an extra potential market to which inner-city service providers and caterers, formal and informal, in principle have daily access. In addition, there is potential office-related business – such as printing and publishing – generated by the provincial government.
- *Council revenue base*: in the short term, the increased use of council services such as water and electricity will boost council revenues. Over the medium to longer term any improvements in property values will increase rate revenues.

The following observations provide some indication of the likely scale of these effects.

First, as at March 1995 the provincial government's estimated requirements for new office space in the inner city may reach $100\,000\,m^2$. This is a relatively large office space requirement in relation to there being a 17.4% ($367\,000\,m^2$) vacancy level in A and B grade office space in the inner city (including Braamfontein). The provincial government therefore appears likely to take up approximately 27% of the vacant A and B grade office space in the inner city, a sizeable proportion of such vacant space. The creation of a provincial government precinct will also have important effects on the distribution of office vacancies in the inner city. Much of the prospective precinct will be located in the mid-town district, where the total of vacant A and B grade space[5] is $62\,000\,m^2$. Vacancy rates in this district will therefore fall to very low levels over the next few years, while there will be some additional take-up of space in these grades in the commercial and financial districts.

To the extent that the take-up of office space shores up property values in the mid-town district and leads to an increase in the consumption of services, council revenue will be bolstered.

Secondly, the number of government staff who will be taking up inner-city employment over the next two years will be of the order of 8000 persons. On a base of 293 000 existing formal-sector jobs in the inner city, this is a welcome but not overwhelming gain for the inner city.

---

5. The different types of office space are defined and discussed in the section on physical decay.

Third, potential spin-offs for inner-city commerce and catering are especially difficult to estimate at this stage. For example, although it is true that most of the well remunerated management echelon of the provincial government will be working from the inner city, this comprises only 130 people; and high income earners probably spend only a small amount on inner-city commerce and catering enterprises. The potential extra market for such firms is unlikely to be large. Greater long-term benefits are probably to be found for the accommodation and conference industries.

The indirect effects are also potentially important.

* *Boost in confidence in the inner city*   While few inner-city companies regarded the new proximity of government as in any way affecting their direct business operations, almost all suggested that the associated confidence boost would necessarily help the inner city. Such a perspective is presumably to some extent self-fulfilling. It should be noted, however, that the boost in confidence has no effect on firms that have already left the inner city. At best, therefore, the confidence boost slows the departure of firms.
* *Increased policy attention*   Possibly one of the more important effects of locating the provincial government in the inner city is that the area is likely to be the subject of substantially increased policy attention. Given that some of the important problems of the inner city are susceptible to policy decision (crime, cleansing, housing), this is all to the good.
* *Triggering of private sector investments*   Investments plans that have been on hold pending an improvement in inner-city market prospects, or new investment plans could be implemented following the announcement.
* *Improved physical environment*   Improvements in the physical environment could make the inner city more attractive for some users.
* *Easier access to credit*   Private banks could re-evaluate their credit risk assessments for inner-city residential and other loans, particularly for public servants.
* *Attraction of international organizations*   Possible location in the inner city of the permanent offices of major international organizations such as the UN, the Commonwealth, and the Organisation of African Unity.

Business and financial services

The inter-metropolitan pattern of the location of the top 100 companies, listed by the *Financial Mail* and shown in Table 10.2, shows the changing role of Johannesburg and the inner city as the location of the leading business enterprises in South Africa. It is evident that the Central Witwatersrand has always been South Africa's leading location for company headquarters offices and that its position over the past 30 years has strengthened markedly. In 1965 the Central Witwatersrand was home for the corporate head offices of

46 of South Africa's leading business enterprises, by 1994 this figure had grown to 65 of the country's leading enterprises, which, together, control over 72% of the country's listed assets. (There are, in addition, unlisted companies and there is also the government, which controls approximately 50% of the

Table 10.2 The location of headquarters offices of the top 100 leading enterprises, 1965–94.

Company headquarters	1965	1970	1975	1980	1994
Central Witwatersrand	46	51	56	52	65
Durban	19	15	8	9	9
Cape Town	13	8	9	13	12
East London	7	5	7	2	8
Stellenbosch	5	5	5	5	4
Pretoria	4	3	4	5	1
Vereeniging	4	5	3	4	0
Port Elizabeth	2	2	0	1	0
Rest of SA	0	6	8	9	1

country's productive assets.)[6]

The increasing inter-metropolitan dominance of the Central Witwatersrand has not, however, translated into benefits for the inner city. This conclusion can be demonstrated through considering the intra-metropolitan changes in corporate office location of:

• giant companies and the top 300 industrial listed by the *Financial Mail*
• the leading mining houses, banks and life assurance offices
• leading retail organizations and building concerns
• producer services, in terms of advertising, accounting and legal services.

South Africa giants and the top 300 industrials

The category of South African corporate "giants" includes all economic sectors of activity. The table of "giants" is headed by the country's leading life assurance companies, mining houses, banks and organizations such as the state pension fund and South African Reserve Bank. In terms of this category of enterprises, in 1994 Central Witwatersrand was the base for 19 of these 30. The inner city is the location for 13 of them, the balance are located in Johannesburg's northern suburbs.[7] Indeed, in total, only six moves were recorded across the top 30 enterprises. Of these moves, only two were inter-metropolitan shifts of offices (both from Pretoria to Johannesburg); the

---

6. I am assuming that the top 100 companies are all listed on the stock exchange.
7. The major decentralized notes of new activity are Sandton, Bedfordview, Rosebank, Parktown and the newly emerging foci of Dunkeld, Illovo and even Midrand. These areas are what is referred to as the "northern suburbs" or decentralized locations.

remainder were minor shifts taking place within a short distance. A different picture emerges, however, when the focus is placed upon the listing of the top 100 industrial enterprises. As indicated above, Central Witwatersrand is the home for 65 of the top 100 enterprises. Nonetheless, among this particular subgroup of enterprises, only a few companies retain head offices in the CBD. Indeed, by comparing the 1982 and 1994 locations of head offices of these 65 firms, a clear picture emerges of a flight from the CBD to decentralized locations elsewhere within the metropolitan region. In total, the CBD lost the head-quarters offices of a remarkable number of 17 of these 65 corporations; in other words, more than a quarter of these enterprises moved their head-office functions from the CBD to decentralized locations within the metropolitan region.

If the analysis is extended to cover the group of the top 300 business enterprises, the picture is confirmed once again of an exodus of head-office functions from the Johannesburg inner city to emerging decentralized nodes of activity, particularly in Sandton. Among the group of top industrials ranked between 101 and 300 in the *Financial Mail* listings, at least 104 (52%) are presently headquartered in the Central Witwatersrand. This finding underscores, once again, the significance of the city as a corporate location centre. The importance may be greater even than indicated, for undercounting may have occurred due to the fact that it was not possible to identify the location of the company head offices of 14 of this group of 200 companies. Of this total of 104 enterprises, only 28 had head offices situated in the CBD.

As with the top 100 industrial concerns in Central Witwatersrand, there was again a strong trend for established companies ranked between 101 and 300 to leave the inner city for the northern suburbs and beyond. Included in this category are many of South Africa's new, growing enterprises, which chose to establish their corporate headquarters in the Central Witwatersrand but outside the inner city.

The broad trends that appear to emerge from this analysis are of a greater degree of stability in location of head offices among the group of "giants" than among the next tier of large, particularly industrial, enterprises. A clear trend is evident for an exodus of the headquarters offices of established top industrial firms from the inner city of Johannesburg. In addition, the groups of growing, often newer, enterprises have shunned the inner city in preference for locating their new head offices in the decentralized office nodes.

Mining houses, life offices and banks

Many of the group of eight major mining houses fall into the category of the South African "giant" enterprises analyzed above. Of the eight mining houses listed by the *Financial Mail* survey in 1994, seven are based in Johannesburg. Not surprisingly, therefore, Johannesburg is the control centre for the mining sector of South Africa. Typical of the experience of the "giant" enterprises as a group, the category of mining houses is stable in terms of head-office location. A comparison of the location of these head offices in 1983 and 1994 reveals that six of the seven mining houses have remained in the Johannesburg inner city.

Of the big five life assurers, only one is headquartered in the Central Witwatersrand. However, in total, metropolitan Johannesburg is the base for 10 of the leading 18 life assurance concerns. In terms of their present location, nine of these Johannesburg-based life assurers are headquartered in the CBD. This pattern of corporate office headquarters is almost unchanged from the situation in 1983.

The corporate offices of South Africa's leading commercial and merchant banking institutions exhibit a similar pattern of stability rather than change. Johannesburg is the leading national centre for banking, with the headquarters offices of seven of the top ten banking institutions. In overall terms Johannesburg is the headquarters for 11 of the leading 16 banking institutions in the country. It is notable that nearly all these institutions cluster their corporate head offices within the inner city. This pattern was established by the early 1980s and remains unchanged since that time.

Overall, among this important cluster of organizations relating to mining, banking and life assurance, the prominence of Johannesburg nationally is once more in evidence. Moreover, these sectors of economic enterprise, with three prominent exceptions, have remained committed to headquarters office locations in the inner city of Johannesburg.

Retailing and construction

Although the retailing outlets of these organizations are well represented in Johannesburg, the headquarters offices of the retail sector are predominantly situated outside the city. In total, of the top ten retail organizations, seven are headquartered in either Cape Town or Durban. This pattern was established by the early 1980s and has not changed in terms of the inter-metropolitan location pattern. Of the three organizations within the Central Witwatersrand, none is presently situated in the inner city.

Unlike the retail stores sector, the building and construction sector is firmly concentrated nationally in Central Witwatersrand. In 1994, Johannesburg was the headquarters base for ten of the leading eleven enterprises in this sector and eleven of the top eighteen enterprises. Of the eleven leading Johannesburg-based enterprises, however, only two in 1994 were situated in the inner city. The majority of these firms have preferred to locate their business headquarters in the northern suburbs. In the 12-year period covered by this investigation, there were two cases of relocation of building and construction firms from the Johannesburg inner city.

Business services: accounting, advertising and legal

Given the close linkages of major accounting firms to the groups of South African industrial giants and of the leading industrial and financial enterprises, it is not surprising that there is a close relationship as regards their locational arrangement. All the group of seven leading accounting firms in national terms are based in Johannesburg. In respect of their locations within Johannesburg, there has been a notable shift. Only three of the seven largest accounting companies retain head offices in the inner city, as compared to the situation twelve years earlier when all seven were housed in the Johannesburg CBD.

The advertising sector is perhaps the most fluid in terms of the rise and fall of particular agencies and in terms of merger activity. The pattern of the 15 leading national advertising agencies in 1994 showed the importance of metropolitan Johannesburg for this sector: 14 of the largest 15 agencies are based in Johannesburg. This dominance of Johannesburg was established already by 1981 when a similar listing of the leading 15 agencies showed all to be situated in Johannesburg. In terms of the locational preference within the metropolitan area, the 1994 data shows that all 14 agencies have their headquarters in decentralized office areas. The most important node for advertising headquarters is that of Sandton. By contrast, a 1981 listing of the then parallel top 15 agencies showed 7 agencies situated in the inner city.

Lastly, the legal services sector has exhibited a slightly different trend to that of the accounting or advertising agencies. The location of the courts in the inner city has necessitated that the major legal firms retain a presence, if not a head-office function within or close to the Johannesburg CBD. However, by 1994 decentralization pressures were affecting even the location of legal enterprises. Only six of the top ten legal firms were situated directly in the CBD; the other four were again located in the northern suburbs. Moreover, some those firms that retained an inner-city office were also expanding their branch offices in decentralized locations, most importantly, once again in Sandton.

Explanations

Two major conclusions are evident. First, at the inter-metropolitan scale of analysis, the Central Witwatersrand is by far South Africa's leading headquarters office location. Since the mid-1980s this control function *vis-à-vis* other South African cities has greatly strengthened. In terms of banking institutions, finance, mining houses and leading industrial corporations, Johannesburg's dominance is unchallenged. In the light of this, it is not surprising that the metropolitan area is also the major national cluster for such business services as accounting, law and advertising.

Secondly, at the intra-metropolitan scale of analysis a more complex picture emerges. The overall trend is for a weakening hold and attractiveness of the CBD as a head-office location for virtually all sectors of the economy. Indeed, with the sole exception of the "giant" enterprises, decentralization has been taking place in almost every segment of finance, banking, mining houses, construction, industrial and business service sectors. Broadly speaking the overall trend is therefore one that might be described as "dispersion within concentration".

An explanation of these trends centres on six factors:

- infrastructure requirements
- convenience factors
- deterrent factors
- corporate restructuring
- issues of prestige
- corporate coercion
- sunk investments (being "locked in").

These are not listed in order of importance; indeed, they may have different importance to different companies.

The main infrastructural advantage, from the point of view of head-office location decisions, is undoubtedly its public transport system. This becomes a determining factor if the head office concerned employs many people who rely upon public transport to get to work. For example, South Africa's four largest retail banking groups account for nearly 10% of formal employment in the inner city. The bulk of this staff are women; in one bank they constitute more than 70% of total inner-city staff. Most of these women are clerical and administrative staff whose pay is such that they rely on public transport. In contrast, for smaller head offices, the bulk of whose staff commute by car, this factor alone tends to encourage decentralization to the north. The inner city has further infrastructure advantages, however. In at least one case, this was a crucial point. A major bank's decision to stay in the inner city was based largely upon its advantages in respect of transport, power and communications infrastructure.

Secondly, convenience factors relate to the supposedly greater convenience of operating a business from the inner city, because of more immediate access to customers, suppliers, business service providers, tax authorities, local and provincial government, the stock exchange, the courts, and so on. This is a traditionally cited advantage of the inner city, with publicity and property brochures constantly extolling these benefits. However, interviewees suggested that, although such factors may have been important once, they are no longer significant (Tomlinson 1995). It should be remembered that the province has become an extensive urban region, and a location in the inner city does not necessarily optimize convenience in this broader context.

Thirdly, the standard set of reasons advanced by all interviewees for the flight of certain categories of head-office companies from the inner city include street attacks, a lack of street hygiene (including the question of street trading), poor conditions for vehicles (poor road access, traffic congestion and a lack of parking), and "inner-city decay" more generally. Inner-city crime is clearly the single most important aspect. Several inner-city head offices keep statistics relating to attacks on staff, and several indicated that further attacks on staff could be the swing factor forcing them out of the inner city.

Fourthly, several interviewees indicated that corporate restructuring played a role in head-office location decisions. For example, changes in management philosophies and practices in respect of the centralization of management authority, and the location of group functions, operational divisions, and other corporate segments, had a distinct bearing on the nature and location of head offices. In one case, a company decentralized its headquarters as part of a comprehensive restructuring process intended to centralize head-office departments that were previously scattered across several buildings, and to shift head-office functions away from an operational site in the CBD. In other cases, changes resulting from mergers and from unbundling had implications for the spatial distribution of corporate head offices, which were not immediately attributable to the characteristics of the inner city itself. The approach has been to house the factory-type operations in the CBD while moving the prestigious functions to Sandton.

Fifthly, concern with corporate identity and visibility may cause companies to seek a prestigious location. In some cases, concern with company history and tradition has become important. The fact that there has been a South African Breweries presence at 2 Jan Smuts Avenue for over 60 years is clearly important to the company. The inner city benefits from such tendencies.

Sixthly, companies with large commitments in the inner city naturally have a substantial interest in taking steps to protect their assets. Companies wishing to leave the inner city stand to face certain pressures to stay. Two forms of pressure in particular were described by interviewees:

- from owners: dominant shareholders in a company who also have extensive inner-city property investments can and do instruct their subsidiaries to remain in the inner city, as a means of protecting their investments
- from clients and customers: large property interests can and do threaten to withdraw their accounts from business service providers, as a means of forcing them to stay in the inner city.

Last, it is worth paying special attention to the inner-city financial sector, which is locked into the CBD by virtue of its large investments there. Despite the manifest advantages arising from public transport and other infrastructure, one bank executive indicated that his corporation would walk away from the inner city were it possible to let their offices for rental income. Three of the four banks are adopting the contrary route of investing in inner-city complexes and of centralizing many of their corporate functions. In the process, all three groups have made substantial investments in the inner city. One bank's complex, for example, represents an investment of R1.25 billion. Functions performed in these offices include management services, accounting, computing, human resources, marketing, communications, technology, property and merchant banking.

Commerce, catering and accommodation[8]

The retail mix of the inner city has shifted to accommodate the African consumer and changed business climate of the area. Over a decade ago, the inner-city retail economy was conditioned by the consumer demands of a White buying public. To satisfy these particular consumer demands and tastes an array of high-order, specialist retail functions existed alongside a wide range of more general retail outlets headed by major chain stores and a mass of small independent line shops. One aspect of the changing retail economy is the disappearance or run-down of these specialist, high-order types of retailing activities. Examples would include the departure from the inner city, mainly to new suburban shopping malls, of exclusive ladies' boutiques and jewellery outlets, specialist medical retail outlets, and a range of other shops that cater primarily for a White consumer clientele, such as hobby and toy shops and interior design establishments. Another loss from the inner city has been the run-down of the retailers that cater for the tourist market; examples would be certain jewellers and curio outlets, which again have sought the suburban locations. This aspect of the changing retail landscape thus links to the general downgrading of the inner-city hotel and tourism industry. For example, although most hotels within the inner city have continued to do business, most have reduced their star rating and some have reduced their room capacity.[9] Luxury hotels are now mostly found in the suburbs of Sandton and Rosebank. Upmarket restaurants, also, have tended to relocate; although the fast food industry, mirroring changes in the retail sector, has grown in the inner city.

Underpinning the "downgrading" of inner-city retailing is the rise in crime; one property manager observed that "every single retailer has been robbed, held up or had an attempted break-in". One index of the escalating effect of crime on the landscape of inner-city retailing is that, whereas a decade ago most shops had open display windows, now the majority have security roller shutters.

"Downgrading" has impacted clearly on streets where departmental stores have been replaced by small general dealers, many of which link to the informal retail economy. Behind this shift was the recession of the late 1980s, which saw the closure or relocation of many traditional White retail outlets leaving vacant retail space that the property sector was willing to fill with new tenants geared more specifically to low-income markets. In the slow economic upturn since the elections in April 1994, the property sector is beginning to replace a segment of these downgraded retail sites in the more prestigious areas with higher-grade tenants.

The "downgrading" of the inner-city retail economy should not, however,

---

8. I am especially indebted to Jayne Rogerson for her contribution to this section.
9. The five-star Carlton hotel, once South Africa's foremost hotel, now has a 20% occupancy rate.

be associated with a collapse of the retail sector. Indeed, the retail vacancy pattern in the CBD has remained constantly low as new types of retail operations have immediately replaced those departing enterprises. The emergent and growing types of formal retailing activities are clearly those geared to the mounting purchasing power and tastes of the African consumer. Significantly, the sector of the retail trade engaged in furniture has remained situated in the inner city, experiencing no significant downturn. A growing area of the retail economy that is definitely associated with new African purchasing power is that of men's outfitters. This sort of development is linked to the growth of a new professional class of African (mainly) male middle management working in the inner city with relatively high disposable incomes. The small number of African professional women accounts in part for the much weaker position of ladies' outfitters in the inner city and the flight of the high-class boutiques to the suburbs in search of the affluent White woman consumer.

The role and responses of the major retail chains to the changing complexion of the inner city has been a key factor in altering the retail landscape. A few high-class retail chains have left the inner city entirely. The majority, however, have re-adjusted their operations and re-geared themselves to the changed market environment. Another form of response has been to focus the store's mix of merchandise in the inner-city stores to their most basic and reasonably priced items. A further common adjustment made in most of the clothing chain stores is to stock up and expand their range of children's clothing, a major purchase of African consumers. Beyond shifting the range of their goods, many of the chains offer cards that allow consumers to purchase goods on a six-months interest-free payment scheme. In turn, this has had a negative effect on smaller retail establishments. In common with the clothing stores, the food retailing sector has adjusted also to accommodate African tastes, introducing, for example, the sale of chicken. It is significant that those fast food retail establishments that have failed to readjust their product mix to the African consumer are suffering in financial terms.

Accompanying the changes in the formal retail sector has been a tremendous growth in the informal sector. In the early 1980s, during the heyday of official repression of African street traders in the ostensibly White city, there were fewer than 300 hawkers functioning in the Johannesburg inner city. Nowadays, perhaps the best estimate of the size of the informal sector is drawn from the former Johannesburg City Council's Health, Housing and Urbanization Directorate, which suggests that in 1993–94 there was a total of roughly 15000 hawkers operating in the Greater Johannesburg area. Of this total, the number of hawkers regularly trading in the inner city is unclear; nonetheless, one commonly quoted statistic is 4000 (*The Star*, 31 August 1993). In addition, there has been the establishment and expansion of several flea-markets in the inner city; such markets include both independent hawkers and many traders who are linked to formal retail establishments in the city.

The three key factors that underpin the growth of informal retailing are:

- the changed official policy environment from repression to one of greater tolerance and even, through certain initiatives, the limited promotion of street vending
- problems with labour absorption in the formal economy
- the growth of poverty in the context of an expanding city population, particularly with the demise of influx control regulations, and more recently with the arrival of considerable numbers of international immigrants.

One important dimension of this contemporary informal retail economy is the substantial number of traders other than South Africans on the pavements of inner-city Johannesburg. The most widely quoted estimate of the number of foreigners engaged in hawking activities is 7000 of the total of 15000 in Johannesburg as a whole (*The Star*, 18 August 1994). There are several suggestions that a major segment of these foreign hawkers are communities of illegal immigrants who originate variously from China, Korea, Zimbabwe, Mozambique, Nigeria, Zaire and even eastern Europe (*The Star*, 10 March, 18 August, 13 October 1994). In addition to these hawkers, there are also many traders who originate in Swaziland, Ghana, Ivory Coast, India and Pakistan. Fragmentary evidence points to the fact that there are distinct specialities in informal retailing, which are the domain of particular immigrant communities.

The vast majority of informal retailing taking place in the inner city of Johannesburg falls into the category of "survivalist enterprise". The characteristics of the informal sector are that 52% are male, more than three-quarters are in the 25–49 age category, and 96% are African. In spatial terms, although retailing occurs almost as a ubiquitous activity throughout the inner-city zone, there are notable concentrations of informal traders, particularly around the taxi and bus termini and the major formal retailing streets of the CBD. By contrast, the tempo of hawking is much lower in other areas of the inner city, most notably in the financial district, which is dominated by office functions of the mining houses. In the industrial areas of the southern strip of the inner city, hawking activities are dominated by food vending operations.

The beginnings of physical decay

Johannesburg's CBD is experiencing a declining office function with high vacancies and poor rental performance, a downgrading of its retail environment, increasing demand for inner-city housing, a loss of manufacturing enterprises and jobs,[10] and rapidly increasing use of the CBD by emerging[11] entrepreneurs. This contraction of the past functions of the CBD is particularly significant in the case of the office market since it is because of the vacancy levels and low rentals achieved in this market that physical decay is beginning.

189

From a comparative point of view, rentals for A, B, C and D grade space[12] within the CBD lagged behind those of both the Cape Town and Durban metropolitan areas. Further comparative evidence of the weak performance of office space within the Johannesburg CBD is furnished by Rode (1993), who computed growth in demand for office space (grades A, B and C) for the period 1981–92. In addition to calculating the growth in demand as a growth rate for the entire period, it was also expressed as the compound growth in demand over the 12-year period. The results revealed major inter-city variations in patterns of office demand, with growth in Johannesburg's CBD described as "dismal". Rode (1993: 7) argued that "even buoyant demand for office space in the decentralized nodes was insufficient to pull up demand for the entire Johannesburg metropolitan area to the levels achieved for the Durban or Cape Town metropolitan areas". Thus, while the demand for decentralized office space has been climbing steeply for over a decade, demand for CBD space in the latter half of the 1980s exhibited a declining trend.

Tables 10.3 and 10.4 show that it is only in the exchange and finance districts that there is little vacancy among A and B grade office space. The commercial and mid-town[13] districts are experiencing an inexorable relocation of the focus of prestige office functions to the former districts. The additional large availability of marginal C and D grade office stock within the city, coupled with the protracted economic recession, has meant that rentals have not increased and tenants are able to negotiate them from a position of strength. This over-supply of low-grade stock, together with low rentals, has meant that in many cases the rentals achievable are lower than the building's basic operating costs (rates, refuse, security and cleaning), and landlords have seen no other way out than to board up or demolish buildings to either retail or ground level. These disused or razed buildings have led to increasing blight.

---

10. Surprisingly, given the manufacturing trends already noted, Rode (1994) illustrates that, although the industrial townships within the southern strip may lag slightly behind the average industrial rentals for the Witwatersrand, the difference falls within a 10% margin and on a large space of $5000\,m^2$ in fact achieves a higher rental. The industrial southern strip comprises mainly old multi-storey industrial stock, yet its locational advantages ensure that rental levels are sustained.

11. This is a reference to micro and small African entrepreneurs.

12. A Grade: prime space, generally not older than 15 years, prime location/high quality finished, on-site parking (unless special circumstances pertain), air-conditioned; market rentals near the top of the range.
    B Grade: generally older buildings, but accommodation close to modern standards, prime location, air-conditioned, on-site parking (unless special circumstances pertain).
    C Grade: an older building but in good condition, although finishes not up to modern standards, good location, may or may not have on-site parking, unlikely to be centrally air-conditioned.
    D Grade: all remaining buildings.

13. The mid-town district will obtain some relief from the new provincial government's requiring approximately $100000\,m^2$ of A and B grade space.

Table 10.3   Office space within the CBD (m^2).

District Grade	Exchange	Financial	Commercial	Mid-town	Station	Braam- fontein
A	242 588	391 622	287 667	34 680	5 635	261 260
B	116 541	275 143	120 067	115 479	80 586	177 843
C	54 513	271 135	114 645	264 116	164 172	282 207
D	46 115	34 100	156 642	69 597	80 798	88 122

Source: Ampros 1994a–f.

Table 10.4   Office vacancies within the CBD and Braamfontein (%).

District	A Grade	B Grade	C Grade	Total
Exchange	5.8	30.4	32.4	16.2
Financial	8.9	33.3	30.9	22.4
Commercial	19.0	27.0	41.3	25.8
Mid-town	65.8	33.6	42.4	41.9
Station	0.0	2.7	18.0	12.7
Braamfontein	8.9	9.3	16.6	12.0

Source: Ampros 1994a–f.

Emerging enterprise[14]

Broadly speaking, a distinction can be drawn between three kinds of small businesses. First, *survival enterprises* of the informal economy, which are a set of activities undertaken primarily by unemployed African people unable to find regular employment. In this group of enterprises, incomes usually fall short of minimum standards, little capital is invested, skills training is minimal, and there is little prospect for upward growth into a viable small business enterprise. Examples of such survivalist enterprise in the inner city would be garbage scavengers, itinerant hawkers, car-parkers and car-washers. The second category of businesses are *micro-enterprises*, which are very small enterprises often involving the owner, some family members and, at most, one to four employees. Although such businesses often lack the trappings of "formality" such as licences or formal premises, and entrepreneurs sometimes have only rudimentary business skills and training, many micro-enterprises will make the transition into viable small businesses. Currently, the best prospects for micro-enterprise development are seen in the spheres of production-related activities. Finally, small enterprises constitute the basis of the *formal small business economy*, with employment levels between 5 and 50 workers. Such enterprises usually are generally owned by Whites (albeit

---

14. I have again to acknowledge my debt to Chris and Jayne Rogerson.

with a strong segment of Asian-owned business), owner-managed, operate from fixed premises and fulfil all the trappings associated with formality.

In this section the focus is on emerging enterprise, defined as micro and small African enterprise. The majority of such enterprises are micro rather than small: they involve only the owner, some family member(s), and at the most one or two paid employees. The information on these enterprises is based on surveys of property brokers and letting agents, and 85 emerging entrepreneurs.[15] A sample of 85 interviews is obviously not statistically representative; nonetheless, every effort was made to make the sample broadly representative through instructing interviewers to undertake questionnaires in a range of inner-city commercial properties. The majority of the properties were C and D grade offices.

It was found that the major segment of present-day emerging African enterprise in the inner city is composed of production micro-enterprises. Indeed, the group of manufacturing micro-enterprises formed 53% of the total sample of enterprises. Within the cluster of manufacturing enterprises are a range of activities that, with the exception of one furniture manufacturer and one leatherware concern, would all be classified as falling within the clothing and textiles sector.[16] Beyond these production operations, the next most significant sphere of activities relates to training and skills upgrading serving, in particular, dressmaking. This again underlines the importance of an emerging African clothing production sector within the inner city of Johannesburg. A group of offices for NGOs, trade unions and trade associations, including traditional healers, formed another prominent group of ten interviewees; however, such organizations do not constitute emergent small African enterprise *per se*, albeit some of them may function in a supportive role. If this group of interviews is excluded from the total, the share of production enterprise in the overall sample rises to 60% of all African enterprise in the Johannesburg inner city. Outside these leading spheres of activity, the other African enterprises operating in the inner city were highly diverse in their activities. These included a small group of legal professionals, retail outlets, repair services, property and insurance sales, a modelling agency, hair salon, computer agency, car hire facility, photographic studio/video hire outlet, and a photocopying/typing centre.

The interviews conducted with property brokers and letting agents revealed that distinct shifts have occurred in the nature of inner-city African enterprises in Johannesburg. Historically, there had always been a few African professionals (mostly lawyers) working in the CBD. Beginning in the late 1980s, however, a fresh phase of African enterprise development was marked by an exodus of businesses from the violence-wracked townships. Former

---

15. The surveys were conducted by Chris and Jayne Rogerson.
16. Male and female employees were represented approximately equally in this stereotype area of "women's work".

home-based enterprises, in activities such as light manufacturing, particularly of clothing production and sewing, led the march of new African enterprises into the inner city. This locational shift of enterprises coincided in the phase of late apartheid with a more relaxed official legislative environment concerning where African people could live and establish formal businesses in the city.

It is evident that during the past two years in particular there has been a noticeable upturn in the number of African enterprises establishing within the CBD. This situation underscores the fact that, although violence was the initial trigger for an influx of enterprises into the Johannesburg CBD, this is clearly no longer the case, and the growth of such enterprises has gained a cumulative momentum within the inner city. Indeed, the expansion of African enterprise has reached the point that it is now recognized by the institutional property sector as a "feature" of the Johannesburg inner city. Nevertheless, it must be acknowledged that African enterprise still represents only a minority segment of the overall business profile in central Johannesburg. The property sector estimates that African enterprise constitutes "still well under 20% of the tenant profile".

Overwhelmingly, business owners (59%) were residents of Soweto commuting to their inner-city businesses by taxis, private car and only occasionally by train. When questioned as to whether or not the business was growing, only a minority of enterprises responded that they were either living "from hand to mouth" or that profits were falling, often blamed on high rentals. Nevertheless, clear signs of economic health were evident, as 61% of respondents indicated elements of growth. New expansion was indicated variously in terms of increased office space, new machinery and equipment, growing numbers of employees, and a wider customer base.

The picture presented above of a growing community of African entrepreneurs in the Johannesburg inner city must be qualified by an appreciation of the extraordinarily high failure rate that occurs among these emerging businesses. It was estimated by the property brokers and managers that, of the new African businesses that opened in the inner city, "between 50–60% fail to survive". The high failure rate was emphasized in one interview, where it was observed that "If a hundred companies moved in, 40% would have died within two months". The reason why most of these emerging African enterprises fail is probably related to lack of business skills and lack of access to credit facilities, factors that have been widely identified in small enterprise research in South Africa.

In this respect, few African enterprises in the inner city were receiving any support from development agencies or banks. Most had not applied for assistance or they indicated that they had been discouraged from applying from the dismal experience of others. Nevertheless, a significant proportion (roughly one-third) of (particularly manufacturing) micro-enterprises had tried to secure financial support for their business enterprise from banks or organizations such as the Small Business Development Corporation. None had been successful, with interviewees perceiving that they were "refused because we are African", "because the business was too small" or "they did not want to help us". The disappointment was expressed strongly by one woman clothing entrepreneur who thought that "Jo'burg was the place in which the SBDC could provide support, unlike Soweto". Refusal from banks was normally explained as due to the enterprise's lack of collateral. Of the sample of manufacturing enterprises, only in one case out of 45 was any financial support forthcoming from development agencies.

The property sector assists African enterprise development only through the facility of a monthly lease agreement. Such a lease is viewed as both simpler for tenants to understand and also not a long-term commitment. Only after, perhaps, a period of one year of continually renewed monthly leases and after exhibiting clear signs of economic survival of an enterprise would the institutional sector enter into a longer-term lease agreement (normally one year).

It must be appreciated that the major property companies do not set aside specific buildings for use by African tenants. Nonetheless, by the very nature of their space requirements and ability to pay, African tenants are inevitably limited to and channelled towards several low-grade buildings, tending to group together in surplus C and D grade office space. It was disclosed that landlords are apprehensive about leasing retail space to new African tenants because of the particular visibility of retailing and the consequent deleterious effects that a bad tenant may have on the image of a building. More specifically, if tenants have low standards or (as is commonly the case with many new African businesses) exhibit a high failure rate, resulting either in shop vacancies and occupation by a succession of new and different ventures, then it is seen as negatively reflecting on the image of both the building and the property landlord.

The perception of African entrepreneurs and organizations in locational choice of the inner city was highly revealing. Questioned as to the advantages of an inner-city location, most respondents gave more than one factor. Nevertheless, issues concerning the advantages of the inner city as a market or access to suppliers were paramount considerations. The role of the inner city as a potential zone for enjoying economies of agglomeration was evident in the majority of responses. Overwhelmingly, entrepreneurs stressed the vital attractions of the inner city as a market for both African and, in some cases, White consumers, its accessibility in terms of transport facilities and, finally, its advantages as regards access to suppliers of inputs for both production and retail types of enterprises. The sheer availability of premises and of space in the inner city was a factor noted also by many entrepreneurs (18%), particularly by those who had searched unsuccessfully in other areas and who could not be accommodated in crowded home premises or townships.

One striking finding was the high number of African entrepreneurs who stressed the advantages offered by the security of the inner city. Indeed, a remarkable 40% of survey respondents indicated the positive security advantages of business locations in the inner city, with the low number of burglaries cited as a major advantage, especially in relation to the problems of operating former township-based businesses. One respondent even added that they saw the inner city as a "clean" environment. Available water and regular electricity supplies "with no power failures" were added advantages for some enterprises. It is significant that the cheapness of business premises in the inner city was a factor mentioned by only two respondents.

Overall, what these findings underscore is the radically different perceptions of the inner city offered by emerging entrepreneurs as compared to the views of White business enterprise, the popular press or officials concerning the state of the inner city. Commonly, business enterprise and the popular press stress images of lawlessness and of the "hawker problem" in explaining the "miserable death" of the Johannesburg CBD (*The Star*, 22 December 1994). In addition, city officials raise issues of "insecurity" and of problems caused by the growth of informal employment in terms of "the general housekeeping and image of the inner-city area". Such views were supported also by the property sector, which argued that the competition offered by pavement hawkers was a negative factor for retail activities, resulting in some tenants vacating premises and instead trading on the street. In marked contrast to these views offered by the property sector, city officials and the popular press, such factors were not apparent in the responses of African small enterprise. Rather, the survey findings underlined the fact that African entrepreneurs in inner Johannesburg do not perceive the city in the same manner as large (primarily White) business enterprise or city officials. In sum, most African entrepreneurs expressed considerable satisfaction with their choice of location in the Johannesburg inner city. When questioned whether they had plans for future relocation, the vast majority indicated a desire to retain business premises in the inner city. In a few cases entrepreneurs, however, expressed a desire to move to other locations. However, the most common preference was expressed as a move back to suitable township business premises, which might offer the advantage of closeness to place of residence.

The partiality for an inner-city location also arises from the fact that it is the source of the inputs for virtually all the production micro-enterprises. Overwhelmingly, the pattern is for these African clothing producers to secure their inputs from Indian retail suppliers or wholesalers. Indeed, there is a symbiotic set of linkages between the Indian retail and wholesale clothing trade and the African inner-city manufacturers. Several producers were clearly involved in forms of subcontracting to primarily Indian-owned retail outlets (in one case the linkage was to a White-owned retail outlet).

Apart from sales of produce back to the Indian retail sector, most clothing producers sold their outputs independently to hawkers. This network of linkages of inner-city producers to a community of pavement sellers clearly accounts for the overall lack of negative feeling expressed towards the hawker community by the clothing entrepreneurs. Other supply outlets included selling in township areas, around mines, specialist networks such as the Zionist Church and, in two cases, of bulk sales to Swaziland.

In conclusion, the inner-city area has functioned to support and nurture the development of primarily White small enterprise. The question now is whether the inner city will retain this traditional role as a small enterprise hatchery, transferring that function to foster the upgrading and capacity of communities of emergent African entrepreneurs. Particularly relevant is the finding that most African entrepreneurs fall outside the network of development support agencies.

Development policy

Johannesburg's economy has undergone considerable change in the past decade or two. Manufacturing output has declined in absolute terms. The service sector has grown, with the exception of commerce, catering and accommodation, but it has done so more slowly than the national average. The growth that has occurred in business and financial services is increasingly inaccessible to the mass of the country's low-income population. Not only is the city's economic position ebbing, its ability to contribute to the relief of poverty is also waning. What is government doing about it?

Central government has historically promoted Johannesburg's economic misfortune. This policy goes back to the turn of the century, when Paul Kruger, president of the Transvaal Republic, distrusted the "uitlanders" (outsiders) who arrived to develop the goldfields. In more virulent form, the National Party opposed employment creation in Johannesburg as it would abet African urbanization. The country has experienced decades of controls on industrial development in Johannesburg and growth centre policies that favoured the country's periphery. These policies never had much effect (Tomlinson 1990), but in revised form they are still "on the books".

The central government Department of Trade and Industry is currently (late 1995) reviewing the decentralization policies and one can only speculate as to the conclusions it will draw. The reason for apprehension in this regard is that the Interim Constitution provides the provincial governments with particular powers with respect to trade and industry and regional planning. Apparently the meaning and implications of this divestiture of powers is somewhat contested, and it may well be that the Department of Trade and Industry employs its Regional Industrial Development Programme to control the flow of resources. The Department of Trade and Industry is also responsible for small business promotion and has formulated detailed policies in this area.

In the interim, on the basis of their Schedule 6 powers, provinces such as Gauteng have established agencies to promote trade and industry and to assist small business. Gauteng has two departments, Development Planning, and Economic Affairs and Finance, which exercise responsibility for aspects of economic development and location, and they are trying to co-ordinate their policies, which at this point are in the process of formulation. The provincial government itself subscribes to twelve "possible growth and development objectives", but these consist of statements such as "ensure coordination", "address areas of economic decline", "support areas of greatest need", "streamline regulations", and "develop coordinated information systems". In the interim, the provincial government is showing an interest in inner-city development, to the discomfort of city government. However, Johannesburg's Schedule 2 powers in terms of the Interim Constitution leave it with little economic responsibility (aside from efficient administration and the creation of cities with an efficient form).

Perhaps inevitably, one has to draw the reader's attention to the fact that South Africa has a new government and its central government line departments are reviewing and redirecting policy; and newly created provincial governments are presently employing staff, building capacity, and are themselves reviewing and redirecting policy in terms of newly assigned powers.

At the same time, the country anticipates local government elections in November 1995. At this point the boundaries of local governments have been redrawn (previously we had a checker-board of racially defined local governments) and the governments are redirecting their budgets in favour of low-income areas. There is little coherent thinking likely on local economic development strategies for another six months. It is nonetheless interesting to consider the previous Johannesburg City Council's efforts at local economic development.

The City Council:
- marketed the city
- hosted trade missions
- worked with the police to enhance public safety
- invested in sports stadia
- pedestrianized streets
- promotes hotel, conference, casino, and office developments in the inner city
- is reviewing the feasibility of a light rail system
- provided informal sector market areas and associated facilities and also supplies training.

This list is no doubt very familiar. Much of it is directed at preserving property values and the inner-city rates base. In fact, perhaps the most visible product of the Central Johannesburg Partnership (comprising the public and private sectors and community groups) is a Business Improvement District where the private sector funds security services and cleaning around the Carlton Hotel and the pedestrianized area of the commercial district.

The benefits for those with few skills and who are under-employed are hard to discern. It is unclear, though, that this scepticism will describe the future. A democratic local government, which will be reliant on the state of the local economy, will seek to regain Johannesburg's lost ground. The effect will be to thrust it into the already contested terrain between central and provincial government!

Table 10.5   Delimitation of the metropolitan areas and secondary cities.

Urban centre	Magisterial district
Witwatersrand	
Central Witwatersrand	Johannesburg, Randburg, Roodepoort
East Rand	Germiston, Alberton, Benoni, Boksburg, Kempton Park,
West Rand	Brakpan, Springs, Nigel, Delmas, Heidelberg
Durban Functional Region	Krugersdorp, Westonaria, Randfontein, Oberholzer
Metropolitan Cape Town	Durban, Pinetown, Inanda
	Cape Town, Wynberg, Simonstown, Belville,
Pretoria	Goodwood
	Pretoria, Wonderboom, Soshanguve, Brits,
Port Elizabeth	Bronkhorstspruit–Cullinan
Bloemfontein	Port Elizabeth, Uitenhage
Pietermaritzburg	Bloemfontein
Welkom Goldfields	Pietermaritzburg
East London	Welkom, Odendaalsrus
Klerksdorp	East London, Mdantsane
Newcastle	Klerksdorp
Potchefstroom	Newcastle
Kimberley	Potchefstroom
Witbank/Middelburg	Kimberley
Mmabatho	Witbank, Middelburg
Pietersburg	Mmabatho, Ditsobotla
Nelspruit	Pietersburg, Seshego
	Nelspru

References

Ampros 1994a. *Report on the letting market of the Exchange District, Johannesburg: July 1994*, Research Department of Anglo American Property Services, Johannesburg.

Rode, E. 1993. *Prospects for the property market and the building industry with special reference to falling inflation*, Unpublished paper presented at Rode's Annual Conference, Breakwater Lodge, Cape Town, 27 August.

—1994. *Rode's Report on the South African property market, 1994*, Volume 7 No.3., Rode and Associates, Bellville.

Rogerson, C. & J. Rogerson 1995. The decline of manufacturing in inner-city Johannesburg, 1980–1994. *Urban Forum* (forthcoming)

Tomlinson, R. 1990. *Urbanization in post-apartheid South Africa* London: Unwin Hyman.

—1994. *Urban development planning: the economic reconstruction of South Africa's Cities.* Johannesburg: Witwatersrand University Press.

—1995. *Johannesburg inner-city strategic development framework: economic analysis.* Consulting report commissioned by the Johannesburg City Council. The consulting team consisted of Roland Hunter, Marzia Jonker, Jayne Rogerson, Chris Rogerson and Richard Tomlinson (Project Manager).

Further reading

Ampros 1994b. *Report on the letting market of the Financial District, Johannesburg: July 1994*, Research Department of Anglo American Property Services, Johannesburg.

—1994c. *Report on the letting market of the Commercial District, Johannesburg: July 1994*, Research Department of Anglo American Property Services, Johannesburg.

—1994d. *Report on the letting market of the Mid-town District, Johannesburg: August 1994*, Research Department of Anglo American Property Services, Johannesburg.

—1994e. *Report on the letting market of the Station District, Johannesburg: September 1994*, Research Department of Anglo American Property Services, Johannesburg.

—1994f. *Report on the letting market of Braamfontein: November 1994*, Research Department of Anglo American Property Services, Johannesburg.

Bell, R. T. 1983. *The growth and structure of manufacturing employment in Natal, Occasional Paper no.7* Institute for Social and Economic Research, University of Durban-Westville.

Development Bank of Southern Africa 1994. *South Africa's Nine Provinces: A Human Development Profile*, DBSA, Halfway House.

Fallon, P. R. 1992. *An analysis of employment and wage behaviour in South Africa*, (Draft) Southern Africa Department, The World Bank.

Hofmeyr, J. F. 1990. *The rise of Black wages in South Africa*, Paper delivered at the biennial conference of the Development Society of Southern Africa, University of the Witwatersrand, 5–7 September.

Industrial Development Corporation 1994. *General equilibrium analysis of proposed tariff reform.* Johannesburg.

Ligthelm, A. A. & L. Kritzinger-Van Niekerk 1990. *Unemployment: the role of the public sector in increasing the labour absorption capacity of the South African economy, Development Southern Africa* 7(4): 629–41.

Manning, C. 1993. Dynamo or safety net: can the informal sector save the day?. *Work in Progress* 87, 12–14.

Urban Foundation 1991. *Policies for a New Urban Future. Urban Debate 2010, Income distribution model.* Johannesburg.

Urban Foundation nd. *Policies for a New Urban Future. Urban Debate 2010*, Johannesburg.

CHAPTER ELEVEN
Sheffield: restructuring of a city economy over two decades

Peter Townroe

Introduction

There was no policy agenda for the economic regeneration of Sheffield after the Second World War. The war-time economy of the city contributed to the national war effort from its strong base in alloy steels and in related manufacturing activity in tools and engineering. And then from the late 1940s and through the 1950s, demand for the outputs of the Sheffield economy did not slacken.[1] Unemployment was low, wages were rising and companies were profitable. (Binfield et al. 1993).

In the 1960s the story changes. Strong competition emerged in special steels as well as in hand tools and in cutlery as other national economies recovered from war time. The continuing stream of advances in product and process technology that had maintained Sheffield as a leading world city in steel production for over 200 years either no longer came from Sheffield, or the new technologies required major investment that was not always forthcoming, or they resulted in rises in process productivity and a reduced labour force. The quality premium and the sheer variety of products that Sheffield had offered in cutlery and cutting tools of all description for over two centuries were no longer demanded. Craftsmanship, the hallmark of the Sheffield metal trades and of its steel-making, was giving way to automation, mass production and flow-line quality control. The myriad of small family businesses and the complex matrices of interrelationships between alloy steel-making, cutting tools, cutlery and engineering products in the city were slow to change. At the same time, export demand fell, a demand not made up in that decade by a sluggish performance in the national economy.

In 1967 the British steel industry was nationalized. The British Steel Cor-

---

1. In 1960 Sheffield-based companies manufactured over 1 million tonnes of alloy steel and 3 million tonnes of ingots and castings.

poration was formed from an amalgamation of 14 companies and some 200 subsidiaries, with a total workforce of 270 000. The government of the day felt that the private sector steel companies were not doing enough to restructure the industry and that investment was inadequate. The technology of the time was pointing towards bulk steel production requiring considerable economies of scale in large integrated plants, preferably on coastal sites with good access for both iron ore and coal. This seemed to be the lesson to be learned from Japan, the USA and elsewhere. The new Corporation launched into a very large investment programme, creating, in the event, a capacity that was never fully used. The world demand for steel took a sharp downturn in the 1970s, especially after the two worldwide oil-price rises.

Nationalization had positive and negative impacts on the steel industry in Sheffield. Through the BSC Special Steels Division Sheffield was able to secure the investment necessary for the competitive mass production of stainless steel. But one-third of the national alloy steel production of nearly 2 million tonnes, concentrated in Sheffield, was left in private hands, involving some 50 companies. So, steel production in the city entered the 1970s with the three largest local companies very much under threat from their new owner, the new Corporation, and with its small specialist producers insufficiently rationalized. And the industry as a whole was in political dispute with the government over a climate of uncertainty of policy and over subsidies being granted to competitors in other nations.

Therefore, although Sheffield entered the 1970s still recognizably a "Steel City", the firmness of the foundation of its growth and prosperity over 200 years was being called into question (Tweedale 1995, using the framework of Porter 1990). In terms of its economic base and of the employment prospects for its citizens, the Sheffield economy needed to diversify, both within its manufacturing sector and away from manufacturing and into service activities. That requirement was little appreciated in 1970. It took a bitterly severe recession at the end of the 1970s for the lesson to begin to be learnt. Then, ten years later, by the end of the 1980s, a range of policy instruments from central government, local government and the European Union were being deployed in Sheffield to secure the required diversification and a subsequent economic regeneration. The policies have had mixed success, as described below.

The need to adjust

Sheffield remains one of the largest cities in the UK that is not a major regional centre. Its geographical location, backed up against the Pennines and the Peak District National Park to the west, did not provide for a large city–region hinterland. The rail links, north–south and east–west were slow and have been difficult to upgrade. (By rail, London may be reached from Leeds, 50 km farther north than Sheffield, more quickly than from Sheffield). And road links were inadequate, until the north–south M1 motorway passed on the eastern boundary of the city in 1980. Sheffield is tucked down into the southwest corner of the Yorkshire and Humberside administrative region of 5 million people; and, by 1970, Leeds, a city then of similar size, was very definitely wearing the crown of the regional centre. Over the next 25 years, regional service-centre functions of both the public and the private sector have been concentrating in Leeds to the north; and also in Nottingham, a smaller city, to the south. Nottingham is centre for the East Midlands, a region that abuts to the southern boundary of the city of Sheffield.

In 1970, Sheffield was a manufacturing city. Its economic base was almost exclusively in alloy steels, cutting tools and cutlery, and in associated engineering. Other major employers bringing in income from outside did include a couple of food companies, a large university and a growing polytechnic, and laboratories for the national Health and Safety Executive. But other employment in the economy was locally focused, in both producer and consumer services and in smaller manufacturing companies selling to the larger manufacturing companies. The resident population in the administrative city was 573 000 in 1971, and the number of employees in employment in the slightly larger travel-to-work area was 287 000, 44% of whom were engaged in manufacturing. By 1989, this employment total had fallen to 233 000, with only 27% engaged in manufacturing. By the time of the 1991 census of population, the number of residents had fallen to 501 000. In terms of its workforce, Sheffield could no longer be characterized as a manufacturing city (Tables 11.1–11.3). The number of jobs in manufacturing had halved over the decades.[2] And the city was not a regional centre. It had not experienced a major influx of new service sector jobs as had many cities of similar size. Even so, its levels of unemployment in the early 1990s were comparable with major regional centres in Britain, all being somewhat above the national average figure. However, with relatively low incomes and a falling population, the Sheffield economy was proving to be barely sustainable, in relation to many other British cities.

The pattern of contraction across the two decades was at its most dramatic in the 1980–83 period, when there almost seemed to be a whirlwind blowing in the Sheffield economy, as factory after factory closed down. This was during the Thatcher administration, which came to power in 1979. A misjudgement in macroeconomic policy-making at that time (as seen in retrospect) was based on three understandings held by that government. One was the belief that the rapid rise in oil exports (and oil import substitution) from the British North Sea would support the international balance of payments. It did, but it strengthened the pound sterling at the same time, pushing many British exporting companies into uncompetitive pricing at a time of world recession

---

2. In 1964 the largest eight steel companies employed approximately 54 000 people in Sheffield. In 1994 this total was below 10 000 and still falling.

Table 11.1 Population of the City of Sheffield.

Year	Census	Census-based estimate
1971	520000	
1981	537000	548000
1991	501000	529000
1992	–	531000
1993	–	532000

Source: Census of Population, OPCS.
Notes:
– The 1971 figure predates the 1973 reorganization of local government, which expanded Sheffield's geographical area.
– The estimate figures are assessments made by Sheffield City Council of the actual population of Sheffield taking into account under enumeration and students.

Table 11.2 Employment trends in the Sheffield travel-to-work area, 1971–89.

	1971		1981		1989	
Economic sector	No.	%	No.	%	No	%
Primary	19354	6.7	16684	6.5	5611	2.4
Manufacturing	125824	43.8	81649	31.8	52317	26.7
Construction	16266	5.7	12391	4.8	13577	5.8
Services	125641	43.8	145546	56.7	151929	65.1
TOTAL	287085	100.0	256522	100.0	233414	100.0

Source: Sheffield City Council, Department of Employment and Economic Development.

Table 11.3 Employees in the City of Sheffield, 1981–91.

	Totals		Percentage change	
Division	1981	1991	Sheffield	gb
0 Agriculture	339	288	−15	−22
1 Energy/water	6069	3005	−15	−39
2 Steel/chemicals	27072	7314	−73	−29
3 Engineering	42503	28792	−32	−28
4 Other manufacturing	16246	13143	−19	−18
5 Construction	11233	9736	−13	−11
6 Distribution/catering	44540	44509	−0.1	−13
7 Transport/communication	13600	12930	−5	−5
8 Finance/business services	15885	22103	39	51
9 Other services	64248	69944	9	15
TOTAL	241735	211764	−12	1

Source: Census of Employment (NOMIS).

induced by the 1979 oil shock. A second belief was that the priority given to reducing the high rates of price inflation of the 1970s was to be achieved through monetary measures rather than by fiscal policy or corporatist prices and incomes policies. Consequently, interest rates rose dramatically, pushing many smaller companies, reliant on their bank overdrafts at variable interest rates, into insolvency. And a third belief of that government was that the economy would benefit by shifting the burden of taxation from direct to indirect measures. Income tax was reduced, value added tax was increased, prices therefore rose, and the demand for domestically produced goods and services, already dented by cheaper foreign competition, then fell. Together, these three thrusts of national policy hit Sheffield particularly hard.

In any recession, suppliers of investment goods and elements of infrastructure, and manufacturers of producer goods, suffer as investment falls and stocks are run down. The Sheffield manufacturing sector was concentrated in these kinds of markets. The unemployment rate in the city rose from just over 4% of the workforce registered as unemployed in 1979 to nearly 15% in 1983. It then dipped, but then rose again to nearly 17% in mid-1986 (see Figure 11.1). It is currently (1995) just over 10%, with many potential workers having left the workforce (the "disguised unemployed"), a situation very different from the real, albeit fragile, prosperity of the early 1970s.

The drama of the economic recession of the early 1980s can be illustrated with a few key statistics (from Tweedale 1995). Between 1980 and 1983 the steel-making and engineering sectors in Sheffield lost about 20 000 jobs. This happened in a city that in 1981 was the urban area in the UK with the third highest dependence upon mining, iron and steel and the other metals sectors. Exports of alloy steels fell from 359 000 tonnes in 1979 to 236 000 tonnes in

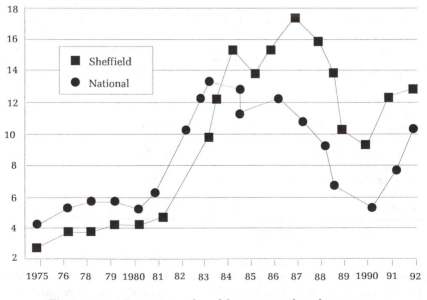

Figure 11.1 Percentage of workforce unemployed, 1975–92.

1980, while imports rose from 218 000 tonnes to 274 000 tonnes. Deliveries of finished alloy steel to the motor vehicle industry fell from 80 100 tonnes in 1975, having been 121 200 tonnes in 1970, to 35 200 tonnes in 1985. Sheffield was the major British producer of these steels. In the city's cutlery industry, employment fell from 12 000 in 1960 to 7800 in 1971, to 5000 in 1980 and 2000 in 1993. In hand tools, the fall was from about 8000 jobs in 1971 to 3650 in 1989. The empty factories and the emerging associated physical dereliction underlined the plight of the unemployed and those on low incomes in the city. A policy response was required.

Public policy intervention

The major industrial intervention of government in the 1960s of relevance to Sheffield, as noted above, came in 1967 with the nationalization of bulk steel production and the formation of the British Steel Corporation. Under a government of a different political complexion, the Corporation was then sold back into private ownership in 1989, having achieved considerable rationalization, a reduction in capacity, and a huge improvement in labour productivity. But neither of these moves was designed to help the Sheffield economy. Both were probably unhelpful at the time they took place. The public policy initiatives that were focused on the city, and were helpful, were those that had a primary ambition of job creation, and normally job creation in the context of a partnership in investment between a government agency and a private sector investor. These policy initiatives were developed through the 1980s in an uneasy alliance between the central government and the Sheffield City Council and (eventually) between the City Council and local business interests.

As the chronology in Table 11.4 indicates, Sheffield become a borough in 1843 and achieved the status of a city 50 years later. In 1974, following a review of the structure of local government in the UK, the city of Sheffield became a Metropolitan District Council within a new County of South Yorkshire. This new status limited the tax-raising and expenditure powers of the City Council and in particular its ability to involve itself pro-actively in policies of economic development and urban regeneration. The Council was unable to do much more than to use its land-use planning powers (which were essentially negative), the significance of its large payroll (of 27 000 plus employees), and a relatively small marketing budget (to attract inward investors). When the national economic recession hit the city from 1978 onwards, the City Council had no mechanism or financial capability to intervene significantly in any process of industrial restructuring or of supportive investment in the economic base of the city. In 1981, formation by the City Council of the Department of Employment and Economic Development provided additional analyses of the destruction of manufacturing jobs then occurring

Table 11.4   Chronology.

1843	Sheffield incorporated as a borough with a town council.
1893	Granted a charter to become a city (with a population of 330,000, a trebling in 50 years)
1974	Became part of the new County of South Yorkshire, as Sheffield Metropolitan District Council, with boundary extensions.
1981	Steel strike
1981	Department for Employment and Economic Development formed.
1981	Refusal by the City Council to apply for Enterprise Zone status.
1984/85	Coal strike.
1986	South Yorkshire County Council abolished, with Joint Boards formed for police, fire services and transport.
1986	Sheffield Economic Regeneration Committee formed.
1986	The Meadowhall Shopping Centre development approved.
1986	Bid for the World Student Games approved.
1988	Urban Development Corporation established.
1990	Training and Enterprise Council established
1990	Meadowhall opens.
1991,	Unsuccessful City Challenge bids.
1992	World Student Games
1991	City Liaison Group formed.
1992	Technopole established
1994	Supertram operational
1994/5	Success in bid for the Single Regeneration Budget

in the city; but it did little, and could do little, to provide replacement employment for those made unemployed (Dabinett & Ramsden 1993).

The City Council placed the blame for what was happening to the Sheffield economy on the Thatcher government. The socialist majority on the Council sided with the local trade unions in a damaging strike in the steel industry in 1981, a strike that hit the state-owned British Steel Corporation at a difficult time. And the same group of local politicians sided with the National Union of Mineworkers in their bitter and violent year-long dispute with the National Coal Board (and effectively with the government) in 1984–85. The national government at this time saw local governments in the major British cities as spend-thrift with tax-raised revenue and as challenging in their views on economic and social policies.[3] And Sheffield was seen as a particular centre of political opposition. For example, Sheffield City Council refused to join 23 other local governments across the UK in applying for Enterprise Zone status, at a time, in 1981–82, when such a status for an area within

3. The "municipal socialism" response of the early 1980s, seen in Sheffield as in some other British cities, was based upon very limited resources. It was a mixture of demonstration projects to support economic development, the formation of municipal enterprises to help protect employment in the public sector, support to improve the quality of jobs in the private sector, and campaigning for new policies from central government (Lawless 1990, Binfield et al. 1993, Dabinett 1995).

the Lower Don Valley (the steelworks area of the city) might well have accelerated industrial conversion to new activity. But the Sheffield City Council was out of sympathy with the mechanisms within the Enterprise Zone policy (Lawless 1990, Binfield et al. 1993).

By 1986, central government had once again changed the structure of local government in the city, abolishing the South Yorkshire County Council and giving powers over the police service, the fire service and the bus service to joint boards, while also further restraining the revenue raising and expenditure powers of Sheffield, as in other cities. The ability to undertake any sort of major initiative in economic regeneration came to require the city to bid for funds from an appropriate government agency or department. Very little could be, and still can be today, achieved by the City Council acting unilaterally (as in other cities: Eisenschitz & Gough 1993).

In the mid-1980s the frost between the local business community and the ruling group of elected politicians on the City Council began to thaw. From an initiative by the President of the Chamber of Commerce and Industry, a Sheffield Economic Regeneration Committee was formed. The intention was to provide a base of local partnership between the private and public sectors from which to bid for nationally available funding, and simultaneously offering a neutral forum for the exchange of views on local issues. The Committee also informed and supported a promotional campaign for the city. A science park and a technology park were built and a cultural industries quarter, was identified for economic activity in music, design and media. A new optimism slowly started to return to the city, although the national economic boom of the late 1980s, largely property-led, had a limited impact in Sheffield.

Three further important local policy decisions from this period stand out. The first, in 1986, was the approval given by the City Council for a major shopping centre development; this was Meadowhall, a £200 million investment. It has been built on the site of a redundant steel-works (Hadfields, one of the largest local steel companies in early twentieth-century Sheffield). The site was alongside the M1 motorway, with a reported 90 minute driving time catchment of nearly ten million people. Parking was provided for 12000 cars. It was, and is, the largest shopping centre of its kind in western Europe. And it is nearly 5 km from the city centre. Trade in the city centre has fallen by an estimated 25–30% since Meadowhall opened in 1990, and many of the 7000 jobs offered are, effectively, re-positioned from retailing in the city centre and from other competing centres (Rotherham, Barnsley, Doncaster, etc.). However, the development has provided a stimulus to redevelopment at the outer end of the Lower Don Valley. (The 1996 turnover is forecast to be £210 million.) More widespread redevelopment and regeneration has followed, with a considerable time-lag, from a second policy decision of the City Council: to support the creation of an Urban Development Corporation for the Valley.

In an agreed understanding, the Urban Development Corporation was established in 1988 with an initial £50 million grant from central government, and a Board made up of local private and public sector leaders. The Corporation gained jurisdiction over 800 ha to the northeast of Sheffield city centre.[4] It has considerable expenditure powers for infrastructure projects of land clearance, contaminated land improvement, roadway improvements, and so on. It also has a large marketing budget and powers to buy and to sell industrial land. It will be dissolved in 1997, having spent some £110 million of public money to lever £550 million of private sector investment and having supported the creation of an estimated 11 200 jobs in the Lower Don Valley. Some 260 ha of industrial land have been reclaimed, 11 km of roads constructed, and 3.5 million ft^2 of floorspace generated. The Corporation was a central government creation, regarded with some suspicion initially by the Sheffield City Council, especially as the Corporation was given land-use development-control powers within its designated area. But the agreed understanding eased this suspicion, as did the membership for the Leader of the Council on the Board of the Corporation. The greater problem for this initiative actually turned out to be the national property development recession of the early 1990s. This hit just at the time the Corporation was beginning to bring forward prepared sites for industrial and commercial development. A major scheme for a short take-off and landing airport also ran into financial problems when the partner developer went into receivership. Only now, in the past two years or so, has new private sector investment in the Lower Don Valley started to gather some momentum.

The third key initiative for economic development in Sheffield of the late 1980s was the decision in 1986 to press on with the successful bid by the city to stage the World Student Games in 1991. This was an extremely ambitious project. In the event, the Games were a sporting success involving some 7000 athletes. However, because of limited television interest, they were a commercial failure. The budget of the city government of Sheffield had to bear the cost of a large subsidy to the running cost of the Games, as well as the continuing interest charges on the large capital projects put in place for the Games. These projects include a major international standard swimming pool complex, a large 12 000 seat covered arena, a new open-air athletics stadium, a tennis centre and a second smaller swimming complex. With the existing facilities for sport, in 1995 these facilities prompted the Sports Council to bestow on the city the accolade of "The City of Sport", Sheffield being the only British city to receive this title. Sheffield can see sporting activity, for participants and spectators and for suppliers of goods and services, as one further and significant contribution to economic regeneration in the city. The run up to the World Student Games also had a local benefit of creating a new

---

4. Of which 35% was derelict or vacant at that time. The Lower Don Valley was home to over 800 companies, employing 18 500 people in metals and metal-related manufacturing. There were only 300 residents in the area. The development strategy of the Corporation was very dependent upon a strong demand for land and property.

optimism: that investment was once again taking place in a city that was feeling very battered and bruised from the previous 20 years.

One further local policy initiative deserves mention. This was the creation in 1990, in line with central government policy and with some 100 other towns and cities across the nation, of a Training and Enterprise Council. The Council has a remit to support training activity for the unemployed, and to assist skills development for employees within companies, particularly smaller companies. It also has a remit to support business development and entrepreneurship and the formation of new companies.[5] It provides a liaison between the secondary schools and the very large further education college in Sheffield (the Sheffield College), and the world of work. It also provides the local bridgehead for a range of initiatives supported by central government and the European Commission in training and small business development. The European Commission is especially significant in this respect, as it is in areas of grant aid for infrastructure investments, because Sheffield is both in an area of "Coal and Steel Conversion" and in an Objective 2 "Restructuring Region" under the European Union classifications.[6] The development of the activities of the Training and Enterprise Council in Sheffield have been complementary to the local industrial linkages formed by the two universities, Sheffield Hallam University and the University of Sheffield. The former, as an ex-polytechnic, has a long tradition of education for local industry, as well as providing applied research support from both academic staff and research students and from testing facilities, specialist equipment, and so on. The tradition goes back further with the University of Sheffield. Its Department of Metallurgy, for example, played a very significant role in the early decades of this century in the development of new alloy steels and of new production processes, as well as in training graduates for both research and management positions in the steel industry. Both universities now strive to have a clear "outreach" mission to local industry, to support progress in both the manufacturing and the service sectors of the Sheffield economy. Both universities have considerably increased their total student numbers, the range and scale of their national and international research activity. With a combined turnover of some £240 million, and a large local labour force, they form an important component of the economic base of the city.[7] From the 1980s, measures led by the public sector of economic restructuring in British cities

---

5. The budget of Sheffield TEC is approximately £20 million per annum (see Bennett & McCoshan 1993 for a full discussion of the role and operation of TECs).

6. European Union assistance comes from Structural Fund Programmes, directed at economic restructuring. Between 1988 and 1992 about £140 million was spent across South Yorkshire in what was termed as an "Integrated Operational Programme". The expenditure went on infrastructure, training, business support and environmental improvements.

7. The two universities and Sheffield College currently enrol over 55 000 full-time and part-time students.

have been very dependent upon central government funds being passed down, either to the local city government or to local agencies (Atkinson & Moon 1994, Blackman 1995). Sheffield has had less success in attracting these funds than other major British cities. The Urban Programme resources, for example, have amounted to only £4.5 million per annum in Sheffield since the early 1980s, a very small amount when set against the total annual City Council expenditure (in 1994) of over £250 million. And in the competitive bidding "City Challenge" regime introduced by the central government in 1990, Sheffield was unsuccessful in the first two rounds, then gaining £38 million for a seven-year expenditure urban regeneration package early in 1995 in the third round, under the "Single Regeneration Budget". The city has also not been successful in the first round of bidding for the Millennium Fund. Overall, it has been very difficult over two decades for the City Council to pursue a programme of significant support of restructuring of the city economy with its restricted ability to spend on either its recurrent account or its capital account. And, unlike some other British cities that act as regional financial and commercial centres, the forces of the market have not worked in Sheffield's favour either.

A current assessment

As a major manufacturing city in western Europe, Sheffield has not been alone in experiencing a generation of apparent relative economic decline as its industrial sectors have had to meet the challenge of major restructuring in the face of new competition (Healey et al. 1995). Cities in the Ruhr area of Germany, for example, have faced similar cold winds of change. Whether a more enlightened or more interventionist set of policy measures from both central and local government could have achieved an easier transition remains an open question. What is now clear is that, although the Sheffield economy is now more diversified and prospectively resilient than it was in the early 1970s, casualties of the process of economic restructuring remain. The unemployment statistics provide one measure of the current position.

The recorded unemployment in 1995 of 10.5% – 20% higher than the national average – is probably only two-thirds of a "real" figure, and in some inner-city wards the figure is over one-third (Lawless 1995). Also, one-third of the unemployed are under the age of 25, and 40% of registered claimants have been unemployed for more than one year. There are about 18 unemployed people in the city for every officially recorded job vacancy (although "officially" recorded vacancies are probably only one-quarter of the underlying real totals). These figures are against a backcloth of trends of rising participation in the workforce by women and falling participation (at all ages, but particularly aged 55 plus) of men. A reflection of the move to a service-

210

sector dominated economy is seen in the increase in temporary and part-time employment. Half of the official vacancies in 1994 were of this nature. The low incomes that go with both long-run and intermittent unemployment are also reflected in indicators of poor health. Recognition of this has caused the new spirit of partnership among the leadership of the city to plan simultaneously for both economic and social regeneration.

The Sheffield Economic Regeneration Committee, the initial partnership forum of the mid-1980s, has developed into the City Liaison Group. This Group brings together relatively few leaders, from the City Council, the two universities, the Development Corporation, the Chamber of Commerce, the Training and Enterprise Council, Sheffield Health Authority and the Cutlers' Company. It has created a series of working subgroups, resulting in the publication of what the Group claims is an integrated economic and social regeneration strategy and plan for the city: *Sheffield: growing together*. This document, published in 1995, builds upon two earlier outputs in 1994: *The way ahead: an economic regeneration strategy*;[8] and *Shaping the future: a social regeneration strategy* (Sheffield City Liaison Group 1994).[9] The "integrated strategy" has a vision, a set of targets, linked to a set of objectives. It is therefore seen as an action-orientated plan, setting out clear milestones. Considerable efforts have been made to ensure that development of the documents has been based upon both the technical and analytical expertise available in the city, but also upon wider processes of consultation. There is a firm commitment by the parties involved to ensure that the City Liaison Group is more than a talking shop and more than mere civic boosterism.

Economic restructuring of a city economy requires investment, from both the public and the private sector. Ten years ago in Sheffield there seemed to be little of either: no sound of cement mixers, no construction cranes on the skyline. Today, in the mid-1990s, the prospects are much brighter. Since 1990, building upon the expenditures related to the World Student Games and investment by the Urban Development Corporation, it is possible to point to ten major projects:

- new law courts
- new offices for the Norwich Union Insurance company
- new offices for a division of the Abbey National Building Society
- new teaching buildings and
- student accommodation supporting the expansion of both universities
- the redevelopment of an old canal basin immediately to the northeast of the city centre into an office complex called Victoria Quays

8. *The way ahead* document was a development of the economic development strategy of the Sheffield Economic Regeneration Committee, published as *Sheffield 2000* in 1990.
9. A "Healthy Sheffield" partnership was formed in 1992. It has established a "Framework for Action", bringing together policy initiatives in health awareness, environmental improvement, housing, leisure provision, healthcare facilities and education of health professionals. (See also Dabinett & Ramsden 1993.)

- several hotel projects
- a new retail park in the Lower Don Valley, close to Meadowhall
- a new bus station
- a major combined heat and power scheme, using municipal waste as a fuel source.

The tenth project is of particular significance. This is the Supertram. This is 29 km of a new urban light-rail tramway system, with three arms of line running out from the city centre, to the southeast, the northeast and northwest. It is a £240 million investment, complemented by three major road schemes. The Supertram investment is certainly not above criticism, in its routing, its scale, the spacing of stations, its interchanges with other transport modes, and so on. But it has been taken up as a symbol of the "New Sheffield", a clear commitment to the future.

In contrast, where Sheffield has been unsuccessful since the mid-1980s is in attracting significant industrial projects, new companies locating locally from elsewhere in the UK or from overseas. There has been no equivalent in the manufacturing sector to the 1300 job arrival of the Norwich Union between 1989 and 1994. Until recently, Sheffield could not provide large industrial sites of serviced land. Projects in the city have also not been eligible for Regional Selective Assistance, the subsidy package offered in the Assisted Areas of the UK by central government. The realization has grown in Sheffield that economic regeneration has to be largely home grown.

One key facet of home-grown economic growth, alongside encouragement to local entrepreneurs, access by investors to funds and availability of sites and premises, rests in the knowledge and skills of the labour force. Arguably this is *the* key facet, particularly in an advanced First World economy such as the UK. Sheffield has therefore been coming round to see itself as a "knowledge-based city". Of course, in a sense, it has always been this, for 250 years, as Tweedale's history of the steel and related industries makes very clear (Tweedale 1995). But a new policy emphasis on education and training and knowledge transfer underlines the point.

The expansion of both higher and further education in the city has already been noted, as has the creation of the Training and Enterprise Council. There is currently in the city a new emphasis on achievement levels in secondary schools, using the new National Targets for Education and Training based upon the revised secondary school curriculum and the new framework of National Vocational Qualifications. This is complemented by, on the one hand, a new emphasis on pre-school education, and on the other one on lifetime learning. This latter is being encouraged through employers by the national standards of Investors in People, a commitment to the continuing training and education of employees. This in turn links across to employers taking up the challenge of becoming accredited for quality assurance under schemes of total quality management.

In knowledge transfer, the significance of the two universities has already been noted. Sheffield has had a long history of deep investment in research and development in steel, but that is not a tradition seen in other sectors of the city economy, particularly in smaller companies. A technopole was established in 1994, under the leadership of the Cutlers' Company, with funds from the European Union, to stimulate and to facilitate the transfer of metals and materials technologies within Sheffield.

With the support of the various initiatives described here, the Sheffield economy should once again be able to pursue sustainable economic growth. Adding to the expenditure powers of the tiers of both local and regional government would assist this, a subject of current debate. But Sheffield competes with other cities. Its fortunes are very much tied in with the economic performance of both the UK economy and the wider EU economy. Local policies and initiatives directed at economic development in the city, as in other similar older industrial cities, are directed as much at catching up to the average performance of competitors as with establishing a clear lead.

References

Atkinson, R. & G. Moon 1994. *Urban policy in Britain: the city, the state and the markets*. London: Macmillan.

Bennett, R. J. & A. McCoshan 1993. *Enterprise and human resource development*. London: Paul Chapman.

Blackman, T. 1995. *Urban policy in practice*. London: Routledge.

Binfield, C. et al. (eds) 1993. *The history of the city of Sheffield, 1843–1993* [3 vols]. Sheffield: Sheffield Academic Press.

Dabinett, G. 1995. Economic regeneration in Sheffield: urban modernisation or management of decline? In *The British economy in transition: from the old to the new?*, R. Turner (ed.), 218–39. London: Routledge.

Dabinett, G. & P. Ramsden 1993. An urban policy for people: lessons from Sheffield. In *British urban policy and the Urban Development Corporations*, R. Imrie & H. Thomas (eds), 123–35. London: Paul Chapman.

Eisenschitz, A. & J. Gough 1993. *The politics of local economic policy: the problems and possibilities of local initiative*. London: Macmillan.

Healey, P. et al. (eds) 1995. *Managing cities: the new urban context*. Chichester: John Wiley.

Lawless, P. 1990. Regeneration in Sheffield: from radical intervention to partnership. In *Leadership and urban regeneration: cities in North America and Europe*, D. Judd & M. Parkinson (eds), 133–51. Newbury Park: Sage.

Lawless, P. 1995. South Yorkshire: policy responses in an era of substantial economic change. Paper presented at conference on "Transition of older industrial regions", Oviedo, Spain, May.

Porter, M. E. 1990. *The competitive advantage of nations*. London: Macmillan.

Sheffield City Liaison Group 1994. *The way ahead: plans for the economic regeneration of Sheffield*. Sheffield: Sheffield City Council.

Tweedale, G. 1995. *Steel city: entrepreneurship, strategy and technology in Sheffield 1743–1993*. Oxford: Oxford University Press.

CHAPTER TWELVE
Santiago de Chile:
the second turning point

Antonio Daher

Introduction

Santiago de Chile, January 1994: a central hypothesis is formulated that Chile's capital city faces a surge of growth and (re-)concentration, forming the basis for a proposal to modernize the city's economy.

Why a second turning point? A shift in a secular trend towards concentration of national output and population in Santiago was first registered in 1973. Since then, with only a brief exception, Chile's capital city has grown more slowly than the rest of Chile in terms of geographical product, employment and investment.

At the beginning of the 1990s, almost two decades later, Santiago had probably reached a turning point, this time towards an increased concentration. This reversed the tendency for slower growth in industrial production and overall employment, as well as promoting a greater dynamism in the non-tradable sector (i.e. services: electricity, gas and water, construction, transportation and communications, commerce and general services).

The unemployment rate is a singularly significant indicator of this change in tendency, both for its economic and for its social implications. From the crisis of 1982 until 1990, this rate was invariably greater in the metropolitan region than in the rest of the country. In 1993, in the midst of an unprecedented fall in national unemployment, the metropolitan rate of unemployment was lower than the rest of the country by more than 1%.

What can explain the two turning points? This is certainly not the product of chance: the years 1990 to 1993 have been characterized by a fall in the real exchange rate and by lower international prices for practically all Chilean exports. In the midst of a recession in developed countries, Chile has observed sustained growth in its products, particularly in the non-tradable sectors. These have a predominantly urban orientation.

The results of the success of Chile's export model have been reflected in the dynamism of the most important urban economies in certain regions, activating its secondary (manufacturing) and tertiary (services) sectors, which contribute to export production; the development of industry orientated to foreign trade begins to take place. This is partly linked to raw material production, but increasingly to the manufacture of higher value-added goods. This, along with the sale of international services, initiated the so-called "second phase" of the export economy (Ominami & Madrid 1989).

This second phase, geographically situated in the metropolitan areas and associated with the second turning point, is registered particularly in the cities of Valparaiso and Santiago (on the other hand, a third metropolitan area in Chile, Concepción, shows a different performance attributable to the highly diversified nature of its regional economy).

Cities are the economic product of market forces. They offer agglomeration economies and locational advantages, which should in principle lead to greater productivity and, hence, to greater competition. Agglomeration economies – both of scale and external – constitute the fundamental economic reason for the existence and growth of cities. Such economies benefit producers as well as consumers, and are produced in the markets for factors, goods and services. Size and urban complexity involve increasing degrees of specialization, so that the significant sectors of the economy (secondary and above all, tertiary) become located mainly and sometimes almost exclusively in cities.

In an open economy such as Chile's, which is part of an increasingly globalized external market, natural comparative advantages cannot avoid complementing socially produced ones, among which the urban advantages occupy a very important place. If the recent national economic boom is associated with success in the export of natural resources, then its consolidation and development will depend by and large on growing value-added and production diversification. Cities play an crucial role in this process.

Cities that were formerly headquarters of import-substitution industrialization have been converted into real export platforms by industrial and services exports, as well as by the increasing competition for more qualified human capital. Metropolitan areas are highly complex and they concentrate capital-intensive economic infrastructures. These areas, apart from sustaining urban enterprises, serve the national economy as a whole in political and economic terms.

In this context, the Macro Central Zone (MCZ) of Chile (made up of three highly interactive adjacent subregions: Valparaiso (V), O'Higgins (VI) and Metropolitan) acquires a role of potentially great significance, both for its demographic and economic relevance and for its strong degree of metropolitanization, and hence quantitative and qualitative infrastructural endowment.

The following section will describe and explain, from a territorial-economic perspective, the declining tendency – in terms of product – of the metropolitan region (and of Valparaiso) after the first turning point at the beginning of the 1970s. The hypothesis will foreshadow the second turning point, characterizing the adjustments and changes demanded by it.

The analysis and its qualitative projection result is indispensable for future study. Above all, it serves as the groundwork for policies and investment decisions on a medium- and long-term basis, both in infrastructure and other sectors. This chapter will propose a re-conversion of the metropolitan economy in accordance with the challenges of a globalized market and a growing industrialization of national exports.

Santiago, first turning point

Santiago's economy has not only grown more slowly than the rest of the country but it has done so at the country's expense (Daher 1993a). Santiago de Chile represents approximately 40% of the economy and population of the country. It has been growing for almost 200 years. Contrary to common belief, Santiago's economy grew more slowly than the national average after 1973, with the sole exception of a three-year period between 1977 and 1979 (ODE-PLAN 1990a: 17).

In fact, in the period between 1970 and 1990, while the country was growing annually at an average of 2.7%, the metropolitan region was growing only at 2.3% (Region V presented an average of 2.1% and Region VIII, with Concepción as its capital, was identical to the national rate). As a consequence, the percentage contribution of the economy of the metropolitan region to the national gross geographic product fell by 9%, from 47.4% in 1973 to only 38.4% in 1985, with an estimate of 40.4% for 1990. (The contribution of the Valparaiso region fell by almost 4%, from 12.1% in 1974 to 8.2% in 1990) (Silva 1994.)

Simultaneously, in the 1982 census, the metropolis revealed a deceleration in its demographic growth. Furthermore, the gap between the population growth rates of the capital city and the country as a whole was reduced to only one-third in 20 years, making the rhythm of the demographic concentration decline persistently.

In 1992, although the census registered an inter-census variation for the metropolitan region (RM), with respect to 1982, over the Chilean mean, other regions – I, II and XI – presented a higher relative growth, and two others – II and IV – a similar percentage. Additionally, while the RM was growing by 19.7%, if we include the province of Santiago it was growing by only 11.4%. Since Santiago represents 81.9% of the regional population, its high relative weight hides very high growth in the rest of the region.

While unemployment in most regions was decreasing after the recession of the early 1980s, in the capital city the situation was more difficult; from

216

1982 to 1990, the unemployment rate was higher in the metropolitan region than in the rest of the country (ODEPLAN 1990b: 6). It is not by chance that the relative income for most employees improved more in rural areas that in the city, thus reversing the geography of poverty. The fastest growing sectors were no longer located in the capital city but increasingly in provincial regions and rural areas.

What was there to be done with Santiago? For many, this question became how to stop metropolitan growth and centralization. What had seemed impossible became a fact; Santiago was facing a turning point in the mid-1970s.

What happened? Why did Chile's capital city lose its leadership? Why did its economic and demographic rhythm decline? This situation is not one where the city exceeds a supposed optimal size and enters into a phase of decreasing returns, where negative externalities, or congestion and pollution have slowed its growth.

What made this possible was the market economy, liberalization, export promotion and foreign investment. What is more surprising is the fact that the neoliberal model achieved this unintentionally with macroeconomic policies designed for different ends.

In fact, the lowering of import tariffs in the second half of the 1970s ended decades of protectionism for an industry geared to import substitution and located mainly in urban and metropolitan areas. In this process, the urban consumption subsidy, which discriminated against agriculture, was corrected. Chile's capital city was greatly affected by the reduction in the size of the state, as well as by the decrease in fiscal deficits and establishment of monetary equilibrium.

During the 1980s, the low real exchange parity – along with the opening of capital markets – was translated into an excess of imports, consumption and indebtedness. This led to a disproportionate growth of markets and services, and a decline in productive sectors, and favoured the urban and metropolitan economy over the regions. Nevertheless, this transitory privilege made the recession in Santiago, Valparaiso and other large cities stronger, greater and longer lasting.

The tariff phase of the new economic opening ended the subsidy to the metropolis, which had been typical of the inward development model. After the crisis, this was followed by an exchange phase, which favoured the export-orientated regional economies (Daher 1990, Escobar & Repetto 1993). Therefore, while Santiago's growth was decreasing, the rest of the country was, in general terms, growing rapidly.

If economic growth rates have been positive for Chile, they have been even greater for some regions within Chile. If the rest of the country as a whole has not grown faster, it is because the metropolitan economy was falling behind; with its national weight of 40% of the national economy, it did much to lower the national average. In a macroeconomic equilibrium context, tariff and trade policies inverted the relative prices and the dialectic between the trad-

217

able areas (fishing, forestry, farming, mining and industrial sectors) and non-tradable ones (services) setting up a process of sectoral and geographical resource re-assignation, including human resources. The state did not act by omission in these changes. Although the market and free enterprise appear as the protagonists, state policies sustained the framework and often itself intervened, promoted, subsidized and protected with the aim of liberalizing and privatizing.

The somewhat centralist behaviour of the state, expressed in the territorial distribution of fiscal expenditure, in the location of productive and social infrastructure investment, in the proportion between regional budget collection and distribution, and in its per capita distribution, is still being explored. Certain figures reveal a growing concentration tendency in Santiago, somewhat more serious in comparison to the observed economic results. However, other indicators would show that the proportions have reverted in favour of the regions. By no means would this be a cause for metropolitan depression.

In terms of sectoral state investment, which concentrated over 90% in public works, housing and urbanism, the metropolitan region received less in the past 15 years. In public works, it took 33% during the 1976–9 period, 20% between 1980 and 1986, and only 8% in 1990. On the other hand, in housing and urbanism, the percentages were 42.48% and 35% during the same years, respectively (ODEPLAN 1990a).

The public works sector *deconcentrated* more (in geographical terms) than housing and urbanism. Whereas the latter responded to existing demand, the former tended to supply future demand. One is rather an historic indicator, the other a forecaster.

Except for the Ministry of Housing, Urbanism and the Municipalities, total effective per capita public investment in the MR was always lower than the national average between 1986 and 1992. In 1992, public investment for each Chilean averaged $30 708 and for each Santiago resident only $21 748 (MIDE-PLAN 1993).

When considering effective public investment by regions between 1980 and 1992, the MR reached its peak in 1981, with 36.6%, to fall to only 28.2% in 1992 (SUBDERE 1994). Obviously, both percentages are much lower than the demographic and economic share of the MR.

However, the most relevant indicator and, at the same time, the most surprising one, is the total multi-sectoral investment – public and private – for the 1990–5 period. Chile's capital city obtained only 12% of this investment, a very low proportion in comparison to its share of the national gross geographic product (Aninat 1990). This indicator anticipated a near future of lesser growth for the metropolitan region. The relative "de-investment" does not allow a different conclusion, even after we allow for the fact that the figures overvalue some sectors, such as agriculture and construction, and do not in general include less important projects.

Moreover, in terms of financial capital – another key indicator for development – the MR has a radically lower share in real terms than it is nominally assigned. In fact, after allowing for the pro-metropolitan bias associated with the location of headquarters, financial management and transactions, the final geographical investment obtained favours the non-metropolitan regions. As a matter of fact, a study of the largest debtors of the leading investment banks arrives at the conclusion that 32.4% of bank credits can be assigned to the capital region.

Finally, from the AFP (pension funds administrators) investments in company bonds, similar conclusions were reached. These funds – which constitute the greatest investment capacity in the country – by and large feed financial intermediation; in terms of company bonds the MR took 24.5%, although it provides 45% of the AFP revenue flows. This shows a geographical contrast between obtaining and investing, which is also a transfer of resources between regions (Daher 1993b).

In 1990, the MR received only 26.8% of total financial capital from bank credits and share issues. However, this low percentage is greater than the mere 12% that the MR received from investment projects. In both cases, it is an extremely low proportion compared to the city's output and population. Why would the per capita investment in Santiago between 1990 and 1995 reach only US$451 while in the rest of the country – including Santiago – it reached US$1495, and, excluding the MR US$2305: five times as much? The answer is clear: because Santiago is a more closed economic region. The new market economy model – whose essential features are the reassessment of the private sector, and liberalization – was imposed from the capital city on the rest of the country, but that same model was initially contradicted by the MR itself.

Between 1970 and 1990, while the tradable sector in most regions either remained stable or grew in real terms, in the capital region it dropped from 35% to 27% of regional geographic product, the lowest percentage in Chile. The capital region's contribution to the national tradable GDP decreased from 40% to 29%, during the same period (Behrens 1990). This occurred regardless of the fact that this region made a lower contribution to national agricultural and industrial output, and held an important second place in the projected mining investment (1990–95) in the country.

In terms of exports, having declared the model as pro-export, the MR contributed only 7.3% of its regional GDP (the lowest number after the Araucana region, which had the highest relative level of poverty). Although the figures for the regionalization of exports required a few adjustments, as in the II region, in the case of the MR the statistics are more trustworthy (Servicio Nacional de Aduanas 1990).

The MR contributed only 11.2% of national exports in 1990, whereas its output was close to 40% of GDP. In per capita terms, the MR exported US$182 in 1990, while the figure for Chile – including the population of the MR – was

US$646. Thus, it is clear that Santiago is a region with a more closed economy, and that it has continued to be so in the years of open economic policies.

The MR had lesser economic growth and a lower capacity to obtain investment because of its position, which in principle diverges from the dominant policy model. In fact, the model favoured the rest of the country, where profitability higher than in the capital can be achieved because of the important endowments of natural resources and investments.

The MR not only has a more closed economy; the state there has a larger presence. In fact, 69% of the projected investments in infrastructure for the whole country (public and private sectors) in the 1990–95 period were by the private sector and 31% by the state, whereas in Santiago 52% of such investment originates in the public sector (construction and infrastructure represent more than half of the national total investment).

One can therefore speak of state and private regions in Chile (Daher 1993c), since neither has privatization been homogeneous in the territory nor has the investment of both sectors.

If the contribution of each region towards national GDP is an historic indicator relative to the economic territorial disparity, its share of international trade, and above all in investments, will determine the preservation or alteration of those disparities. Moreover, whereas per capita GDP is 8 times higher in the richer than in poorer regions, investments are 29 times larger and exports 280 times.

Santiago, second turning point

The greatest challenge confronting Santiago is its low productivity and low social profitability. The per capita product of the metropolitan region (in thousands of 1977 pesos) was 42.8 in 1971 and only 31.9 in 1985, while the national figure remained virtually unchanged. Therefore, in relation to the national mean, the GDP index per capita of the MR fell from 1.3 in 1970 to 1.1 in 1985 and in 1990 (Silva 1994).

The MR's productivity is dramatically contrasted with its invested capital, its operational costs and the proportion of fiscal revenues it receives. This is so because Santiago is, above all, the main endowment and the most important stock of fixed capital in the country.

According to the Internal Tax Services department, in January 1991 the value of non-agricultural real estate for the whole country was equivalent to US$20 billion. From that total, US$11 billion, 55% was in the MR. The figures contrast with an agricultural valuation of only US$3 billion for the whole of Chile (SII 1991). Santiago represents the scarcest resource of a developing country: capital. As well as being a "millionaire" in capital, it is also many times a "millionaire" in terms of population and labour force.

220

Regardless of its crisis, the annual product generated supersedes any other sector in the economy. CODELCO is not the top company in Chile: Santiago is. Santiago's economy surpasses in size (and complexity) that of many medium-size and small countries. Santiago has the best infrastructure and capital equipment, and represents the most strategic economic resource and, administratively, the most important and complex challenge.

The management of Santiago affects economic agents positively or negatively, as well as the whole of society in macroeconomic terms. The metropolitan administration is surely a challenge to national efficiency; and efficiency makes equity more possible. Confronting the future of Santiago necessarily implies political and economic choices.

The implementation of political and financial decentralization is relevant for this study. This could be a process that will reduce further the role of the government in the economy, particularly in the capital. Its direct participation in the metropolitan economy is not only minimized; its multiplier effect is also lessened, particularly its influence in centralizing and assigning resources, including especially those of infrastructure as a support for development.

In the second case – the economic options faced by Santiago – the central issue is, on the one hand, the locational tendencies of the non-tradable sector and, on the other, the evolution towards greater diversification of exports and, above all, of greater value added; that is, the export of increasingly industrialized goods and of services.

In fact, during the greatest export boom in Chile, from 1985 to 1990, while the tradable sector grew by 29.2%, the non-tradable grew a surprising 38.3% (Banco Central de Chile 1994: 1575). Moreover, exports were equivalent to 11.7% of the national GDP in 1970 and 20.9% in 1980 (de la Cuadra 1988: 34), reaching 27.5% in 1990. Therefore, along with the dynamism of the export sector – regional and rural based – went high non-tradable sector growth, much of it urban and metropolitan.

The questions are evident: Will the industrialization of raw materials be followed by a phase of greater value added in manufacturing, less tied to the rural areas and more to the metropolitan? Will the dynamism of production of non-tradable goods and services benefit Santiago and Valparaiso, or will it be expressed, on the contrary, in a decentralization and *deconcentration* of the infrastructure, transport, construction and services? Furthermore, is it possible for the metropolis to compete with the regions when its environmental crisis not only decreases the quality of life but also make the activities that are developed there more expensive, monetarily and non-monetarily? Large-scale industry is located in the regions, but a more numerous and diversified but principally small and medium-size industrial sector is on the rise in Chile's capital city.

A recent study of the territorial impact of manufacturing growth during the 1985–91 period (De Mattos et al. 1993), a stage of greater activity in traditionally metropolitan-orientated sectors, concludes that the MR is the most diversified, dynamic, productive and value-added generator in the industrial field, considering that establishments there, which develop with greater independence of natural resources, find the most appropriate institutional and infrastructural conditions in such regions.

However, the same study recognizes that, inside the MR itself, a dispersal of industrial activities is taking place outside the Province of Santiago. This tendency is expressed in the sectoral statistics, and, above all, in the industrial consumption of electricity: while falling in the province from 21.9% to 20.9%, in the region it increased from 21.9% in 1985 to 29.8% in 1991.

The authors also identify changes relevant to the MR in the regions of Valparaiso and Concepción, both significant metropolitan areas. In the first case, relevant to the Macro Central Region and adjacent to Santiago, although there was a significant decline in the number of places of work, the regional contribution to industrial value added increased from 13.3% to 14.6%. The MR, moreover, increased this contribution from 37.2% in 1985, to 38.6% in 1988 and 43.8% in 1991. The strongest increase in the last period coincides with other indicators, generally reflected in employment. This allows identification of the multi-sectoral breaking point or second turning point, occurring probably around 1990.

Recent official figures indicate that, between 1985 and 1992, the national GDP grew by 55.2% and the GDP of the MR by 72.5% (Banco Central de Chile 1994). Santiago's greatest dynamism, until 1990 – in order of growth – was in construction, transport, communications, manufacturing industry, commerce, financial services and agriculture. All of these activities, in the same order and preceded by fishery (with a low absolute significance), grew more than the average for the metropolitan economy. The sector with least dynamism was public administration, which is strongly established in the capital.

The turning points of Santiago's growth show themselves clearly in considering a broader time period. From 1960 to 1972, the MR's share of the national product was always increasing – from 41.5% in the first date to 48.2% in the latter. From then on, the share has fallen strongly, reaching a minimum of only 41.3% in 1976 – only four years later – and a lesser rise in share in 1981 to 45.5%. It is only from 1986 onwards that there has been a sustained growth, reaching 46.7% in 1992 (Vial & Bonacio 1994).

These turning points are certainly confirmed by the annual rates of growth of the metropolitan product. In 1975, it decreased by –15.2%, in 1982 by –16.0%, and in 1992 it grew by 12.2% (SUBDERE 1994).

In the Vial & Boracio (1994) study, CIEPLAN concluded that "it is not good that the MR is each time absorbing a greater proportion of the national GDP" and that "during the boom periods, the MR grows more than the rest of the country; but during the adjustment or recession periods the consequences are greater". The same study adds that "the 1985–92 period is marked by strong recovery and growth, following the 1982 crisis; therefore it should not seem

222

strange that the MR recovers part of the relative importance lost at the beginning of the 1980s".

If the economic tendency of Santiago and the MR in general face a change
moving away from industrial activity, which is obvious, it would then be convenient to anticipate, through statistical projections and probable scenarios,
the behaviour of the principal variables for longer-term horizons.

A prospect of the future of Santiago, and of the Macro Central Zone (MCZ),
surrounding the capital and the heart of Chile, was recently developed by an
Interministerial Infrastructure Committee.

The MCZ study (MECSA–INECON 1993) is not only a sectoral one: it is also a
study of and a proposal for territorial development. It is of great interest to
evaluate its results, not only in terms of infrastructure but also in geographical concentration–deconcentration, land use and consumption, spatial distribution of the population, and other regional and local effects.

The study was initially undertaken at a regional and even macro-regional
level, without zone desegregation. However, the strong metropolitan concentration in Santiago and Valparaiso compelled the study to make long-range
inter-urban proposals.

In the Macro Zone, and particularly in the V region, ports determine the
particular specialized infrastructure, and also the roads and interregional and
inter-urban transport. Additionally, ports generate location factors and land
use that can be decisive for urban development contained in the zone.

It is surprising the study did not manage to predict or even suggest Valparaiso and San Antonio port movement. In fact, one projection until the year
2010 suggests a 69% decrease for the first against a 1058% increase for the
second. Other results of the same document offer completely opposite figures. Certainly, the study's scenario suggests less deconcentration in favour
of the V and VI regions, compared to the MCZ, and in favour of smaller cities
in the case of the MR (an already verified tendency in the two most recent population census). However, this lesser deconcentration translates into an enormous extension of trips, both in terms of passenger-kilometres (144% more)
and in terms of cargo/km (178% more). The possible explanation for this phenomenon would be a functional specialized deconcentration that, far from
translating into more self sufficient zones, would lead to longer trips.

This result is controversial. In fact, if after having implemented the proposed policies (regulations and introduction of tariffs) and the important
investment in transport infrastructure there is such a result, then the policy
could be reassessed to establish the "increase" in journey time, cost and con-
tamination.

At a more urban scale, the fact that the study makes the assumption that
land demand is elastic with respect to prices – without considering location
inertia and normative restrictions – ensures that there will be some projected
non-desirable and improbable territorial effects.

In the first case, there could be a critical worsening of central Santiago's depopulation and a parallel phenomenon in the VI region (associated with the decline in agricultural employment, the workers that supposedly are to be absorbed by the cities of the same region). In the second case, an "eastern bias" should be noted in the increase in product, employment and, to a lesser degree, households. In fact, the study assigns the eastern Santiago zone greater growth in production and employment, not only in the capital but in the MCZ as a whole. Much of that growth would be linked to the industrial sector. However, the same document recognizes that the greatest endowment of industrial land would be in the northern, southern and western zones (the last being equivalent to the other two combined). Moreover, it is recognized that most unused land is concentrated in the southern, western and south-western zones. This conclusion is pertinent to the theoretical base and purpose of the study. It is also related to the disequilibrium in transport and use of land. In fact, the study – on certain elasticity and non-restriction assumptions – assumes that the most scarce resource is not land but infrastructure. As a consequence, the model and reality adjust themselves to the infrastructure variable. This situation leads to an overvaluation of the relocation options – through land policies – which would alter demands on infrastructure and transport.

More than half the proposed investments in infrastructure are assigned to the roads subsector, and of this almost 50% is devoted to the Santiago orbital highway and to completing the Americo Vespucio ring road. The total proposed investment in the Macro Zone (57.5%) is assigned to Santiago, only 10.2% to Valparaiso, and the rest – less than a third – would be distributed to the whole Macro Zone.

The challenge remains of finding an adequate response to the development and infrastructure requirements of the Macro Central Zone. This is indicated in terms of production distribution, land consumption and demographic growth; the depopulation of downtown Santiago contrasts with the high growth of the eastern zone, the growth of the urban area of the VI region, the elongation of the area extending trips of cargo and passengers, with its economic and environmental consequences, the failure to decide the relative roles of ports between Valparaiso and San Antonio, with its road, urban and regional implications, and the high concentration of proposed investment in the Metropolitan Area of Santiago (Daher 1994).

The projections, along with the record of recent economic history and its territorial impact, set two imperatives for Santiago: one, its greater privatization; the other, increased economic opening. Both are directed at making the metropolitan economy more dynamic while reducing the serious burden of capital costs to the state and hence to Chile. The largest possible opening of the MR's economy supposes: a growing integration in the export model through more development relative to its important agricultural and mining sectors and to a greater industrialization of such primary resources; the acceleration of the manufacturing–industrial export-orientated reconversion and absorbing of higher technology and qualified labour (in biotechnology, pharmaceuticals, home appliances, etc.); and the development of export services (university, banking, computers, etc.), including tourism as a generator of foreign exchange. It is in these sectors that the MR, and particularly the city of Santiago, will have comparative advantages. The Valparaiso region would present similar advantages.

Likewise, greater privatization of Santiago is related to: growing state decentralization and the regional transfers in imports; state withdrawal from certain public enterprises (some responsible for action in the MR only); and, very importantly, the absorption of the real marginal costs of urban growth by the private sector. Today these costs are subsidized by the rest of Chile as they are by and large being assumed by the state. This process deals with privatizing costs, in particular infrastructural costs.

The privatization of the greatest and most complex enterprise in Chile – reducing the state and making it more competitive by continuing to open the economy – is an efficiency and equity mission, which is still unfinished in Santiago.

The second export phase therefore demands a real reconversion of Santiago – in its economy, its structure and urban management. The reconversion tendency of the old import substitution industrialization city and the inward developing model, along with the metropolitan effects of the regional and rural export sectors, imply a process of economic *(re-)concentration*, which will probably be registered as a second turning point in Santiago's dynamism.

This outcome will depend, by and large, on the more or less sustained behaviour of the macroeconomic variables, both national and international. In fact, by mid-1994, the recovery of the developed economies has strongly increased the prices of commodities. This increases substantially the profitability of the regional and rural export sectors. At the same time, unemployment in Santiago has once again beaten the national average.

Conclusions and challenges

A strategic sector is a strategic territory. It is around these concepts that this chapter has been structured: infrastructure and Chile's Macro Central Zone. The first refers to a *sine qua non* condition for economic growth and social development. The second alludes to a greater demographic and economic concentration for the country in Santiago.

The V, VI and metropolitan regions represent, in fact, more than half of the national population and close to 60% of the geographical product of the country. The MCZ not only has a large share in industry and services (63% and 75% respectively) (MESA-INECON 1993), but it also generates over one-third of the agricultural and mining output of the economy as a whole.

Moreover, infrastructure has enormous macroeconomic importance: together with the construction sector, it represents over 50% of fixed capital investment in Chile. The real estate economy contributes a fifth of the geographical product and a quarter of all services.

Although the economic importance of both infrastructure and the MCZ are undeniable, their social implications call for a certain reflection. The populations of the MCZ and the metropolitan areas constitute a large part of the social demand, in health and housing as well as in terms of general infrastructure and transportation. Furthermore, such regions include geographical areas of extreme poverty and a large number of the poor of the country. The problems of social equity are worsened, additionally, by the lower quality of life associated with urban problems and environmental damage.

Infrastructure is not unrelated to the social dimension of development. A significant part of infrastructure – particularly roads – is heavily subsidized. This implies distortions, with a loss in economic efficiency and a clearly regressive character in distributive terms. It should be noted that the sectoral investment of the ministries related to infrastructure represents close to 90% of total public investment in Chile, making it one of the main tools for government action in the socio-economic field along with the social expenditure.

The infrastructure sector and the MCZ further raise another issue related to institution-building in terms of both inter-sectoral relations – public works, transport, and so on – and the management of interregional, regional and local links. Moreover, strengthening institutions for the infrastructure sector and spatial management requires close coordination; every time problems and issues arise in one field or another, they overlap considerably and often become inseparable (Majluf et al. 1991).

A series of significant advances has taken place in the infrastructure sector, regarding the privatization of some subsectors – especially within the energy and telecommunications sectors; in the port and more recently in road sectors; and a move towards greater economic rationality through bidding and introduction of user-charges – for example in mass urban transport. However, there is still much to be done in these fields in terms of funding and investment policies, of regulation and prices, and of public–private cooperation. Such a task is more urgent as the country's economy grows.

However, this challenge lies beyond immediate actions and responses, establishing a qualitative change that is possible only through urgent institutional modernization. In this respect, there are certainly valuable achievements in terms of inter-ministerial coordination, in investment planning, in the excellence of technical secretaries, in the organization of public enterprises, in the sectoral–regional coordination, and in other matters. However, there is a consensus regarding the need for an institutional redefinition with a strategic vision, which demands simultaneously greater integration and coordination, and greater decentralization, a normative and regulatory framework, and an organizational redesign that could include incorporation, regulatory bodies and highly qualified technical units. Although there is a consensus on the need for an institutional modernization, this does not seem to exist in terms of a specific project of strengthening institutions in the infrastructure sector.

The challenge of the modernization of local and regional government is by no means small nor less urgent. In fact, the processes of strengthening municipal governments, and the regional reforms, have created the basis for what is potentially a new face of public management. Municipalities and regional governments – sometimes with citizen participation – are certainly resetting the traditional sectoral agenda and ministerial management. However, in relation to territorial development, a greater institutional vacuum co-exists, with entities and norms of obsolescence. This is particularly so in relation to urban management, at the level of both the municipality and the metropolitan regions. From the ministerial sphere to the local administrations, the policies, tools and public action show that the governance of cities is critical and that lack of adequate urban management generates economic inefficiency, social inequity and a lower quality of life for a majority of people. Given the high degree of urbanization of Chile's population, and the strong metropolitanization in the Macro Central Zone, urban problems end up being those of the majority, and urban management becomes decisive in economic growth and regional development. If infrastructure contributes significantly to the formation of fixed capital, cities – and metropolitan areas to an extreme degree – become the main contributors of fixed capital formation for the country. Large cities are, in fact, true enterprises – great and complex – whose management is poor.

In addition to the close relationship between infrastructure and cities, and of both with regard to economic growth and social development, cities are in themselves, infrastructures –for production, consumption and exchange. It is in this relationship that urban management and infrastructure management are linked.

The infrastructure sector and the MCZ are in a doubly privileged location, when it comes to testing and implementing state modernization policies that deal with decentralization, regionalization and strengthening of local government. Obviously, this cannot be done at the expense of the rest of the country. Chile requires its central regions to gain efficiency and competitiveness, ceasing to be a drag on the national economy, and to contribute to raising national averages of economic growth and general development.

A second turning point in Santiago's growth would allow for a restored equilibration between the capital and regions, within the development model. However, the new metropolitan boom should not respond to a simple quantitative increment, but to a qualitative reconversion; it would not constitute a regression to the past but a contribution to the future.

References

Aninat, E. 1990. *Investment opportunities in Chile: results form a survey of projects 1990–1995*. Seminario Oportunidades de Invesión en Chile, Comite de Inversiones Extranjeras, Comisión de las Comunidades Europeas, Stgo., Chile, Marzo, 1990.

Banco Central de Chile 1994. *Boletín Mensual* N° 760, Junio, Chile.

Behrens, R. 1990. *La estrategia de desarrollo en Chile y el papel capital extranjero: 1974–1989*. Unidad Conjunta CEPAL-CET sobre Empresas Transnacionales-Santiago, Chile.

Daher, A. 1990. *Ajuste económico y ajuste territorial en Chile* in *Reestructuración Ecónomica Global. Efectos y Políticas Territoriales*, 113–28, E. Laurell y J. Lindenboim (comp.) Ediciones CEUR, Buenos Aires.

—1993a. *Santiago estatal, Chile liberal* in *Metropoli, Globalidad y Modernización*, 181–204. A. Bolivar et al. (Coords.), FLACSO-UAM Azcapotzalco, México DF.

—1993b. *Territorio del capital bancario y provisional* in *Desafíos de la Descentralización* 245–72. I. Irarrazaval (ed.), CEP, Santiago.

—1993c. *Infraestructuras: regiones estatales y privadas en Chile*, in *Estudios Públicos* N°49, 137–74. CEP, Santiago.

—1994. *Infraestructura en la Macro Zona Central, Asesoría con la colaboración de J. Pablo Muñoz y Edmundo Ruiz, a la Contraparte Técnica del Estudio Análisis sobre el Desarrollo de la infraestructura en las Regiones V, VI y Metropolitana* (MECSA-INECON, 1993) del Comite Internacional de Infraestructura. COMINF, Santiago.

De la Cuadra, S. 1988. *Necesidades de inversion en el sector exportador*, in *Estudios Monetarios* X, sept. Banco Central de Chile.

De Mattos, C., M. Guerra, F. Riveros 1993. *Impacto Territorial del Crecimiento Industrial Manufacturero durante el período 1985–1991*, Contrato mideplan-puc. IEU, P. Universidad Católica de Chile, Santiago.

Escobar, B. & A. Repetto 1993. *Efectos de la estrategia de desarrollo chilena en las regiones: una estimación de la rentabilidad del sector transable regional*, in Colección Estudios CIEPLAN. N° 37 5–36. Santiago.

Majluf, N. Daher A. et al. 1991. *Diagnóstico sobre la problemática institucional del sector infraestructura*, Proyecto INDES, Convenio P. Universidad Católica de Chile-Comite Interministerial de infraestrucura, Santiago.

MECSA–INECON 1993. *Análisis sobre el Desarrollo de la Infraestructura en las Regiones V, VI y Metropolitana* (cuatro volumenes). COMNIF. Santiago.

MIDEPLAN 1993. *Serie Regionalizada de la Inversión Pública Efectiva 1986–1992*. Ministerio de Planificación y Cooperación. Santiago.

ODEPLAN 1990a. *Estadísticas Regionales. Información macroeconómica*. Oficina de Planificación Nacional, Santiago, Chile.

—1990b. *Estadísticas Regionales. Población e indicadores sociales* Oficinal de Planificación Nacional Santiago, Chile.

Ominami, C. & R. Madrid 1989. *La inserción de Chile en los Mercados Internacionales*. Dos mundos, Soc. de Profesionales, PROSPER, CLEPI, CESOC, Santiago.

SII 1991. Subdirección de Avaluaciones, Unidad de Análisis y Sistemas, Servicio de Impuestos Internos, Santiago, Chile.

Servicio Nacional de Aduanas 1990. *Memoria 1990*, Servicio Nacional de Aduanas, Chile.

Silva, I. 1994. *Inversión y crecimiento regional en Chile 1970–1990*, Instituto Latinoamericano y del Caribe de Planificación Económica y Social, Naciones Unidas, CEPAL, Santiago.

Sociedad de Fomento Fabril (SFF) 1989. *Catastro Proyectos de Inversión*. Gerencia de Estudios, Sociedad de Fomento Fabril, Santiago, Chile.

SUBDERE 1994. *Producto Interno Bruto Regionalizado, Región Metropolitana*. Subsecretaría de Desarrollo Regional. Santiago.

Superintendencia de AFP 1990. *Boletín Estadístico Mensual* de la Superintendencia de Administradoras de Fondos de Pensiones, Diciembre, Santiago, de Chile.

Vial, J. & C. Bonacio 1994. *Tendencias del Desarrollo Regional 1960–92* CIEPLAN. Comunicado de prensa. Santiago.

CHAPTER THIRTEEN
"La Métropole du Nord": a frontier case-study in urban socio-economic restructuring

Annick Loréal, Frank Moulaert & Jean-François Stevens

Introduction

Lille is the capital of the region Nord–Pas de Calais, located on the extreme eastern border of France with Belgium. It is the main municipality of the agglomeration that is often designated as the "Métropole du Nord". Since the end of the 1960s, the Nord–Pas de Calais region has been badly affected by the structural crisis of traditional manufacturing industries: coal-mining, steel, metals and textiles. As a consequence of its sectoral specialization, Lille–Roubaix–Tourcoing lost tens of thousands of jobs in textiles and infrastructure industries. More than half of this loss was counterbalanced by the creation of service jobs. But unemployment continued to increase and the abandoned manufacturing sites and deteriorating neighbourhoods became gloomy spots on the urban redevelopment scene.

The challenges for urban redevelopment – which is interpreted here in a multi-dimensional way, including different policy domains – were massive: job creation, education and training, (re-)development of urban space for new activities and functions, attraction of new industries, and neighbourhood revitalization and improved security.

In the face of these many and growing problems, the local authorities have only limited competencies. For a long time, some parts of economic policy had been in the hands of the municipalities, but the finance had to come first from the central state and later, as regional decentralization became effective, from the central and regional authority. Specific tools for improving the efficacy of local action were developed: the APIM (Agence pour la Promotion Industrielle de la Métropole) for coordinating investment policy, by the Communauté Urbaine, chambers of commerce and the Professional Union of Employers of the Lille metropolis, the Contrat d'Agglomération, and so on.

230

Along with the development of new tools and institutional frameworks, views of development changed. In Lille–Roubaix–Tourcoing, one could characterize these developments as a transformation from a scattered "friches industrielles" (re-use of derelict industrial sites) strategy to a more integrated "logique tertiaire" policy (service-orientated policy, taking into account different agents and strategy domains). This development goes along with a difficult shift in decision-making power from the municipalities to the reorganized APIM and the Communauté Urbaine. But frictions with other institutions such as SOREX (Société Régionale d'Expansion Métropole Nord) and the SEMs (Sociétés d'Economie Mixtes) remain. Moreover, the ultimate political power rests with the municipalities constituting the Métropole du Nord. Given their large number, different views of socio-economic priorities and party-political differences, concerted action is not easy. If some progress has been made in integrating economic agendas and spatial planning objectives, it remains quite removed from the integration of economic and social policy approaches. In the light of growing poverty and social inequality, this may become the most important challenge for the years ahead.

The Lille metropolis and its boundaries

What is commonly called "the Lille metropolis" covers an urban entity with variable boundaries. Its meaning varies: the 60 communes clustered at Lille, Roubaix and Tourcoing (and urban unit, as defined by Institut National de la Statistique et des Etudes Economiques, INSEE); the 87 communes of the Communauté Urbaine de Lille (CUDL), i.e. an intermunicipal public body created in 1968 by order of the state; the 100 communes that form the employment zone (i.e. travel-to-work area) of Lille, as defined by INSEE on the basis of the intensity of the alternating commuting flows; or the 125 communes of the Arrondissement de Lille, which is an administrative territorial area. Finally, the term "metropolis" may also refer to COPIT, an association that regroups the CUDL and the neighbouring Belgian intercommunal bodies, to a vast binational territory straddling the frontier, organized around the cities of Lille, Roubaix, Tourcoing and Armentières in France, and Courtrai, Mouscron and Tournai in Belgium. COPIT was established in 1990.

Within the framework of this study, statistical analysis will concentrate on the perimeter of the arrondissement of Lille, which includes an area wide enough to study the relations between the economic restructuring phenomena, and the roles and intervention strategies of local urban authorities.

231

The urban framework

The Lille metropolis consists of several cities with different characteristics, whose urban fabric was progressively reshaped during the twentieth century (Loréal & Van Staeyen 1995; Fig. 13.1).

Lille, the main city, grew considerably in the nineteenth century, thanks to the development of the linen and cotton industry. Confined by narrow administrative boundaries, it has only 172000 inhabitants (compared to 415000 in Lyon and 600000 in Marseille).

The development of Roubaix and Tourcoing came later, and was more radical. Within a few decades, at the end of the nineteenth century these two large villages were transformed into industrial towns, specializing in the wool industry. Today, they have just under 100000 inhabitants each.

The fourth major urban centre in the agglomeration is a new town, Villeneuve d'Ascq, created in 1970 by a decision of the state (Laborie et al. 1985). From its inception, most of the local university establishments were installed there. Today, its population is 70000. The other communes of the agglomeration, of slightly or considerably smaller size, are either juxtaposed to or are very near to these four main urban centres (CEDRE 1992).

Within this complex conurbation, one must distinguish clearly between the towns situated around Roubaix and Tourcoing, backing onto the Belgian

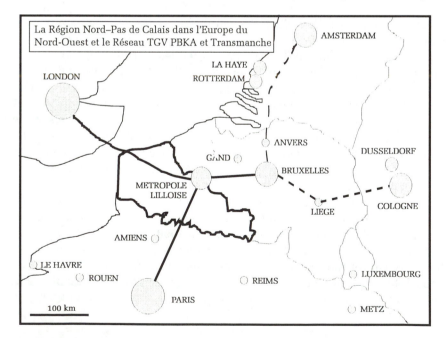

Figure 13.1 The Nord–Pas de Calais region, situated in north west Europe, the TGV network and the Chunnel.

frontier, burdened by an old industrial heritage and regrouped within a "North-East Slope" association, and the rest of the agglomeration, which has been more favoured by the recent economic and urban evolution.

This particular urban organization distinguishes the Lille conurbation from the other great French metropolises, mostly built concentrically around a large urban pole (Lyon, Marseilles).

The following section of this chapter provides a summary of key statistics concerning demography, migration, economic structure and employment, as well as land use. The section is written from a restructuring point of view: What were the features of the economic structure that suffered so badly from the economic crisis? And what are the main features of the restructuring dynamics? Of course, to obtain a full understanding of the transformation processes in the Métropole du Nord it is also essential to set the geographical context.

The third section explains how public responses and public–private institutional organization have changed over the years. The increasing impact of the socio-economic situation and a better understanding of the potential of public initiative caused significant shifts in the latter. These shifts include a stronger emphasis on services instead of manufacturing, attempts to increase the spatial scale of intervention (from the municipal to the level of the Communauté Urbaine) and to diversify policy instruments.

The fourth section focuses on the past ten years of local development policy in the agglomeration of the North. The challenge of the Channel Tunnel and the TGV (high-speed train) transportation network have undoubtedly driven the different municipalities towards renewed collaboration. The main dynamics are generated in the context of the Communauté Urbaine de Lille. But many contradictions remain and the growth of a strategic approach is hampered by several difficulties.

Economic crisis and structural changes

This section examines the evolution of some key variables for the arrondissement de Lille in the period 1975–90 or, when earlier data are available, 1968–90. As pointed out in the introduction, the arrondissement de Lille does not completely coincide with the agglomeration or the perimeter of the Communauté Urbaine. But as a proxy the arrondissement, which is the territorial denominator for more refined statistical data, is certainly acceptable (for details on these statistical problems see Bruyelle 1986).

Compared with the overall evolution in France, the structure of employment shows a more than average tertiarization, an unnoticed rapid deindustrialization and a virtual disappearance of the primary sector (Table 13.2.)

These spectacular changes in sectoral composition, especially in the

Table 13.1 Number and shares of employment in the "Métropole du Nord" (head-count)

	1975		1982		1990	
	Number	%	Number	%	Number	%
Primary sector	7980	1.72	7084	1.54	5516	1.21
Secondary sector	213485	46.07	174912	38.03	131766	28.99
textile	80265	17.32	53340	11.60	29704	6.53
agro-industry	18195	3.93	18036	3.92	13996	3.08
Service sector	241950	52.21	277952	60.43	317300	69.80
market services	167980	36.25	195204	42.44	224326	49.35
non-market services	73970	15.96	82748	17.99	92974	20.45
TOTAL	463415	100.00	459948	100.00	454582	100.00

Source: Agence de Développement et d'Urbanisme, 1994, AII–3.

Table 13.2 Structure of employment by sector (% share for metropole and France)

	1968	1975	1982	1990
France primary	18.3	10.0	8.2	5.7
Lille primary	7.4	1.7	1.6	1.2
France secondary	35.6	38.5	34.2	30.1
Lille secondary	45.6	45.9	37.3	29.0
France tertiary	46.0	51.3	57.5	64.1
Lille tertiary	46.8	53.0	61.0	69.7

Source: Agence de Développement... (1994). Données INSEE.

1980s, are also visible in the shifts in job profiles. The job profiles, which were very strongly linked to textile and infrastructure industry, only slowly transform into innovative service job profiles. In fact the compensation for massive manufacturing job losses happens predominantly in low and inter-mediately skilled service jobs. The growing commercial function, with its intermediate skill levels, is far more important than the rise of superior skills in the advanced producer services sector. Tables 13.3 and 13.4 show the relative performance of the metropole du Nord in the job creation and destruction process, according to skill levels and in comparison with the other regional metropolises. Table 13.3 makes a distinction between the dynamic and the structural effect in the job creation/ destruction process for all French regional metropolises. The structural effect refers to the correspondence with the average composition of the national job creation process; the dynamic component refers to the proper dynamics of each metropolis. From the table one can see that Lille scores poorly both for the structural and the dynamic effect. This is mainly attributable to the fact that it loses huge numbers of traditional manufacturing jobs whereas it is only partly capable of compensating these losses by a reinforcement of employment in its business service activities. Table 13.4 provides an explanation of the job losses and gains for the

Table 13.3 Structural and dynamic effects in the job creation process, 1982–90 (%).

Metropolis	Job growth rate of the metropolis	Structural effect	Structural effect excluding farmers	Dynamic effect
Reims	2.18	−2.10 (13)	−1.33 (14)	1.26
Amiens	−4.53	−4.42 (20)	−3.19 (20)	−3.12
Rouen	−3.33	−0.13 (8)	−0.6 (12)	−6.22
Orléans	5.88	−0.46 (10)	−0.41 (11)	3.32
Caen–Bayeux	1.13	−3.87 (19)	−2.61 (19)	1.98
Dijon	6.90	−0.32 (9)	−0.40 (10)	+4.2
Lille–Rbx–Tcg	−4.04	−0.84 (11)	−1.85 (17)	−6.22
Nancy–Toul	−4.04	1.87 (4)	1.26 (5)	−8.93
Strasbourg	7.42	1.87 (4)	1.01 (7)	2.53
Besançon	5.08	−2.77 (16)	−1.65 (15)	4.83
Nantes	3.68	−1.04 (12)	0.17 (8)	1.70
Rennes	5.75	−3.36 (17)	0.00 (9)	6.09
Poitiers	2.92	−2.67 (15)	−0.88 (13)	2.57
Bordeaux	7.63	1.97 (2)	1.65 (4)	2.65
Toulouse	20.53	1.23 (7)	2.09 (2)	16.29
Limoges	−4.91	−3.37 (18)	−1.87 (18)	−4.56
Lyon	6.16	1.66 (6)	1.02 (6)	1.49
Clermont-Ferrand	−3.89	−2.51 (14)	−1.73 (16)	−4.40
Montpellier–Sète	20.22	1.93 (3)	2.21 (1)	15.27
Marseille	−0.54	2.93 (1)	1.84 (3)	−6.50
Average metropole	3.02			

Source: INSEE/ IFRESI 1995
Figures in parenthesis show ranking of metropolises.

most important professional categories in the agglomeration, in comparison with the "average regional metropolis".

With over a 1.1 million inhabitants in 1990, the "arrondissement de Lille" represents the fourth agglomeration of France, and the largest north of Paris. Figure 13.1 shows its location vis-à-vis the regional territory, but also with respect to the neighbouring or nearby countries (Agence d'Urbanisme et de Développement de la Métropole Lilloise 1994). The proximity to Brussels, London, Amsterdam, Rotterdam, Antwerp and Gent is gradually losing its symbolic value in favour of effective economic relationships. These relationships intensify gradually as a consequence of overall European economic integration, but also because of the privileged position of Lille–Roubaix–Tourcoing in the transportation networks of northern Europe, especially its nodal role in the TGV networks (access to the Channel Tunnel, main node in the connection between London, Paris and Brussels) (CEDRE 1992) and the innovative strategies of public and private agents have affected the integration of the agglomeration in the northern European economy.

Remarkable in the economic geography of the metropole is its position *vis-à-vis* the region. Topographically, it appears as a real border city, but one whose size and economic weight still affects the economies of the smaller cities and

Table 13.4   Socio-professional categories in the "Métropolis du Nord" (=LRT): major losses or average gains

Socio-professional categories	Metropolises gaining or loosing more jobs than Lille–Roubaix–Tourcoing
Socio-professional categories with more than 10% job loss in LRT between 1982 and 1990:	Metropolises losing more than LRT:
– artisan workers	none
– shopkeepers and assimilated	none
– drivers	none
– skilled workers	Rouen, Nancy–Toul
– unskilled manufacturing workers	Rouen, Nancy–Toul, Limoges, Cl-Ferrand, Marseilles
– unskilled artisan workers	none
Socio-professional categories with at least 30% job increases between 1982 and 1990:	Metropolises with higher job gains than LRT:
– personnel of liberal professions	Reims, Amiens, Orléans, Dijon, Besançon, Rennes, Bordeaux ét., Toulouse, Lyon, Montpellier–Sète, Marseille ét.
– academics, scientific professions	Caen–Bayeux, Dijon, Nancy–Toul, Nantes, Bordeaux ét., Limoges
– engineers and technical managers	Rouen, Orléans, Dijon, Strasbourg, Besançon, Nantes, Rennes, Poitiers, Bordeaux ét., Toulouse, Limoges, Lyon, Montpellier–Sète, Marseille ét.
– intermediate administrative and business professions (public sector)	Caen–Bayeux, Strasbourg, Besançon, Poitiers
– intermediate administrative and business professions (private sector)	Orléans, Caen–Bayeux, Dijon, Strasbourg, Besançon, Rennes, Poitiers, Bordeaux ét., Toulouse, Limoges, Lyon, Clermont-Ferrand, Montpellier–Sète, Marseille ét.
– personnel of personal service activities	Reims, Orléans, Caen–Bayeux, Dijon, Strasbourg, Bordeax ét., Toulouse, Montpellier–Sète.

Source: INSEE/ IFRESI 1995
Et. = agglomeration.

towns located to the northwest, south and east of the agglomeration. In terms of share of innovative activities, especially business services, its economic dominance over the smaller cities keeps growing (Moulaert & Gallouj 1995).

Demography and migrations

The population of the "arrondissement de Lille" has been virtually stagnating since 1968. The agglomeration gained only 45 123 inhabitants between 1968 and 1975, 55 (fifty five!) from 1975 and 1982, and 14000 from then until 1990 (Bruyelle 1991: 15) This slow growth is attributable to a negative migration balance, which is nevertheless more than compensated for by a relatively strong natural increase in population. In rough terms, one can say that, between 1968 and 1990, net outmigration was 90000, while net natural growth amounted to 130000.

These sloppy growth figures hide relatively significant intra-metropolitan shifts. Between 1968 and 1975, the zone of Lille gains almost 1% a year, zone Roubaix–Tourcoing only 0.6%. In the two following observation periods (1975–82 and 1982–90) Lille kept growing very slowly (0.1–0.3% a year) while Roubaix–Tourcoing slowly declined.

At the more detailed statistical level of the municipalities, the population of the central communes (and maybe particularly Lille) declined in relative terms. In the period 1975–82 there is also an absolute decrease, absorbed by the peripheral or new municipalities (such as Villeneuve d'Ascq). Even the municipalities in the "first fringe") of the agglomeration ceded population to the outer localities, but recently migration to the suburbs has slowed down.

Important for the sequel of the analysis are the following two demographic observations. First, the Métropole du Nord is the most densely populated of all the regional metropolises in France. In 1990, compared to Lyon and Grand Marseilles, the northern metropolis was only 30% of the extent of these urban areas, with a population density of about 2.5 times larger. Moreover, its population is spread over 125 municipalities, with the main commune representing only 15% of the overall population (Grand Marseilles: 51%; Lyon: 27%) (INSEE/IFRESI 1995). This territorial patchwork quilt may cause political fragmentation as well. Secondly, the population of the Métropole du Nord is the youngest of all regional metropolises: almost 40% of the population is younger than 25 years of age, whereas the French average is 33.1% (INSEE/IFRESI 1995). This means a tremendous challenge with respect to education and employment.

Economic performance and sectoral economic structure

The Lille arrondissement shows one of the saddest stories of deindustrialization in France. Against the background of a general loss of employment, the share of manufacturing has been decreasing significantly. The number of people employed was 433884 in 1975, down to 425037 in 1990. Over a period of 15 years this result is no worse than for the Lyon agglomeration. However, the decline for Lille is concentrated in the past decade: Lyon benefited from an increase of some 13000 jobs, whereas in Lille there was a decrease of about 7000. Looking at the numbers and the distribution of jobs in the agglomeration, the spectacular deindustrialization becomes quite apparent (Table 13.1).

When considering this gloomy picture of restructuring in activities and jobs, one begins to gain the impression that the Métropole du Nord has severe

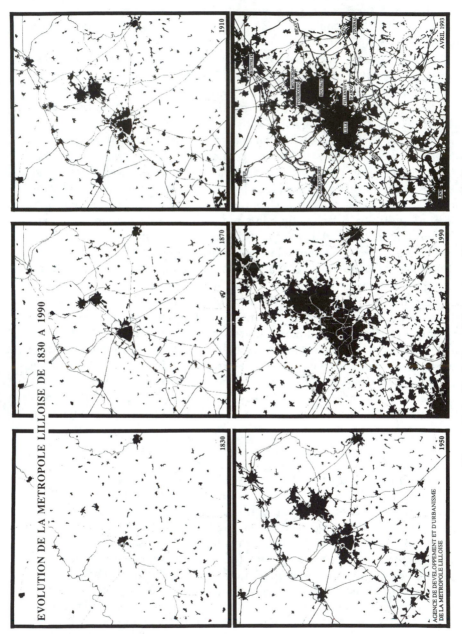

Figure 13.2 Evolution of the metropolitan area of Lille.

problems in overcoming the restructuring crisis. However, some sectors are doing well, for example, agribusiness, business services and trade-related activities show promising growth, value added and international trade figures (Stevens 1992).

Land use

The physical appearance of the agglomeration reflects the painful socio-economic struggle that it has been undergoing for the past 20 years. But the municipalities and the Communauté Urbaine, in collaboration with the regional authorities, have actively used local policy instruments to renovate the traditional centre, to lead a social housing policy, and perform a policy of rc-utilization of abandoned industrial sites and derelict manufacturing land. Poor-quality housing and environmental problems remain, however, but hope exists that these can be tackled in the near future (Agence de Développement . . . 1994, Stevens 1992).

Elements of restructuring

The rise of different service activities   The rapid tertiarization of the Métropole du Nord was pointed out before. It was shown how the intermediate service skills are rising fast, while top-level qualifications remain behind. An activity or branch-wise approach to the tertiarization process shows a more optimistic picture. In terms of "business services", compared to the regional metropolises, which had a significant yearly increase in their overall employment in the period 1982–90, the Lille metropolis did very well, with an average yearly increase in business service employment of 6.8% (see Table 13.5). This encouraging figure points at the business services sector as a main factor in development for the future.

Table 13.5   Employment growth in business services (1982–1990).

Metropole	Average yearly rate of change in business services	Average yearly rate of change in overall employment (%)	Number of business services jobs in 1990	Share of business services in total employment in 1990 (%)
Toulouse	+9.7%	+2.1	17 496	4.8
Nantes	+6.9	+0.8	11 261	4.0
Strasbourg	+6.8	+0.9	8692	4.1
Lyon	+6.7	+0.8	33 344	5.2
Lille–R'baix–T'rcoing	+6.6	+0.0	14 560	3.5
Grand-Marseille	+5.9	+0.9	22 208	3.9
Strasbourg	+6.8	+0.9	8692	4.1

Source: INSEE/ IFRESI 1995

Education and skill levels The educational background of the salaried active population (private sector) in the Métropole du Nord has progressed significantly between 1982 and 1990; but the share of those with a higher education certificate remains lower than that of the average metropolis and, for example, significantly less than that of Toulouse (9.6% in 1990), Montpellier (8.6%) or Lyon (8.1%); moreover, there are remarkable differences between Roubaix–Tourcoing and Lille. In 1982, the share for Lille was 4.2% compared to 2.7% for Roubaix–Tourcoing. In 1990, higher education certificate holders reached 8% in Lille against only 4.2% in Roubaix–Tourcoing (Table 13.6).

Redevelopment of land and activity zones In the agglomeration, as everywhere in France, the first and for a long time the preferred way for municipalities to intervene in the field of economic development has been through the creation of industrial estates, later of activity zones and parks, and today also of sites dedicated to tertiary activity (Legalès 1993).

Table 13.6 Levels of education in the Métropole du Nord as compared to the average regional metropole (%).

	Lille–Roubaix–Tourcoing		Average metropolis	
Category	1982	1990	1982	1990
No diploma declared	30.0	20.3	29.8	18.9
CEP/ BEP	51.1	52.2	50.1	52.4
BAC	12.6	11.7	13.4	12.7
DES1 (BAC+2)	2.7	9.2	2.8	9.1
DES2 (≥BAC+2)	3.6	6.6	4.0	6.9
TOTAL	100.0	100.0	100.0	100.0

Source: INSEE/ IFRESI 1995

For, in spite of employment losses, secondary activities have proved to be greedy in the consumption of land (an average of 50 ha a year for industrial estates between 1980 and 1990 (Agence de Développement . . . 1994). Logistic requirements made some businesses leave their historical urban location. They have sought larger sites, with better connections, especially in the industrial estates connected to the motorway or railway networks that have developed since the end of the 1960s.

With the exception of the Lille Port, created in 1948 by the Lille Chamber of Commerce, the first industrial estates that appeared in the 1960s were often a joint venture of the state and the Communes. But the Lille Chamber of Commerce and Industry soon began to play an important role in the creation of business estates (Agence de Développement . . . 1995). Those days saw the appearance of the great industrial estates in Seclin, Armentières and La Martinoire in Wattrelos, later Tourcoing-Nord and Roubaix-Est, and La Pilaterie in Wasquehal–Marcq-en-Baroeul. Five zones were created in the 1960s with a total surface of 363 ha, 22 in the 1970s (978 ha) and 30 in the 1980s (196 ha).

With the years, the size of the estates has decreased as their number went up.

The sudden acceleration in the 1970s can be explained mainly by the action of the Chamber of Commerce, which saw the increased need for local business to leave urban sites in favour of locations connected to the new motorways. This development took place mainly south of the agglomeration near the A1 (Lille–Paris) motorway, which was opened in 1967. On the North East Slope, where the first symptoms of the textile industry crisis were appearing, the large industrial estates were the attempt by the mayors to benefit from the first re-conversion policies put in place at national level. The creation of the zone of Tourcoing-Nord, for example, where a Rank–Xerox production unit was located, should be seen in this context. But spurred by the crisis, competition between municipalities in the agglomeration increased, and this led to the creation of more or less well planned new estates. For instance, Roubaix-Est was created by the mayor of Roubaix to attract business from outside. But it remained almost vacant for many years because it had no access to the motorway network, built in 1982.

Finally, since the 1982 laws on decentralization gave new powers to mayors, we have seen a multiplication of small activity zones. In this way, each commune hoped to emerge from the intensified deindustrialization crisis without too much damage. The local character of the business location market has caused an exacerbated competition between the communes, with each trying to lure "mobile" businesses from neighbouring communes. Another result from this abundance of initiatives that became manifest was the revision of the urban plan for the arrondissement (a legal and administrative document that indicates the general use of land), as of 1991, which showed a severe shortage of available land.

As the Director of the APIM (Agency for the Promotion of the Lille Metropolis) stated in a public interview, the metropolis cannot fulfil any need for more than 5 ha. This discourages business from outside the area, and especially foreign ones, and may lead, it is feared, to the transfer of local businesses to nearby Belgium or to the ex-mining district on the south of the agglomeration.

This quick survey shows that no authority has planned and managed the development of activity zones at the level of the agglomeration. This contrasts with the view of the local authorities that favoured the creation of activity zones to support the development of the urban fabric. A revealing detail reinforces this point: it is only in 1994 that the Chamber of Commerce, with the backing of the CUDL, published the first directory of available business location zones. The late creation of this planning tool reveals how slowly councillors and local government civil servants became aware of the need for economic development tools and strategies covering the whole of the agglomeration.

Housing In response to the shortcomings of the Lille housing market, an increase in qualitatively acceptable housing is one of the first priorities of the new urban plan for the agglomeration. Depending on the hypothesis, between 45 000 and 60 000 dwellings will be needed within the next 20 years. But this forecast does not take into account the possible qualitative decline in the existing housing stock. Therefore, taking all needs into account, it will be necessary to build between 3500 and 5000 dwellings a year, while also keeping up the quality of the existing housing infrastructure. In order to meet these objectives, the supply of the past six years should be increased by 10% (Agence de Développement . . . 1994: 37). Moreover, the Agence (i.e. the local development agency) suggests some major breaks with the past, by reducing the peri-urbanization of dwellings and using the available downtown space. This means that the residences would reconquer degraded urban areas. Therefore, 35–50% of new construction should be undertaken within the existing urban space (non-used land, re-utilization of derelict industrial land, renovation of old housing). The social dimension of the housing policy should become even more explicit, especially by increasing the accessibility of rented social housing for deprived groups of citizens (Vervaeke & Lefèbvre 1996).

Transportation and communication networks   One of the major development axes of the past few years has been the transportation networks and their links with the rising business- and trade-related services. Improvements in motor- and waterways are on the agenda. But the most important challenge has been the completion of the TGV Nord, the Channel Tunnel and the construction of the new TGV Station, "Lille Europe", together with the EURALILLE services complex (Stevens 1992, Moulaert et al. 1993).

Public responses to socio-economic challenges

Institutional and political organization

In the 1960s, the state instituted a planning policy for the national territory (Laborie et al. 1985). This resulted in, among other things, the definition of "equilibrium metropolises" (métropoles d'équilibre), which received a major development impetus. In the Nord–Pas de Calais region, this role was assigned to the whole of the Lille–Roubaix–Tourcoing urban region.

The creation of the new town of Villeneuve d'Ascq followed from this decision, as did that of the Lille Urban Community (CUDL) in 1968 (Kruczkowski-Deboudt 1991). This new structure is a public body. Its council is elected by the municipal councillors of the 88 communes that are involved. Its aim is to plan, implement and manage the main infrastructures that ensure the development of the agglomeration.

Important powers of the communes especially in the field of town planning have thus been transferred to the CUDL, especially in the field of town planning. Henceforth, it is the CUDL that instigates large urban works, such as roads, public transport infrastructure (underground tramway) and new industrial estates to host business (Bruyelle 1976). For this purpose, it manages considerable financial resources, much larger than those of the largest communes.

The CUDL has rapidly become a major actor in the transformation of the agglomeration (Fleury 1992). And yet, it has no legal power in the economic domain. These powers remain monopolized by the communes. The decentralization law of 1982 has even reinforced this situation.

As a matter of fact, since the reform of 1982 and within the framework of the law of decentralization, the communes have the power to intervene in matters of economic development, either by giving direct grants (for business or job creation) in addition to those given by the regional councils, by providing indirect help (sale or renting of premises, with favourable financing) or by use of direct support for firms in difficulties (Legalès 1993).

In the Lille agglomeration, city councils have taken advantage of these new powers to (re-)shape the economic fabric. However, the financial resources of most cities are small when compared to the weight of the economic actions needed. Moreover, the limited size of the municipal territories, and the lack of training and experience by the municipal civil servants in the fields of economic action, did not really favour the development of strategies.

There is a crucial element that has kept councils from relinquishing their economic powers to CUDL: the structure of the local tax system. The councils receive the professional taxes paid by business located on their territory. These professional taxes correspond to half the fiscal resources of the communes. Keeping, or even attracting business to the territory of the commune is a major objective for mayors, because it is crucial for the city's budget. Hence, it is necessary to keep control of direct economic intervention. Therefore, the more important cities in the agglomeration have, one after the other, put in place an economic development department. The CUDL, on the other hand, did not have any department or service dealing with these matters. In this context, no public intervention strategy for the economic development of the agglomeration was planned or conceived at the intercommunal level until the early 1990s. However, necessity compels, and the responses of the cities to the socio-economic challenges tended, little by little, to be elaborated within a wider framework than the strict communal limits.

Premonitory interventionism in the North-East Slope

In the early 1980s, we saw that the northeast part of the agglomeration (i.e. the cities of Roubaix, Tourcoing, Wattrelos and their suburbs) became strongly affected by the crisis in the textile industry. The job losses and closures of many textile plants led to the appearance of many industrial wastelands, a rise in the rate of unemployment, and deep social and urban disorders.

The rise of tertiary activities at the south of the agglomeration, especially in Lille and Villeneuve d'Ascq, has had little impact on the North East Slope, which remained severely handicapped by a degraded urban and social fabric. In this context of emergency, the communes of the northeast have engaged in active economic development support policies that went beyond local communal divisions.

But their action was limited to the traditional domain of the economic intervention by cities (i.e. business real-estate) which devolved on the SEM du VNE (Société d'Economie Mixte du Versant Nord-Est at the North-East Slope), and the prospection of business opportunities by the SIAR (Intercommunal Syndicate of the Roubaix agglomeration) and the UAT (Union of the Tourcoing agglomeration).

Evolution of the action of the SEM du VNE   The SEM of the VNE was created in 1980. Its capital is shared between cities (Roubaix, Tourcoing, Wattrelos, Roncq, Leers, Neuville, Croix, Wasquehal), the Chamber of Commerce and Industry of Lille–Roubaix–Tourcoing, the Caisse des Dépots et Consignations and the Caisses d'Epargne of Roubaix and Tourcoing.

In the mind of the mayors who founded the SEM, the crisis situation that affected business was momentary. The aim of the SEM was thus to help firms by buying their land and buildings, which would be sold back to them later. It quickly appeared that the crisis would endure, and the SEM found itself owner of $400\,000\,m^2$ of vacant buildings on wasteland. Its mission was altered to treat industrial wasteland and promote its re-utilization for new economic activities. (Agence de Développement . . . 1994).

Three stages can be distinguished in the action of the SEM. A first stage (1980–84), when wasteland was treated at the lowest cost for the relocation, at a very low rent, of vulnerable firms with a quick turnover on the site; a second stage (1984–89), with a more elaborate rehabilitation of the sites, together with a study of the activities to attract to the site; and a third stage (since 1989), stressing the necessity of relocating activities that allow a diversification and consolidation of the local economic fabric.

With time, the managers of SEM and their counterparts in the city councils have progressed. From a scratch approach of economic development (failing business had to be replaced by new business, whatever its nature) they have come to more elaborate practices that combine the needs of patching up the urban fabric and the need to promote an enduring evolution of the economic fabric. Because of the failure to evaluate the complexity of the continuing economic process, this evolution took some time.

It must be pointed out here that only the largest cities (Roubaix, Tourcoing and Wattrelos), had a business department, with a very small staff. These were completely absorbed by the problems in hand and lacked the resources to reflect on the consequences of the continuing economic transformation, and the principal economic development orientations.

The SIAR and UAT   The second direction of municipal intervention is promotion and prospection. In 1987 and 1988, hoping to favour the location of new activities thereby, the cities of the North-East Slope created two tools for the promotion of their territory: the SIAR (Intercommunal Syndicate of the Roubaix Agglomeration) and the UAT (Union of the Tourcoing Agglomeration). The names of these two bodies reflect the competition between the traditional rivals, Roubaix and Tourcoing.

At first, the SIAR comprised Roubaix, Wasquehal and Leers; five other small cities joined the intercommunal syndicate in 1990. The original aim of the SIAR was to promote the territory and the sites that could house outside investors. Very quickly, the syndicate's aim turned to putting up internal relocation operations. It was a waste of time trying to attract external businesses to the rather unattractive Roubaix agglomeration while there were many local firms looking for new premises inside the employment zone.

The SIAR function has been to launch real-estate operations, and to act as a "funnel" to gather grants and aid. These are all financing operations that allowed business in old sites to be relocated. There is no doubt that the action of SIAR has retained activities in the area that would otherwise have moved somewhere else. This was possible because, for the first time in the metropolis, a mechanism of fiscal solidarity was put in place among the member communes to finance the SIAR syndicate. In this way, the communes have grouped together to help local business.

The UAT, created as a response to the SIAR by the communes of Tourcoing, Halluin, Roncq and Neuville-en-Ferrain, is also based on a mechanism of fiscal solidarity between the communes. Whereas the SIAR intervenes directly to undertake real-estate operations, the UAT does it through the SEM of the VNE.

Oddly enough, while these two structures were developing real skills in the field of business needs and became professionals in local development, the cities kept economic units to deal among other things with the needs of trade and craftsmen. Responsibilities are thus partitioned by structure and of course by territory. Given the proximity of the two urban zones, this situation soon produced perverse side-effects.

The Employment Zone Committee (Comité de Bassin d'Emploi, CBE)

Yet another organization has been used by the councillors of the North-East Slope to influence the interaction between demand and supply of jobs in their zone. This novel structure unites municipalities, trade unions and local employers' associations. Always headed by a municipal councillor, the CBE has worked hard to improve training structures, to accelerate the necessary re-conversion of the local workforce, and to improve its skills.

First metropolis-wide approaches to economic development

In spite of the division of the metropolis into small communes, and of the per-sistence of strong rivalries between them, in the 1980s some decisions were made creating structures aimed at overall economic development of the metropolis.

The APIM   In 1985, the CUDL and the Chamber of Commerce and Industry of Lille–Roubaix–Tourcoing created the Agency for the Industrial Promotion of the Metropolis, the APIM. The Agency is meant to discuss prospects for and future plans with industrial firms from outside the metropolis that would move to industrial estates in the metropolis.

In fact, the promotion and actions undertaken by APIM in France and, very soon, abroad, will bear fruit mainly in the fields of distribution and business services. This is the reason why the APIM, while retaining the same acronym, became in 1989 the Agency for the International Promotion of the Lille Metropolis.

The APIM annual report already stated in those days that "economic pro-motion is one of the elements of metropolitan development policy" consid-ered by the APIM as resulting from the strategic public choices made by the new Council of the Communauté, chaired by the mayor of Lille, Pierre Mau-roy (President Mitterand's first Prime Minister of France in 1981).

The breakthrough of the years (1986–90)   The signing in 1986 in Lille, of the Franco–British treaty authorizing the building of the Channel Tunnel, marks a major breakthrough (Stevens 1993). This treaty brought a new awareness into region, and initiated a new strength.

The metropolis and its region stopped considering themselves as a terri-tory undergoing re-conversion, "a dead end", "militarily exposed" (i.e. on a traditional route for foreign invasions), according to notions going back to the beginning of the century. The metropolis began projecting itself as in a state of change, serviced by the most modern European infrastructures. At the eco-nomic level, the transformation to the service sector was seen as a major gain. The re-deployment and rebirth of local economic power is now expected to come from new activities in the service sector.

An agreement was established between economic circles and local govern-ment concerning these ideas. The agreement is embodied in the "TGV–Gare de Lille Association", which acted to secure of the location of the TGV–North Europe railway junction inside Lille, and not, as was first suggested, outside the agglomeration.

Under the Euralille operation (representing FF5 billion investment, of which FF3.5 billion came from the private sector) includes a large-scale busi-ness centre to be built over the new TGV station. It is considered as the "ter-tiary engine" of this strategy. Euralille is to attract head offices and various decision-making centres of (new) French or foreign firms.

The expected inflow of new activities with an international influence is supposed to strengthen the vitality of the local economy and accelerate the shift to the service sector. By diffusing these ideas also inside the metropolis, APIM contributed to the belief that a coherent and unified development strategy was essential for the agglomeration to become a metropolis.

But internal rivalries in the agglomeration did not smoothen the implementation of such a strategy. The mayor of Lille, who also aspired to the presidency of the CUDL, easily convinced the other mayors of the importance of the Euralille project and there were some local councillors who wanted the CUDL to promote and finance projects with an economic impact on their communal territory.

The major projects of CUDL (1989–95)   The election of Pierre Mauroy, mayor of Lille, as president of CUDL was preceded by negotiations leading to a "Charter of the Principal Mayors", which determined seven "major projects", as well as the communes where they would be built: Euralille, the Roncq International Transport Centre, the Roubaix Euroteleport, the Fosse aux Chênes ZAC in Roubaix, the Haute Borne activities park in Villeneuve d'Ascq, the multi-modal platform in Lomme, and the Ravennes-les-Francs activities zone in Bondues–Tourcoing.

Except for the Fosse aux Chênes ZAC in Roubaix (mostly concerned with housing), these projects implied the establishment of business zones or sites. The main economic investments of the CUDL were thus fixed and announced as soon as Pierre Mauroy arrived at the head of CUDL. Having from the start found a consensus on these key points, CUDL was able to work without the chaos and conflicts that had reigned in the agglomeration before.

A first political and strategic approach to metropolitan economic development emerged around these projects, which the principal mayors had wanted, and which together would produce an "orderly development of the metropolis". The development strategy defined mainly what the metropolis could be and wanted to become: a metropolis at the European level with business services reaching out over a wide area of the north of Europe, as well as distribution activities, especially transport and logistics linked to the nodal position of Lille in the rail and motorway networks, and in the longer term, in the canal network. Finally, the CUDL had the ambition to attract new activities linked to research and high technology, through the project of the Haute Borne park, relying on the university located in Villeneuve d'Ascq and close to an important research centre in microelectronics. However, this project is not implemented during the 1989–95 mandate, as the city of Villeneuve d'Ascq gives priority to other actions.

Emergence of a connection between players: the birth of a coherent strategy

From the beginning of the 1990s, under the pressure of various local public and private players, and thanks to the creation of the Planning and Development Agency, the concept of the Lille metropolis has constantly gained strength (Stevens 1993)

A new connection between players

The dynamism of the TGV–Gare de Lille association, and later of the SEM Euralille, made the principal local players increasingly conscious of the importance of more coherent and efficient management of the agglomeration. Economic circles, through the Chamber of Commerce and Industry and the Employers' Unions asked for coherent management of the agglomeration by requesting especially fiscal policy designed at the level of the urban community.

Various initiatives were taken to instigate closer links between economic circles and local authorities. For instance, to accelerate the metropolitanization of Lille, an informal club of decision-makers of all professional or institutional backgrounds, meeting around the Maison des Professions, which houses the Employers' Unions of the metropolis, was established under the name "Great Lille Committee". A "Nord–Pas de Calais Technopole" association, which groups representatives from the "grandes écoles", universities, business circles and local authorities is being put in place to encourage exchanges between the scientific, research and business circles. In addition, a new structure, the European University Pole groups all the university-level education and research establishments, the economic world and local authorities, to lead common action. These organizations will depend on the Planning and Development Agency, which will relay new ideas and widen the horizons of decision-makers.

The development and planning agency of the metropolis

As soon as Pierre Mauroy was elected President of the CUDL, he took the decision to create a Development and Planning Agency, a subdivision of the CUDL, responsible for urban development strategies.

Its first task was to produce the urban plan for the arrondissement of Lille, a legal and administrative document, which indicates the general use of land. This mission was carried out by the agency in an open and strategic way. Elaborating the plan would be, in fact, an opportunity to gather the public and economic actors of the agglomeration around the definition of the major lines of development of the metropolis. It also had the responsibility of carrying out preliminary studies leading to the definition of a "Charter of Objectives" to be signed by the CUDL and the state. This procedure involved about ten large French agglomerations within the framework of the national territorial planning policy. The procedure seeks to determine the poles of economic excellence of the large agglomerations for the next 15 years. For these two missions, the agency will have to carry out a wide spectrum of studies covering past economic evolution, local weaknesses and strengths, to determine the main direction of intervention for the future.

The economic intervention strategy spelled out in the report introducing the urban plan published in 1994, resumes the CUDL's ambitions of internationalization and of attracting new activities. These ambitions are embodied in its large-scale projects, but also bring to light the necessity to improve the quality of infrastructure, as well as public urban assets such as recreation spaces, public spaces, "great events", services to the population. But the main contribution of the agency will be to reconsider its orientations on a wider territory including neighbouring Belgian arrondissements, and to define the future of the metropolis at the level of the Euroregion (Kent, Belgium, Nord–Pas de Calais). This is why one of the major lines of the agency's recommendations is a strategy of alliance and complementarity with the neighbouring Belgian cities of Kortrijk, Mouscron and Tournai, which can be considered as part of the "transfrontier metropolis". But also the support to the evolution of traditional activities (especially textiles) the need to accelerate the use of more sophisticated technological know-how, a better correspondence between the local training system and the needs of business firms, as well as the development of social services, are important priorities in the urban plan. It also brings to light the necessity of anticipating the consequences of the increased effective proximity of Lille and Brussels, which will be only 30 minutes apart by TGV before the end of this century, and between Lille and London with the Eurostar connection. Finally, the analysis preceding the urban plan underlines the necessity of transforming the fiscal system in the agglomeration based on the communal professional tax, and of adopting new measures of fiscal solidarity "to promote the unity of the metropolitan territory".

This urban plan fails to indicate which intervention methods should be used, or how to connect with other public (national) or private structures involved in economic development. Its most significant contribution is that it defines for the first time the main directions for an agglomeration-wide economic intervention programme.

Local bodies and economic development

What lessons can we learn from this quick survey of the long and difficult gestation of economic intervention tools in the Lille agglomeration and from the very slow genesis of an economic development strategy? First of all, the councils and municipal teams were empowered by the challenge of an economic crisis whose scope and structural nature were not understood at first. This may be explained by referring to the "glorious 30" years, when economic development had been "continuous with minor interruptions"; in the eyes of many local leaders, economic expansion was a constant, and the crisis could only be short-lived. The reluctance to install interventionist procedures probably also flowed from some ignorance of economic reality and business life. In fact, in this agglomeration where the Socialist Party has been strong for many decades, there was a wide gap between the world of local business and that of local elected representatives. A revealing detail: the mayor of Lille, a post always occupied by a socialist since the turn of this century, was not invited officially to the Chamber of Commerce and Industry of Lille until 1991. In addition, the regional state services have been strong for a long time. They control public financial aid; this is why, as in the whole of France and in spite of the law of decentralization, not the local authorities but the regions control the financial levers of economic intervention.

In the context of the Lille agglomeration, where public responsibilities are scattered, exceptional circumstances alone have led mayors to overcome communal rivalry and engage in programmes with a global bearing on the agglomeration. The example of the North-East Slope, confronted with a grave economic, social and urban crisis, is illuminating, just as is the new awareness resulting from the hopes arising from the creation of the Channel Tunnel and the opening of the north-Europe TGV.

However, it is clear that the institutional apparatus of the agglomeration is no longer appropriate for today's challenges. The pursuit of a strong strategy of metropolitan transformation presumes the strengthening of intercommunality. But the fear is real that, as long as a body of locally elected representatives, which can only be the CUDL, does not receive official responsibility in the field of economic development, economic interventionism in the metropolis will remain scattered and restricted to projects with solely local interest.

References

Agence de Développement et d'Urbanisme de la Métropole Lilloise 1994. *Schéma Directeur de Développement et d'Urbanisme de la Métropole Lilloise.* Lille.

Bruyelle, P. 1986. Conversion, reconquête urbaine et consommation d'espace: exemples et essai de bilan dans la Région du Nord–Pas de Calais. *Hommes et Terres du Nord* 1, 67–86.

—1991. *La communauté urbaine de Lille. Métropole du Nord–Pas de Calais.* Paris: La Documentation Française.

CEDRE 1992. *Le défi régional de la grande vitesse.* Paris: Syros Alternatives.

Fleury E. 1992. *Partenariat et objectifs du territoire métropolitain,* LARU, May.

INSEE/IFRESI 1995. Lille–Roubaix–Tourcoing. Une métropole régionale. *Dossier de PRO-*

References

FILS. N• 37, June 1995.

Kruczkowski-Deboudt S. 1991, *Les débuts de la communauté urbaine de Lille*. Mémoire de Maîtrise, University of Lille III.

Laborie, J. P., J. F. Langumier, P. De Roo 1985. *La politique française d'aménagement du territoire de 1950 à 1985*. Paris: La Documentation Française.

Legalès P. 1993. *Politique urbaine et développement local: une comparaison franco-brittannique* . Paris: L'Harmattan.

Loréal A. & J. Van Staeyen 1995. *Lille, entre ville industrielle française et métropole européenne diversifiée, Les Pays-Bas Français*. Stichting Ons Erfdeel vzw.

Moulaert, F. & C. Gallouj 1995. Advanced producer services in the French Space Economy: decentralisation at the highest level. In *Progress in Planning* **43**(2–3), 139–54.

Stevens, J. F. 1989/1992. *L'Europe à portée de main. Lille Eurocité. Lille, Préfecture de la Région Nord–Pas de Calais*. Centre d'Etudes et de Prospective du Secrétariat Général aux Affaires Régionales.

— 1993. *L'expérience lilloise, l'aménagement raisonné ou la définition d'un piège dynamique*. Dublin, October 1993

Vervaeke, M. & B. Lefèbvre 1996. Social housing and public policy in the Lille Agglomeration. In *International Journal of Urban and Regional Research*, (in press).

Index